THE NEED TO BE LOVED

BOOKS BY THEODORE REIK

Ritual (*With a preface by Sigmund Freud*)
The Unknown Murderer
Surprise and the Psychoanalyst
From Thirty Years with Freud
Masochism in Modern Man
A Psychologist Looks at Love
Psychology of Sex Relations
Dogma and Compulsion
Listening with the Third Ear
Fragment of a Great Confession
The Secret Self
The Haunting Melody
The Search Within
Myth and Guilt
Of Love and Lust
The Compulsion to Confess
Sex in Man and Woman
The Need to Be Loved

Th

Theodor Re

Need to Be Loved

 The Noonday Press • a division of Farrar, Straus and Company • New York

Contents

Prologue

There are blind dates between thoughts which don't know one another from Adam but which detect concealed affinities at their first meeting. Take the following recent example: I had been engaged in research of one of the basic human needs that had been deplorably neglected by psychology when it occurred to me to look up some lines in Goethe's maxims, so often full of practical wisdom. By mistake I got the volume of the poet's early lyrics. The book opened at the poem "Welcome and Farewell," written almost two hundred years ago. It conveys the emotions the twenty-one-year-old student experienced when he rode from Strasbourg to nearby Sesenheim to see Friederike Brion again. This was the first and perhaps the greatest romance of Goethe's life. I had not read those wonderful verses for more than thirteen years[1] and fell again under the spell of their music. In them, like Sleeping Beauty, the German language awakens and opens wide its eyes. I saw for the first time something new in the poem, so well known to me from boyhood. Certain lines acquired an arresting and unsuspected significance:

> *Ein rosenfarbnes Frühlingswetter*
> *Umgab das liebliche Gesicht*
> *Und Zärtlichkeit für mich-ihr Götter!—*
> *Ich hofft es—ich verdient es nicht.*

> The roseate hues that spring supplies
> Were playing round thy features fair
> And love for me—ye deities!—
> I hop'd for it—but I deserved it ne'er.

And then the farewell:

> *Ich ging, du stand'st und sah'st zur Erden*
> *Und sah'st mir nach mit nassen Blick*
> *Und doch, welch Glück geliebt zu werden*
> *Und lieben, Götter, welch ein Glück!*

> I went—thy gaze to earth first mov'd
> Thou follow'dst me with tearful eye;
> And yet, what rapture to be lov'd
> And Gods, to love, what ecstasy!

It cannot be accidental that the awareness of outgoing love is put into the second line in this stanza. In seeing the charming girl again and in saying good-bye to her the prevalent emotion is not the intense feeling of love, but of being loved, of being the subject of Friederike's tenderness and devotion. Strange that I did not recognize this before, although it springs clearly from the lines! It is the emotional disengagement, that psychological result of the aging process, which now allows me to recognize that indubitable prevailing emotion in the youthful Goethe. Suddenly a bridge is built between the emotional experience, the great romance of the young poet and my research project, the linking of the individual feeling with the general psychological theme. The area that had been neglected by psychological research is the basic need of men and women to be loved.

However, before we shift the emphasis to that subject in general, let's give a side glance at the life history of Goethe. Everyone who has studied his biography from the psychological viewpoint will gain the impression that for him the feeling of being loved had, from childhood to old age, been more important than the need to love, although his poems and plays are full of manifestations of passion and devotion for women.

I have already said that the need to be loved has been neglected as a topic of psychological research. But is this statement correct? A quick survey of the pertinent literature, especially of psychoanalytic books and articles of the last decades, will convince the unbiased reader that the subject was indeed casually treated, if dealt with at all. But do not the writings of Freud and of his most prominent students deal with the psychological problems of love and sexuality? There is, as far as I know, only one article dealing with that distinction between loving and being loved. This is a psychoanalytic paper by Leon Saul,[2] who emphasizes the significance that the difference deserves. It was published more than twelve years ago and tries to include everything in three short pages. Since then, nothing has been added. The matter has been swallowed up by silence.

To give Dr. Saul his due, he energetically tries to press that subject into the Procrustean bed of three pages, but the attempt, however valiant and memorable, falls short. It is remarkable how much of the field is covered by the analytic outline Dr. Saul sketches: not only the psychological distinction between loving and being loved, but also the emotional reactions to the feeling of being unloved, with its repercussions in individual and collective life. He also states that the difference between the receptive need to be loved and the opposed drive of giving love has not generally been made explicit. He mentions too that Freud repeatedly pointed out the importance of being loved and saw this force clearly, but in his clinical writings Freud speaks chiefly of ways of loving "without explicitly making the distinction between loving and being loved." The essential merit of Dr. Saul's paper is that it clearly draws the demarcation lines between the two areas.

This book presents an attempt to trace that basic human need to its manifold manifestations in life, not only in the need of the child—from tots to teens—and in the adult, but also in old age. I shall follow this thread into the tissue of the relationship between the sexes and also between groups.

C. S. Lewis recently published a book, *The Four Loves,*[3] in which he distinguishes between Gift-love and Need-love. The supreme Gift-love is in Lewis' concept of God. God lacks nothing. He has no Need-love that is human and, as Plato says, "the son of poverty." (A side glance at another recent book *The Emperor, the Sages and Death,* by Rachel Berdach,[4] reveals the observation: "O God, if we are Thy image, how lonely must Thou be!")

This book does not deal with the relationship to a divine being. It treats only the relations between human beings, especially between men and women.

2

At this point I had to put aside my writing because of psychoanalytic consultations. (*Je fais mon metier,* you know.) A few hours later, when I returned to my desk, to concentrate once more upon my subject, a tune inexplicably occurred to me. I knew it from somewhere, although I had not remembered it for more than thirty years. But I could not name it. It was like running into a person in the dark, seeing a familiar countenance, without remembering who he was or where you had met him.

I turned my thoughts again to this introduction, but that unrecognized melody recurred and refused to vanish. It was just a waltz tune, and not an especially memorable one. Not by Strauss, nor by Lanner, not even by Waldteufel. Where had I heard it? Was it in an operetta of Lehar, or Eysler, or Leo Fall? No. I was sure only that I had heard it in Austria. It had something to do with Salzburg or the Salzkammergut. When the waltz repeated itself in my mind, I finally caught it, or rather, I got hold of its words: *"Es muss was Wunderbares sein von dir geliebt zu werden."* (It must be wonderful to be loved by you.) Then I remembered, it was from the operetta *The White Horse Inn* by Ralph Benatzky, a Viennese composer, younger than Lehar or Eysler. *The White Horse Inn* is, of course, on the Wolfgang Lake near Salzburg.

Why did that ordinary waltz theme come to my mind? The words of the song contain the answer: "It must be wonderful to be loved by you." I remembered that it was a woman who sang it at the Vienna performance of the *Weisse Rössel*. I recognized then that the haunting melody wanted to remind me of a train of thought I had previously interrupted, namely, of the psychological difference in the emotional life of women and men regarding the universal desire to be loved. I recently read somewhere that a man likes to feel that he is loved, whereas a woman likes to be told. But besides and beyond that, women seem to have a much greater, pervasive need to be loved than men.

This is perhaps the right place to emphasize that the psychological lines of demarcation between the sexes are also often blurred. To repeat a sentence I once wrote: "There is something of the most feminine in a man, and something of the most masculine in a woman."

Another preliminary warning: many of the following pages deal with emotional and mental deviations. Readers may sometimes get the impression that they have similar tendencies, just as young medical students imagine symptoms of diseases they read about in their books. One is not a good judge of himself in this direction. If there is a serious doubt in one's mind, he should consult a psychiatrist or psychoanalyst.

A book treating a subject such as the psychological differences between the sexes is bound to arouse controversy; considering the mores of the times it cannot help being controversial, unless its author is insincere or if its content is superficial. The former is not the case; nor, I hope, is the latter.

Part I : *The Need to Be Loved*

1 : The Sexual Differentiation

Men and Women

Until now we have dealt with the problem of the universal need to be loved as if it were the same for both sexes and as if there were no differences in its forms and aims with men and women. It is high time to consider those emotional variations. Before we even try to find them we must answer the question: Why is it that people, men and women, so much want to be loved? In attempting to study a definite answer, we become aware that the word "loved" is not appropriate in many instances. You wish to be loved by your wife and by your children. You wish to be liked and appreciated by your friends. Maybe you wish to be acknowledged by your community or by the nation, or by the world if you are consumed by an overpowering personal ambition.

Let us then agree that here is a semantic difficulty and that we use the expression "the need to be loved" for many occasions when it would be better to say "to be liked" or "to be admired." This semantic difficulty which besets us cannot be made light of, especially since the expression "to be loved" is restricted to meaning the emotional tie between men and women. In Shakespeare's time and even much later a man could speak of loving his male friend without arousing the suspicion that he was a homosexual. In our time, a man would scarcely use the expression.

Yet in the context of our exploration we have decided to speak of the need of being loved without making those necessary differentiations. We are using this expression because it is the most general and the simplest.

We did not answer that preliminary question, why it is that men and women want so intensely to be loved. Seen from a certain point of view, the answer is self-evident. It was given almost two hundred years ago in the American Declaration of Independence proclaiming that life, liberty and the pursuit of happiness are the unalienable rights of all men. To gratify the need to be loved is part of that pursuit of happiness in which we all are engaged. It is possible to state this condition in negative terms: to be unloved makes one unhappy.

In *Le Livre de Mon Ami* Anatole France tells the story of a little girl called Jessy, an orphan, who was brought to live with her old uncle, the scholarly Dr. Bogus. A few days after her arrival, the little girl said: "Uncle Bog, you are old, you are ugly, but I love you and you must love me." "Why must you be loved, Jessy?" asked the doctor. "Because I am little." The savant asked himself if it were true that one must love the little ones, and he concluded that this was possible (*"il se pouvait"*) because they imperatively need to be loved (*"car, dans le fait, ils ont grand besoin qu'on l'aime"*).

This need is experienced by little boys and girls equally, but very soon the sexual differentiation sets in and boys want to be loved in a different way from girls. They want to be admired and praised for other things than girls and they try to reach this aim differently. A girl just a little older than Jessy in Anatole France's story will wish to be admired because she can dance gracefully; and a boy riding a bicycle will shout, "Look, Ma, no hands!" After a time, the girl wants to be loved because she is beautiful and charming; and the boy because he is strong and tall ("What a big boy am I!").

From then on the boy and the girl part in their ways: the little girl wants to be loved because she is beautiful, the little boy because he is strong and can do things. The dividing line between love for good looks and love for achievement is often plainly seen even before the age of three.

The next question confronting us is this: Is this division or difference determined by physiological and biological factors or does it result from certain experiences? We shall postpone the answer, but not without emphasizing that there is no discernible difference in the need to be loved in infants of either sex before the end of the second year. We would thus be inclined to say that certain experiences of the little girl and of the little boy are determining that psychological variation.

If we now follow the development of those children until the years of maturity, our impression of such a definite difference is sharpened: women in general want to be loved for what they are and men for what they accomplish. The first for their looks and charms, the latter for their actions. There are, of course, remnants from the earliest phases of development besides the proverbial exceptions to the rules, but in general that division can be confirmed by unbiased observations of laymen as well as of psychologists.

We return to our previous question, still unanswered. Clinical experiences of almost all psychoanalysts as well as direct observations of children provide us with information having but one meaning. The experience that determines that variation originates in the little girl's observation of the anatomical difference between male and female. The female child who sees that difference thinks, or rather imagines, that she is physically handicapped compared with the boy. Little Lotte, not yet three years old, for the first time saw a boy playmate urinate and turned astonished to her mother to ask, "Why?" Her mother told her that boys urinate standing up while little girls squat. The child wanted to observe the boy oftener during that activity and asked further questions. Her mother gave her information about the sexual differences. Very soon afterward the girl said: "Lotte wants a silk dress." We see here a shift from mortification to a restoration by vanity.

Psychoanalysis leaves no doubt that the little girl experiences the observation that her genitals are inferior to those of the boy and that she tries to compensate for the resulting humiliation by trying to be very attractive.

So far so good; but the insight is incomplete as long as we do not understand how that compensation comes about. Here we are on the threshold of new insights into the psychology of little girls and of grown-up women. Various cues enable us to penetrate further. A little girl of whom the well-known pediatrician Dr. Benjamin Spock reports complained, to her mother after having seen a boy naked: "He is so fancy and I am so plain!" Let me add a story I heard the other day. An old nurse asked a very young student nurse who worked in the men's ward if she wasn't sometimes embarrassed at seeing male genitals. After the question was answered affirmatively, the old nurse said: "But men are at least complete; women are ugly down there."

The first addition to the analytic theory is thus the information that the little girl, in comparing the vulva with the penis, feels not only handicapped but also thinks that her genitals are ugly compared with boys'.

Freud occasionally remarked that human genitals did not participate in the development of the body's beauty. He might have added that, at least according to the view of the little girl, the female genitals appear to be ugly. He merely stated that the infant girl, comparing herself with the boy, considers herself genitally handicapped. He did not take the next step, the conclusion to the subjective view of unsightliness, although his later assertions clearly point in this direction, for example that the girl consoles herself with the awareness that she appears to be pretty and will be content that her breasts are developing and her figure is becoming graceful.

It is perhaps necessary at this point to state that the relationship of the girl to her mother undergoes a change after the discovery of her different anatomical makeup: she turns away from mother as if she were disappointed in her mother for not bearing her as a boy. In contrast, the little boy becomes proud as the possessor of a penis and emulates his father, whose strength he admires.

We came to the conclusion that there were no inferiority feelings with regard to her genitals in the little girl during the first years of her life. She experiences that inferiority feeling only after the discovery of the anatomical difference—an experience to which we may well attribute a traumatic effect. Mind you, this infantile feminine view is purely subjective. An old psychoanalyst, Dr. Ludwig Jekels, who died in 1954, reacted to complaints of some of his women patients in a picturesque way, saying: "How can you complain? Why, you have an entire department store. You are endowed with eggs, milk, a nest, and soft linings."

This is the place to refer to the part women play in men's lives apart from their function in the perpetuation of the species. Restricting ourselves to the consequences and effect of that great discovery in childhood, we are aware that the care and maintainance of beauty and charm is entrusted to them. I do not mean only the beauty of their own bodies which we all admire, but the creation of beauty in the home, which is an unconscious extension of their bodies. In this aspect we are indebted to women for the comfort we enjoy. The cradle into which the baby is put signifies a recapturing of a situation similar to the one which the embryo found in the womb; the home you live in is merely an extension. The secretions of the female body have the effect that the girl acquires a special feeling for cleanliness not only for herself, but also for her surroundings, a sense which is transmitted to her children in her later role as mother. The mental and emotional transformations during female puberty produce, as Helene Deutsch has shown in her monumental study *Psychology of Woman,* the girl's intuition and tact. The turning of activity inward, in contrast to the direction it takes in the boy, has the effect that the girl becomes more and more feminine in the best sense of the word. We shall not discuss the psychological consequences of pregnancy and motherhood, so as not to deviate too far from our subject. We would thus arrive at the inevitable conclusion that the hand that rocks the cradle rules the world.

Freud has made us familiar with the idea that morality was created by men as a reaction to that mythical crime of primeval ages. But before morals entered society, women were the educators of men, since they are the first educators of the baby. Women taught men how to feel human warmth, conveyed love, secured comfort and beauty for the child as well as for mankind during the period of its first growth. Women still do, for mankind is still in the making.

2 : The Unspecified Form

1. The Irreducible Minimum

Before entering into the discussion concerning the nature of the need to be loved, let us ask a preliminary question: Is the need universal, and is there in all of us an irreducible minimum of that need? We all need certain things from life, not only food, shelter, and so on, but we are all searching instinctively for certain emotional satisfactions. Does the need to be liked, acknowledged, or loved belong to those needed things?

We shall not search for an answer in the area of biology, but in the realm of everyday life. In his introduction to Oscar Levant's *A Smattering of Ignorance,* S. N. Behrman relates an anecdote that is not only characteristic of the musician, but is of a more general psychological interest. Levant once told Behrman that he had encountered a person whom both of them knew, and had walked along with him, finding him pleasant and agreeable. Behrman expressed his astonishment, since this man had always been

Levant's pet hate. "Well," said Levant, "you know, I hate 'em till they say hello to me."

Now the experience from psychoanalytic practice: A patient whom I saw only a few times, a Mr. Hart, was a refugee from Hitler's Nazi Germany. He tried his luck as a Fuller Brush salesman, wandering from door to door, but had no success. Discouraged, he sat in parks and hotel lobbies and felt depressed. Then, by a fortunate accident, he got a sum of money from a relative and opened a small store. Mr. Hart was full of confidence, and soon customers came in to buy his goods. Some of them asked his advice not only about the wares he had to sell, but also wanted his opinion concerning their family difficulties. Mr. Hart felt more than satisfied; he felt happy and functioned well as businessman and adviser. The whole psychological difference was that, before, he had to go to people, and now people came to him. Previously he had felt like a peddler or even a beggar; now he had attained a new feeling of self-importance. With this increase of self-confidence the battle was won, at least for the time being.

What is it that the Levant anecdote and this observation have in common psychologically? What can we learn from everyday experiences with respect to our subject, the minimum need to be loved?

The two experiences, I think, show that every man who does not live in a social vacuum needs a certain amount of acknowledgment or love. Even Robinson Crusoe on his island was dependent on Friday's admiration and certainly anticipated with pleasure the time when, returned to civilization, he would be admired by listeners to his tales of adventure. In Donne's words, "No man is an Island entire to itself"—not even a man alone on an island, because he lives in a society of fantasy.

Oscar Levant, whose hate vanishes when another man shows unsolicited friendliness toward him, and my patient who blossomed when people came to him and asked for his advice—both react with affection when they feel that they are needed. How little is sufficient to make people feel appreciated, welcomed, and liked! An unexpected "Hello" on the street and a casual "Mr. Hart, what is your opinion?" Such random instances show how easily a minimum of that social need to be loved can be satisfied.

That need is, of course, individually variable. It differs according to the society in which a person is born and bred, according to sex, and to various sociological factors. Heredity and environment both have an influence upon how great or small that need in the individual will be. Early education plays an important part. Biological factors also, which we shall discuss later, must be considered as well.

To mention one difference: women usually need more to be needed than men. It is one of their vital psychological necessities. But is it only psychological in character? It has deep biological roots, because any mature woman is potentially a mother who must take care of a child. If she has none another person (or several) will take the place of the child.

Indeed, the need is universal, however variable individually. After having answered that preliminary question concerning the necessary minimum of its satisfaction, may we venture to reach further and ask: what is the maximum? It is certainly a far cry from that small gratification felt when an acquaintance casually says "Hello" to that climax. We can name the maximum satisfaction of that social need. We call it happiness.

2. *The Minimum and the Maximum*

Freud asserted that happiness is contained in the fulfillment of our childhood wishes. (He added that the possession of money does not make one happy because wealth was not among the wishes we have as children.) I am inclined to qualify this statement of my master and friend. I would rather say that we feel happy when the wishes of our childhood *seem* to come true. Not the objective actuality, but the impression we have is decisive. A salesman will, for instance, feel childishly happy when the president of his company expresses enthusiastic approval of his activity and praises his

work in broadening the territory, or when his superior salesman-
ship is acknowledged among other employees. That is not the concept of fame he had as a child—rather a drastic modification of it;
but does it really matter?

The girl who daydreamed (as a child) that Prince Charming
would come on his white steed to marry her is perhaps ecstatically
happy when that flatfooted salesman arrives on the train from
Chicago and proposes to her. He is Prince Charming for her, and no
one derives greater happiness than this girl when she can show off
her engagement ring to her friends. She and her salesman fiancé,
exuberant with joy about his achievement, have experienced the
fulfillment of their childhood wishes, however modified and qualified. They still live in the world of fairy tales.

How little is needed to make people happy! We think of that
minimum of satisfaction of the need to be loved and it makes us
wonder. It sounds like the refrain of a song.

Happiness is restricted to hours, if not to minutes, and can be
sometimes easily achieved; but to achieve enduring contentment
is quite another matter.

3. *Digression on Psychoanalytic Technique*

Do I dare to turn off into a side path at this point after trying to answer the question of the minimum and maximum satisfaction of
that universal need to be loved?

Among the various schools that have departed from psychoanalysis is one that emphasizes that the relationship between the
psychoanalyst and patient is a kind of business relationship. Those
therapists argue that the patient comes to us to get rid of his neurotic troubles and we do our best to help him. There is neither
friendship nor personal connection between him and us. The absurdity of such an attitude in which the transference process is, so
to speak, a superfluous formation is too obvious for discussion. The
positive transference the patient develops from the beginning of
his treatment, wherein he revives his affection for persons near

and dear in his childhood, is the wind that moves our mill. To build such a positive attitude in the patient, to win his trust and make him confide in the therapist, is one of the first important tasks of the analyst.

But I wanted to demonstrate what role that universal need to be liked and to be acknowledged plays in psychoanalytic treatment. It is, for instance, reflected in a seemingly unimportant detail.

Patients are always encouraged when the therapist gives even the slightest attention to their everyday life. Receiving a patient for his or her session, the psychoanalyst usually avoids the conventional "How do you do?" or "How are you?" and asks instead, "How was the dinner party yesterday?" or, "Did you enjoy the theatre performance on Thursday?" In asking these or similar questions, not only does he prove his good memory of what the patient has said, but shows the special attention he has paid to his words. Such trivial features reach beyond the realm of psychoanalytic technique into the region of basic human relations.

While psychoanalysis has, in the words of Freud, to be performed in abstinence, which means in frustrating the most urgent wishes of the patient, that minimum of his need to be loved can and must be satisfied.

4. *An Argument Is Advanced*

I do not intend to present a scholarly and exhaustive treatise on the need of being loved, but to view as many aspects of the problem as possible. The previous chapter dealt with the relation of that need with happiness. Obviously, the frustration of such a pressing need makes us unhappy, but does its satisfaction always make people happy? Is there anything like being unhappily loved?

It is easy to imagine that to be loved does not always make for happiness. Yes, in certain instances it can even add to unhappiness—when, for example, one cannot reciprocate that feeling. There are other situations in which being loved is not the aim of the most urgent wishes of men. One of those situations is found in a little story contained in the charming tale "La Chemise," of Anatole France's *Les Sept Femmes de la Barbe Bleu*.

In that tale, which does not disavow its kinship with fairy tales, two high government officials of King Charles are at his order searching for a happy person among the people of the entire kingdom. Their search is in vain until they decide that the only happiness of men is to be loved. They encounter young and handsome Jacques de Neville, who is loved by all women. This young man then tells them the following story, in which they see his own destiny reflected.

A young merchant in Baghdad awoke one morning and wished with all the power of his soul to be loved by all women. A genie appeared and told him, "Your wish will be realized from now on!" The merchant jumped from his bed and quickly dressed, full of dreams of the many and various pleasures awaiting him. Scarcely had he taken a few steps outside when a terribly ugly old woman, who distilled wine in her cellar, saw him and was overcome by infatuation for him. When she blew him kisses, he turned his head away, but she seized his leg and pulled him into her cellar and kept him prisoner there for twenty years.

We may conclude from this melancholy tale that to be loved does not always bring happiness. Certain circumstances must be present, certain conditions must be fulfilled if happiness through being loved is to be achieved. Finally, it may be that there is something in the nature of being loved that is not completely satisfying. We can guess what this may be. No affection or tenderness compares to the love lavished upon us as babies. Our efforts to recapture mother's love are bound to fall short of those early and indelible impressions. Furthermore, to be loved without loving is not a blessing but a curse in disguise.

3 : Very Early and Very Late

1. *The Life Phases*

It is tempting to explore in which way the need to be loved changes during the seven ages of men and women. Nothing of this kind, as far as we know, has been attempted. The only exception I accidentally found are some humorous lines of Dick Holst of Los Angeles, who delineates the ages of women:

> In her infancy she needs love and care,
> In her childhood she wants fun.
> In her twenties she wants romance.
> In her thirties she wants admiration.
> In her forties she wants sympathy.
> In her fifties she wants cash.

Limitations of space, among other considerations, forbid us to follow that need through the ages of men. We will then restrict ourselves to a discussion of its significance for infancy and to a sketch of its role in old age.

William Menninger justifiably states, "We learn how to love only when we are loved." [5] A child is born with as little of the ability to love as with the ability to read. He or she has to learn both in the most elementary school of life, in the experience of earliest childhood. A child who was never kissed will never kiss anyone.

S. Ferenczi, one of Freud's earliest students, formulated the sentence, "The unloved child dies, and if it does not die maybe it were better that it did." This harsh conclusion can only partly be justified by pointing to the unfavorable vicissitudes of boys who were not loved in childhood. The sociologists Sheldon and Eleanor Glueck of Harvard who wrote the monumental book *The Making of a Delinquent* arrived at the thesis that the difference between the delinquent and the nondelinquent youth is that "the former was brought up in a home lacking a father's guidance and a mother's love while the latter, though living under circumstances equally difficult, did enjoy some social direction from the father and some affection from the mother." Eleanor Roosevelt arrived at the same insight: at a national conference of penologists she said, "Our prisons are full because their inmates' mothers did not know how to love them in childhood."

A noted psychoanalyst, Dr. René Spitz, approached the problem of the unloved child from the clinical point of view. In numerous excellent papers he showed how many of the psychogenic diseases in childhood are to be traced to lack or loss of love. He described a striking syndrome in early childhood, studied the life of infants in a foundling's home, and pointed out what prophylaxis and treatment was possible in cases of psychiatric disorders of this kind.[6]

A psychiatrist, Smiley Blanton, published a book titled *Love or Perish*. In the light of the researches of René Spitz, of Anna Freud, Dorothy Burlingham, and others the more justified alternative should be formulated as "Be Loved or Perish."

Just a few words should be added here about the need to be loved in old age. Old age is an attempt at recapturing youth or even infancy. Old people let themselves die when they recognize that they are no longer needed or wanted. In a very instructive and interesting study K. R. Eissler showed that the influx of unasked for and unambivalent love helped patients in whom cancer had destroyed the will to live.[7] Even the anticipation of near death is mitigated by love. This does not mean that dying is made easier for those patients, but that they are less afraid of it.

4 : The Perverted Form

1. Love At Any Price

Since the publication of my book *Masochism in Modern Man* in 1941, quite a few new psychoanalytic contributions have enlarged and deepened our understanding of the masochistic character, or as the late Dr. Eduard Bergler called it, "psychic masochism." Instead of presenting a survey of writings published in these twenty-two years, I shall point to a contribution which seems to me especially valuable.

I have two reasons for bringing Jules Nydes' lecture on the paranoid masochistic character into prominence, other than its psychological significance. The lecture, given at the New York Society of Clinical Psychologists in 1959, is, alas, still unpublished and thus known only to a small circle of psychologists. Secondly, an essential part of it is of special relevance to our subject, the need to be loved.

Nydes in his lecture compares the attitude of the masochist

and of the paranoid character toward love and points out a very interesting contrast. The masochistic character renounces power and dignity for the sake of being loved. The paranoid character is ready to sacrifice love and affection in order to feel power and carry out his will.

In this context we are most interested in the psychology of the masochistic character which tries to get love "at any price." In a previous book[8] I presented the case of a two-and-a-half-year-old boy to illustrate the emergence of a masochistic character. The child was admonished not to tear pages from books, but did not obey. The father, who finally lost patience, slapped him. The weeping child followed the father, who was pacing the room, and shouted, "Daddy, kiss me, give me a kiss!" The behavior pattern of the masochistic character emerges here clearly. Let me add an instance of the behavior of the same boy, now more than three years old. When the child is frustrated, he sometimes strikes his parents. His father admonishes him: "Don't hit Daddy; don't hit Mummy!" The boy shouts, "I hit myself!" and does so. Impulses of violence turned against oneself are the kind that bring about masochistic perversions.

This character type degrades and humiliates and often ingratiates himself. He has only one aim: to be loved. He is not only willing but eager to sacrifice everything else, to take abuse and punishment of every kind, if he can only gain this end.

Nydes graciously acknowledges that he continues the research into the psychology of the masochistic character which I described in my book, *Masochism in Modern Man*. Since the publication of this work I have arrived at certain new insights that partly confirm the finding of Nydes. In *Masochism in Modern Man* I had already formulated the essence and the concealed aim of masochism as "Victory through defeat."

New psychoanalytic experiences have led me to add another formulation to this previous one: the masochistic character unconsciously aims at a triumph in precisely the area where he has suffered his crushing defeat. In human relations this means the

unconditional surrender of the very person before whom he humiliated himself or who had degraded him. As he once accepted all
kinds of humiliation and shameful disgrace, he, often unknown
to himself, strives to bring the object to full submission and humble
subjection. On rare occasions this secret aim may even become
conscious, as in the following case. A woman whom I observed in
psychoanalytic treatment was a very domineering and strong-
willed person who henpecked her husband, who complied with all
her wishes. Strangely enough, she always complained about his
stubbornness because he was adamant and unyielding concerning
a few issues. It became necessary on one occasion for the husband
to have a consultation with me. Speaking of his wife, he said:
"She always tried to have me under her thumb, but she was frustrated by my compliance."

Another hint along the same path came from the psychoanalytic
observation of another masochistic man who was once rejected by
his wife when he wanted to have sexual intercourse with her. He
remained friendly but aloof during the following years but never
again approached his wife and disregarded her advances. Life
with him became a silent duel of will with the headstrong woman
who argued with him and nagged him; he always yielded and took
her pestering without complaint. In this way he finally broke her
will. Weepingly she asked him to sleep with her. Her unconditional
surrender was thus accomplished.

The new aspect we meet in these and other cases is interesting.
They convey the impression that the masochistic character shows
a bull-headed stubbornness proved not only in obtaining his irksome masochistic aims but also in gaining unconscious or concealed
ends.

We would not have expected this attitude, so contradictory to
the pattern of absolute submission to the will of another person.
We were not prepared to meet with such hidden energy and
scheming of the masochistic character who passively acquiesces in
the wish of his object. It seemed he would think in terms of the

Ninth Beatitude, formulated by Eugene V. Debs: "Blessed be they who expect nothing, for they shall not be disappointed."

Instead of such humbleness we are confronted with an unconscious determination, an extraordinary effort, when the masochist has been thrown into the black pit of despair—just then he is climbing up again. It is as if he said to himself during ascent, "Where you had your worst defeat, there you should have your decisive victory." The ultimate aim of the masochistic character reveals itself only later on—if he becomes aware of it at all.

But our surprise should not overwhelm us when we think of the soil from which the masochist character springs and of the progressive course of his perverted attitude. In a psychoanalytic seminar conducted for students I once compared the opposite attitudes of the sadist and of the masochist with the outside and inside of a glove. Although the inside looks quite different from the outer part, it is made of the same material: in this case the intensity and force of the original drive. We know from Freud that passive drive-aims can also be followed with the utmost energy and stubbornness. In the case of the masochistic character this aim would be to be loved. The final goal, however, is to obtain power over others.

A New York psychoanalyst spoke jokingly the other day of the "power of negative thinking." As a pattern it could be expressed as follows: "I can do anything I want, but I would rather die than do it." This "power of negative thinking" is the essence of the masochistic character with his iron will to fail and his successful attempts of self-sabotage. Masochists are—one would at first think unaccountably—of optimistic temperament. The more you recognize the psychological motives of the masochistic character, the better you will understand that it could not be otherwise. In the background of the masochistic temperament is the unconscious, absolute hope of ultimate victory as reward for so many sacrifices and painful humiliations. With such an outlook, what else can he be but an optimist?

The resistance he encounters in his social and love relations presents a challenge to the masochist. He meets it in his own manner, mostly by submission, but we occasionally discover in the type of person who turns the other cheek one who is ruthless, reckless, and remorseless.

It should not surprise us, then, when we do find behind this defense a great energy, used in reaching the other, positive aim. The need to be loved is vividly experienced by the masochistic character. This ardent wish, "Love at any price," is often fulfilled because it prevails and because that need becomes imperative.

2. *Masochism of Great Men*

Great innovators and original thinkers and artists attract the wrath of the mediocrities as lightning rods draw the flashes. The originality of their thought is as provoking as the prominence of the lightning conductor which directs the electricity to the salient point on the roof. It is not the mob which is concerned, but the mediocrity, the majority of the *Bildungsphilister* (the narrow-mindedness of educated men) as Nietzsche calls them, that is offended by the originality or by the new findings, and will not easily forgive them.

All great men who gave mankind new ideas were ridiculed, persecuted, or worse. The history of ideas, from Socrates and Jesus of Nazareth to Semmelweis and Sister Kenny, confirms the ubiquity of persecution to which those innovators were subjected.

These introductory remarks were stimulated by rereading Thomas Mann's book *Leiden und Grösse der Meister* (Suffering and Greatness of the Masters), and by the memory of a comment by Freud, whose name undoubtedly belongs to the long list of those humiliated and persecuted victims of mediocrity. Freud once spoke of the compact majority that attacked him as a "wolf pack" that falls upon those who want to bestow a benefit upon them. It was said emotionlessly, as an objective statement, rather like a diagnosis and not as an expression of personal feeling.

The impression of Mann's book was not undivided. Some criticism emerged along with admiration. Not all parts of the book show equal psychological penetration, although it is clear that the writer had high ambitions in this direction as in others.

My main objection to Thomas Mann's book, which presents an excellent picture of some highly creative and original personalities, comes from the psychological—properly speaking, the psychoanalytic—angle. My objection does not concern an error but a lack. The presentation neglects to acknowledge and to evaluate a very important though elusive emotional factor in the development and in the vicissitudes of these great men. This invisible but palpable factor, operating behind the wings, is the unconscious social masochism of the masters and great innovators.

That means that a great deal of their suffering was unconsciously stage-managed and sometimes provoked by themselves. Mind you, I do not assert that Beethoven would have suffered less if he had been less rude and conceited. I do not say that Socrates would have had a better fate if he had not been so straightforward in teaching the young Athenians. I merely assert that these great men and most others, aware of the misunderstanding to which their work was exposed and of the hostility it evoked, could have taken those negative reactions of their environment more patiently and more graciously. Well, they were human; they were not supermen. But how about the curses and insults of Beethoven against all his enemies; how about the abruptness with which young Freud broke off with all friends who did not acknowledge his new and shocking findings? Going beyond these to the highest realm, how about the attacks of Jesus against the Pharisees and his offensive actions in the synagogue? Here an agressiveness and violence breaks through, especially while the men were still young, which gave their enemies a plausible justification for personal hostility.

But I wanted to discuss the unconscious masochism of those great and creative personalities. Their behavior in such critical situations as those just mentioned certainly belongs to this sphere, since it must be regarded as self-sabotaging and self-damaging, which means to the acknowledgment and acceptance of their work, since most people do not differentiate between the person and his achievement. There were very few Viennese one hundred and fifty years ago who would say, "That Beethoven is an arrogant and violent brute, but he is a genius."

To those factors pointing to the operating of an unconscious masochism I count the exclusiveness of their statements, their unconditionalness, their unwillingness to allow concessions, and their refusal to compromise. A compliant attitude would perhaps, especially in a certain phase of their life, have paved the way to an earlier acceptance of their original ideas. But that possibility seemed to be precluded by certain characteristic features of their personality. It is, for instance, very significant that Freud, late in life and in the advanced phase of his thinking, made such concessions (e.g., for the role of aggressiveness), allowed concessions which he would have sternly refused a few decades earlier.

One is tempted to guess at some of the characteristics of great men. One trait must have been an intense ambition in childhood, at first vague in its aims; and this early ambition must have been thwarted. It is not important whether the ambition was concerned only with the family or with one member of it, whether it was actually frustrated or merely in the boy's thoughts. That thwarting had definite psychological consequences: it led to masochistic fantasies on one hand, and to a defiant attitude on the other hand. A detailed psychoanalytic investigation into the early life of those exceptional people would show how this twin reaction develops and what different emotional forms it takes in the various individuals.

Among the masochistic fantasies one special daydream is worth mentioning, since it is to be found in different forms in the early life of those men, later considered trail-blazers of civilization. I mean the daydream that the boy is misunderstood by parents and teachers, that he dies, and then the world recognizes that he was someone special and especially endowed. This typical prepuberty fantasy has all the earmarks of a masochistic fantasy: the suffering, the feeling of not being appreciated, the suspense factor, and the final triumph after one's death. To give only two instances which show how long remnants of some of those childhood fantasies are retained: Gustav Mahler used to say: "One need not be still alive when one becomes immortal." Freud predicted the victory of psychoanalysis after his death.

The roots of that unconscious masochistic attitude are to be found in early childhood. Alma Maria Mahler in her memoirs reports that Mahler, as a boy, was once asked what he wanted to become; he replied: "A martyr." In the letters of young Freud to his bride one finds a readiness and willingness to suffer and even to die for his new discoveries. Even much later, in 1927, he used the expression, "defiant courage of truth," to characterize his basic attitude.

Sometimes, as with Freud, those superior minds are sure that after a time in which their original ideas are refused their findings will be rescued from oblivion. The suspense, that inherent factor in the psychology of the masochistic attitude, is experienced by them, in that phase of waiting and that hope for the future, and, not infrequently, for posterity. (No doubt such patient expectancy is also interrupted by doubts and insidious self-criticisms and self-torment—themselves manifestations of the underlying masochistic attitude. They can even take the form of doubt, well-expressed in Arthur Schnitzler's sentence, "Posterity also exists only for the living.")

The general and typical attitude remains the certainty that, once men recognize the originality of their thinking, all the suffering and privations will not have been in vain—a typical masochistic attitude I tried to put into the formula "Victory through Defeat." Some of those daring innovators spend a lifetime in getting their ideas across. Ideas take a very long time to penetrate when they are original and when they contradict the orthodox thinking of the experts. The block in the professional mind seems sometimes to prevent their emergence forever.

The original thinkers or artists are never joiners, and they enjoy for some years their isolation which seems to be a necessary condition for their creativity. (Here, one cannot help thinking of the significant processes of withdrawal and return such as Arnold Toynbee describes in the life of Jesus, Buddha, and others.) Yet this isolation has its pains as well as its sweetness; it is filled with bitterness toward a society that withholds its recognition, a society whose honors are despised and yet passionately desired—a society hated but at the same time loved. The thinker or artist knows how necessary isolation is for him during the most critical period of his life. He might fully accept the wisdom of an Italian proverb: *"Si tu serai solo, tu serai tutto tuo."* Yet his longings are directed to understanding students or admirers, to the company of congenial minds.

The society and its reactions are, of course, replacing the original persons from whom recognition and acknowledgment was desired, namely, the family of the especially endowed child.

The final point I would like to make and drive home is provided by the unconscious enjoyment of that misery and loneliness of the great minds, a bitter satisfaction and acceptance for the time being. Freud explained the negative reaction of his environment, saying, "I had touched the world in its sleep," and declared that one has to be prepared for the unwilling or cross reaction of the slumberer who does not wish to be disturbed.

That bitter enjoyment of one's own suffering is scarcely missed in the life of great innovators in science and art when one listens to their life-melody "with the third ear." Nietzsche himself is a good example of that masochistic attitude when we imagine his loneliness in Sils Maria.

There are, of course, other characteristics common to the men of genius of whom we speak, features of character and of special gifts. It seems to me useful to call attention to the masochistic factor in their attitude and conduct of life—an unconscious factor that has been till now utterly neglected.

5 : The Neurotic Craving for Affection

1. *The Origin of the Notion*

Is there a neurotic need to be loved, clearly discernible and separable from the "normal" need? As far as I can see, Sandor Ferenczi was the first analyst who emphatically asserted the existence of such an abnormal craving;[9] Karen Horney and others followed after him on this track.[10] Around 1927, Ferenczi developed the theory that neurotics are people who have never been accepted or loved as children and experience an abnormal craving for love and acceptance. He believed that children react to the personality of their parents long before they learn the meaning of words.

From these basic ideas a new technique of psychoanalytic treatment resulted for Ferenczi: the patient should have a new experience with the psychoanalyst in an atmosphere of tolerance. The personality of the psychoanalyst thus becomes an instrument of cure. The analyst, proclaimed Ferenczi, should admit his faults and mistakes to the patient, and really has to like and accept him or her. The most significant innovation of Ferenczi's technique was the dramatization of the psychoanalytic technique in treating the patient as if he were three years old and even talking baby talk with him, petting him, and so on.

Ferenczi's new method was severely criticized by Freud and others who denied that offering this kind of love to the patient was appropriate to the analytic treatment. Ferenczi soon found that he could not give enough love to the patient, whose demand for love is insatiable. The psychotherapeutic results of the new method were disappointing. Ferenczi died in 1933 and his method was given up, but the problem of a neurotic need for affection remained unsolved and was often approached by other psychoanalysts.

2. *Is There a Neurotic Craving for Affection?*

The basic question to be answered is, of course: Does a neurotic need to be loved exist? Karen Horney opens the discussion by pointing out that our culture favors such an exaggerated need. She does not deny the normal character of those drives, but asserts that they change their character when anxiety plays the greatest role behind them.[10] Such a craving for affection is so frequent and so easily recognizable in neuroses that it must be considered one of the surest indicators of an existing anxiety. The neurotic person is incapable of loving, yet is in great need of being loved.

Searching for characteristic differences between neurotic and normal need for love, Horney arrives at a recognition of certain significant variations; for instance, that the feeling of affection is primary in normal love, whereas with the neurotic the primary feeling is the need for reassurance; and the illusion of loving is merely secondary. (Horney admits, however, that there are all sorts of "intermediary conditions.") There are other differences, for instance the compulsiveness of the neurotic need that becomes a vital necessity and leads to an overevaluation of the actual significance of being liked. The neurotic feels as if his existence, happiness, and security depend on being liked. This need is attached to everyone without discrimination, and the neurotic is ready to pay any price for the affection he craves. His quest is for unconditional love.

The most important psychological difference is, however, that the neurotic need for love has the character of being a protection against "basic anxiety." Horney,[11] who is occasionally quite imaginative in her presentation, uses a poignant comparison which I shall here adopt. A person walking far off in the country climbs a tree in order to observe something there. This is a situation comparable to the normal need of loving. But the situation is quite different when we imagine the person climbing a tree because he is being chased by a bear. In this situation, comparable to the neurotic craving for affection, anxiety plays the greater role. Climbing the tree is a measure of protection and serves as a reassurance against danger.

What is this tense anxiety that creates that exaggerated need for affection? Horney answers: Anxiety results from hostility. Anxiety and hostility are "inextricably interwoven."

Before starting the discussion, I want to state that there is enough psychological evidence to assume that there is a distinct neurotic need for affection clearly recognizable and separable from the normal need.

3. Discussion

As far as I can see, neither Horney nor any of her students explain the character of that "basic anxiety" beyond saying that it is intimately connected with hostility. This vagueness could easily be identified later with the *"Lebensangst"* of which Existentialism speaks. In what way is it connected with hostility, how does it create the neurotic craving for affection, and how does it offer protection to the patient?

This is not the place to deal with all these problems, but a few critical remarks are called for here. In the theory of Horney and her students, the neurotic need to be loved appears as a reaction to hostility. I doubt that hostility is the psychologically appropriate expression in this context. Following an excellent remark of S. Rado, I suggest that the word "violence" should replace the term "hostility." Only violent tendencies or offshoots of impulses of this kind make necessary such reactions as an exaggerated craving for affection. Hostility, however intensively experienced, remains in the emotional sphere whereas violence pushes the person in the direction of attack and thus gains "the name of action."

The great advantage derived from the replacement of hostility by violence will be recognized immediately when one follows the origin and development of the neurotic need of being loved. The child who is frustrated and reacts in an intensive manner experiences not simply hostility, but wants to strike out, wants to attack those persons who are in his way. Stated differently: he feels violent tendencies, expressed in initial muscular movements. The reaction to his becoming violent, towards his parents for instance, is fear of punishment from them; in a later phase of his development, fear of losing their love.

From this arises the possibility of the origin of a neurotic craving for affection, if other emotional factors are added. The fear of losing the love of those most important persons is, of course, at its core fear of the swift retribution that is anticipated. In later phases of the child's development that fear takes the form of guilt feeling, often of an unconscious nature. We meet that unconscious guilt feeling in most cases of neurosis. It is expressed in various forms, but it reveals its character as social anxiety. At first directed only to the parents and their substitutes, it is frequently generalized and displaced. The basic anxiety against which the neurotic need for being loved is built, is thus of the nature of unconscious guilt feeling, originated as a reaction to intensive violent impulses. I am not in a position to evaluate the progress that would be achieved by tracing the neurotic craving for affection, but it seems to me that a theoretical and technical step forward here is marked by such a novel approach to the psychological problem of the neurotic need of being loved.

4. *Nonviolence*

I mentioned previously a suggestion of Dr. Sandor Rado in a conversation with me[12] to replace the vague term "hostility" or "aggression" by "violence," which seems to me very valuable as a conceptual as well as technical improvement. To give proof of this it provides the most important part of the answer to an essential psychological question: Why do women have fewer and less intensive guilt feelings than men?

The question itself is not controversial: all unbiased observers of women will agree about this difference from men. When you focus on the nature of guilt feeling as moral reaction to wrongdoing, you do not answer the question, but beg it. If you conceive of guilt feeling as reaction to hostility (as is often done in psychoanalytic literature), the answer eludes you. It cannot be denied that there is a great deal of hostility, manifest and repressed, in women, hostility towards other women (some people even assert that this is the basic attitude of one woman to another), as well as toward men.

This psychological situation is, however, radically changed when you substitute the expression "violence" or "brutal force" for the term "hostility." We then confront another question: Are women less violent? Or, to say it in other words: Are they less inclined and able to commit violent deeds than men? The answer is decidedly in the affirmative. We know that there are fewer murders committed by women than by men. Murderous assault and bloodshed, killing and massacres are very rarely committed by women. No doubt some women are capable of it, are bloodthirsty, but they rarely commit homicidal acts. As masculine a woman as Lady Macbeth, who is tempted to murder the king, shies away from it at the last moment. The lines:

> Had he not resembled
> My father as he slept, I had done't. . . .

perhaps does not give the whole story. Something within her resisted the bloody deed.

Are women less violent than men, or do they less frequently resort to violence than males? The answer is that women, for biological reasons and because of their education to the functions of womanhood, do not develop those intensive drives of brutal force. Their physical makeup does not push them to the use of force and to acts of violence. They are perhaps not the weaker sex in the conventional sense, but they use other means than violence to achieve their aims. Girls are early educated by their mothers to suppress such tendencies.

If, as I assume, guilt feeling is the reaction to violent and murderous impulses, it would be easily understandable that women in general experience fewer guilt feelings than men. Lady Macbeth is thus to be considered the exception that proves the rule.

One can assume that the relative infrequency of violent and brutal impulses in woman is biologically determined by the basic function nature has allotted to her, namely, as the perpetuator and guardian of life. Women are delegated by nature to continue the existence of the human species.

"Force," says Abraham Lincoln, "is all-conquering, but its victories are short-lived."

6 : The Moral Climber

1. A Digression

Freud often accused our civilization of hypocrisy. I vividly remember a lecture in which he pointed out that the habitual hypocrisy is not restricted to denial of sexual needs, but also to the disavowal of hostile, aggressive, and violent tendencies. They reside in every one of us and we must learn to live with them. Freud laid the responsibility of that mistake particularly on our education, which gives children the wrong idea that they are surrounded only by good and kind people. In denying the "evil" side of human nature the children grow up with a very exaggerated concept of mankind and feel especially guilty whenever they experience the emergence of hostile and aggressive, envious and malicious impulses—not to mention the inevitable disappointments in social intercourse.

The lecture of which I speak must have been during World War I—perhaps in its initial phases, before I went into the army. Also, I remember it vividly because of a patient whom I treated at the time. She was a middle-aged woman who had several complaints about her husband: the one that concerns us here was that he scolded their two children at the dinner table whenever they did not finish the food on their plates. He repeatedly spoke of the Belgian children who, at the time of the German invasion, had not enough to eat, and he compared their situation with that of his own more fortunate children. The result of his scolding was that the children lost their desire to eat because they felt so sorry for the unfortunate Belgians.

I pursue Freud's train of thought when I add that the education of adults moves even further, beyond the aims of children's education. At least theoretically man is ahead of himself in the moral demands with which he is confronted. This is why I called modern man a moral climber, who lives far beyond his physiological and psychological means.[13] The theory that man is or should be good, kind and noble because this is his original nature sets an impossibly high ethical standard. In accepting this ideal, in trying to conform to it and to measure up to it, he has adapted the thesis of Tertullian, that the soul is *"naturaliter christiana,"* originally Christian. He has become a self-torturer whenever he deviates from that ideal even in his thoughts. The Christians of antiquity were sometimes thrown to the lions; the Christians of our time are often devoured by remorse, a word derived from the Latin *remordere* (to bite). This is especially the case whenever they sin against those too high moral expectations they are supposed to fulfill.

The pedagogical method in this madness was based on the hope that mankind will be wise, kind and noble. We know that the educators overshot the mark. The events of our age, with its wars, gas chambers, menace of annihilation of millions of people by the H-bomb, prove that that program was a fantastic, self-imposed illusion, a colossal unreality. Man refused to give the devil a fair chance. He did not want to believe that men of good will also have malicious and violent impulses. That leap beyond man's shadow— that *salto morale*—failed. A little of moral ambition is a lot, and a lot of it is too much. Pascal recognized that he who tries to be an angel will end in becoming a beast. (*"Qui veut faire l'ange, fait la bête."*)

Western man is like the servant who sweeps the dust under the carpet so that it may not be seen. In denying his true nature man became an inveterate moral climber. There are in our midst millions of casualties of an exaggerated moral ideal that cannot be brought in harmony with human nature. Man does not step over dead bodies he has killed, but stumbles over the bodies of those whom he has murdered in his thoughts. The danger no longer comes from without, but from within.

The moral climber hopes in vain to improve the inner world by exaggerated demands, by waving the flag of high ideals that contradict the human condition. Men would live happier with themselves and with others if they could adopt a more modest concept of their nature. Charity begins at home. A Jewish proverb says, "He who cannot be good to himself cannot be good to others." To injure others is certainly wrong, but it is equally wrong to sabotage and injure oneself. It is not only more realistic, but also more dignified to acknowledge our violent and sexual needs.

At this point I yield to the temptation to insert a few remarks about a typical American attitude, aware of the risk that they will make me notorious rather than popular.

It is very likely that our do-gooders have caused considerable damage, but it is certain that the think-gooders have brought terrible misery upon mankind, especially when they were in the position of statesmen and leaders. The think-gooders are the people who have a very high concept of human nature and believe that only certain forms of government or other institutions of civilization corrupted men. As Abbé Coignard in Anatole France's stories pointed out, people of the think-gooder kind, who are wayward idealists of the purest strain, are bound to be cruel if men do not conform to the ideal picture they have made of them. The French Revolution sent thousands of people to the guillotine on account of such incongruity of preconceived idea and reality; Hitler thrust some million people into gas chambers because they were not what he decided men should be like.

As that gentle Abbé Jerome Coignoird of Anatole France recognized, only statesmen and educators who have a very modest concept of human nature—including their own—will be kind and tolerant toward others. Only leaders who see men as a species of higher ape that can be tamed only so far, will be good to their subjects and will reign wisely. Extreme idealists should be excluded from every influence upon people and kept in reserved areas where they can fight each other. Their zeal should never be unleashed upon people.

The last taboo of mankind, avoiding forbidden and dangerous thoughts, must be removed. There are no illegitimate thoughts. Self-respect demands that we acknowledge also those children of our brain as our own.

Robert Browning demanded that

> . . . a man's reach should exceed his grasp,
> Or what's a heaven for?

Certainly not for aiming at it or for reaching it. Even the biblical legend of the Tower of Babel conveys an earnest warning that should alarm a too ambitious mankind.

The moral climber of Western civilization has overreached himself in his moral ideas. Freud, Anatole France, and other enlightened minds have shown that there is only one way possible for him. He must climb down.

7 : The Psychotic Form

PSYCHOANALYSIS OF EROTOMANIA*

1. The Psychiatric Term

The statements which attempt to make the meaning of the notion of erotomania clearly show how arbitrary and subjective definitions are. The Greek derivation is composed of *eros* (love) and *mania* (madness), and its meaning is clear: it signifies raving love. Usually it is conceived as mental alienation, which is the effect of love or love-sickness. According to Webster, erotomania is an excess of erotic desire, an extravagant affection for some person. *The New Oxford Universal Dictionary* defines it as "melancholy or madness by imaginative love or by sexual desire." The *Nouveau Petit Larousse* defines it as mental disease characterized by the predominance of *"idées amoureuses ou sexuelles."* A new introduction to psychoanalysis by Gerturd Kurth and Hans Herma[14] includes erotomania among the mechanism of defense, "known in the figures of Don Juan and his feminine counterpart Messalina."

* Parts of this essay were published in the magazine *Eros* No. 1, 1962.

All these quoted definitions are either wrong or vague, and all are misleading. Science, including psychiatry, never starts with accurate definitions. It arrives at them only after careful descriptions of the phenomena. It is obvious that these explanations are wrong because they do not include the main characteristic of erotomania, namely, the unshakable, delusional conviction of the patient that he is loved by a certain person. Furthermore, Jean Etienne Esquirol, the most prominent psychiatrist of his time, wrote in 1838 of erotomania as of "chaste love" and of "love in the mind" (*l'amour de la tête*) as opposed to insatiable sexual appetites as they appear in satyriasis and nymphomania. As a matter of psychological fact, all distinguished observers agree that erotomania has in the majority of cases a platonic character. One realizes how mistaken it is to connect the notion of erotomania with excessive sexual excitement or to introduce figures like Don Juan and Messalina as representative erotomaniacs. Whatever can be said of these two great lovers, their passions were certainly not of a chaste nature.

Clinical pictures, however sketchy, speak louder than defining words. Before presenting some cases, I shall introduce them by making two points clear. Pure forms of erotomania are relatively rare: most psychiatrists consider the delusion of being loved as part of the mental disorder called paranoia, or of persecutionary and erotic delusions. Descriptions of representative cases of erotomania in the pertinent English and German literature are scanty and scarce, at least compared with the frequent case histories to be found in French psychiatric books and journals. There cannot, however, be any doubt that the disorder is present in German as well as in British countries, and it would certainly be an absurd mistake to conceive of it as the French psychiatrist Ferdiere did, as a *"syndrome essentiellement français."* [15]

Here are some characteristics of erotomania as they are described by psychiatrists and psychologists. In the majority of cases the patients imagine that a certain person of the opposite sex has fallen in love with them and communicates with them in some way to declare his or her ardent passion. One would assume that the patients who indulge in such fancy or fantasy are mostly women because they certainly are more inclined to develop such images. As a matter of fact, women, especially during the pre-menopause and menopause years, also younger widows and divorcées are frequently victims of erotomaniac imagination. G. Clérambault declared that erotomania is *"le délire professionel de la femme"* who needs security and legitimacy. Yet there are numerous male erotomaniacs, even homosexual ones, who imagine that a certain man is madly in love with them. There is, however, a significant psychological difference between male and female patients of this kind. While a woman daydreams that a certain man who is in love with her wants to marry her, most erotomaniac male patients imagine that a certain woman wishes to have a love affair with them. Since the main characteristic feature of the erotomania is the pervasive illusion that the patient is loved, it is easy to recognize in it a feminine feature which is unmistakably significant. Stendhal had written in 1822, in his *De l'Amour*, "to love means to expect to be loved." But in most cases of erotomania there is scarcely a clear sign that the patient is infatuated with a person and now expects that his love will be reciprocated. The patient is often surprised and sometimes taken aback when he discovers that a certain woman with whom he has never spoken, for instance, has fallen in love with him. But is not this delusion founded on self-deception, and should there not be an original disavowed attraction to the object which is later supposed to be enamored of him? To reach a decision is difficult, especially since, as Eugen Bleuber recently pointed out,[16] the delusion can be developed over a long period of time in the unconscious and enters the conscious mind at a certain moment. Bleuber quotes the case of a 36-year-old woman with a high degree of intelligence—she was a Ph.D., *magna cum laude*—who became erotomaniac and defended herself in legal actions and in the newspapers against the imagined attentions of a man. She herself described the development of her delirious idea in the following manner: "I heard the whole story piecemeal. Soon one person said one word, soon another person, and I put the story together like a mosaic picture." In general the logical processes of erotomaniacs are intact if you once accept the morbid ground from which they unfold. There are, of course, abundant misinterpretations and deceptions of memory, in some cases even hallucinations. To search for the origin of the delusion is often rendered much more difficult because there is sometimes a period of latency for the fixed idea.

Compare with that case another one referred to me by a psychiatrist who diagnosed it as obsessional neurosis. Summer vacation had interrupted the psychoanalytical treatment. After he returned to New York, the patient, a man in his middle forties, appeared greatly disturbed and reported an experience responsible for his state of mind. During the summer he had made the acquaintance of a woman who was not very attractive and with whom he sometimes talked. After his vacation, he got a little package from this woman containing some cakes he had once mentioned as favorites of his. After he had eaten the cakes he was convinced that the woman had fallen in love with him and that the gift amounted to a declaration of her passion. Soon after, he felt a longing for her together with sexual excitement—he had to masturbate several times—and asserted that she had bewitched him by means of the cakes. He refuted all possible arguments against this assumption by referring to the fact that aphrodisiac foods had been known since antiquity. How otherwise could it be explained that he suddenly longed for a woman whom he had not even liked very much? Here, then, is a modern counterpart of the love potion in the form of erotomania. Soon, persecutory ideas emerged in addition to his erotomania. He suspected me, his analyst, of having murderous designs against him; the psychoanalytic treatment had to be broken off.

Other cases will give a better picture of the syndrome that appears in various forms and in connection with other psychiatric disturbances. Since I have seen only a few cases of erotomania—

although I have observed many erotomanic traits interspersed among neurotic symptoms—I draw the following examples from the pertinent psychiatric literature. I shall first concentrate on the morbid misinterpretations that the patients lend to words heard and actions observed around them. An erotomaniac woman (Leroy and Jaquelier presented the case to the Société de Clinique Mentale in 1910) pursued a Catholic priest with love letters, and when the abbé threatened to send these letters to her husband, she interpreted this as a measure favoring her divorce. Everything the abbé had said to her in the confessional was misinterpreted by her. She misconstrued, for instance, his words, "You must have will power," to mean "Continue to love me."

A tailor, one of Maynan's cases,[17] was convinced that a certain singer was in love with him. She glanced at him during a performance of *Lakmé,* observed him, and when her hand was near her mouth it was as if she threw him kisses. She came back early from a starring tour because she wanted to see him. When she did not perform at her theatre once and then appeared again on stage, he explained that she was longing for him. He once saw her photograph in the part of Mignon, in one of the show-windows of the boulevards, and interpreted her tears in it as shed for him.

In another case an erotomaniac woman conceived of a man's pallor as proof of his unhappiness on her account. (The reader will remember here that a certain character in Heine's novel is described as pale: "What women attribute to an unhappy love while the men ascribe it to a happy one.")

In the case of Madame Cavé,[18] Sophie, twenty-five years old, asserted that Dr. X, who treated her, was in love with her and she refused to leave his consultation room. He then had her confined in a mental hospital, as she explained, in order "to have her just for himself." She considered the *certificat d'internement* as a pact that tied them together for life.

Igor, a Russian patient of Jean Fretet,[19] was a married man. He was convinced that Princess Juliana of Holland was in love with him. He received his first communications from her during a walk with his wife. Pedestrians murmured to him, "Regards from the Princess," or "Write the Princess every Saturday." When the princess married and when his numerous letters to her were returned, he did not acknowledge these facts. When he missed two of the letters he interpreted it as proof that she held those two especially dear. Facts are either misinterpreted or ignored.

A homosexual man, imagining that the attendant in an asylum was in love with him, thought that the attendant behaved coolly to him in order to conceal his feelings before others.

There is no insurmountable obstacle, either of an external nature or of an emotional character, which can separate the erotomaniac patient from his object, as, for instance, rejection by the object.

An erotomaniac patient of Ferdiere was under the imperative impression that a man was calling her to him. She traveled from Dresden to Paris, was astonished that he did not meet her there at the East Station, took a taxi to search for him and could not pay the fare. She had hallucinations in which she felt his presence and in which they talked to each other.

Another patient of Ferdiere, a forty-eight-year-old widow, asserted that the assistant chief of a railroad station followed her everywhere, even into the ladies' room, and wanted to marry her. He sent electric rays into her body, she said.

Television, clairvoyance, and telepathy often figure in the symptoms of erotomania. A patient, Mrs. M., forty years old, refused to believe that a man was married and declared, "with a love like his, he can marry only the one he loves," and wrote to him, "Tell me that you are not married!"

In many cases, ideas of persecution soon outweigh the erotomania. A young divorcée imagined that her father-in-law and brother-in-law were against her marriage to the man who loved her. She wanted to kill both of them and then commit suicide.

Another erotomaniac man declared that a certain woman did not answer his letters out of consideration for her eighty-year-old father who would not agree to her marrying him.

An inclination to write letters, often daily (called graphomania by psychiatrists), is frequent among the symptoms of these patients. Some of them declare that they know the thoughts of their imagined lovers better than they. They report that signs are made to reach their attention even before an audience of a thousand people. Some patients are not content with communications and find their way to action. They appear, for instance, in the apartment of their "lovers" and demand to be treated as husband or wife.

G. Clérambault [20] believes that erotomania develops in three phases. First hope, then spite (akin to the *"dépit amoureux"* of Molière), and finally vengefulness or malice. Ferdiere rejects Clérambault's assumption that he calls *"toute une exégese"* and states that there is no unchangeable development of erotomania recognizable. As I have already mentioned, cases of simple erotomania are rare and many psychiatrists deny that it is a psychotic entity, but treat it as a simple syndrome that can be observed in various mental disturbances.

To us, the origin and the psychogenesis of this disturbance should be of more interest than the various labels psychiatric experts put on it.

2. *Psychoanalysis of Erotomania*

It is no longer correct to assert that students of Freud are not interested in the psychoanalysis of a case of erotomania, as Ferdiere stated. The papers of P. Schiff, Mrs. Cavé, and others published during the recent decades prove that there is enough interest in the subject on the part of the psychoanalysts. The fact that the objects of erotomaniac delusions are in most cases socially elevated or highly esteemed persons, often authoritative figures such as priests, physicians, famous actors and actresses, and politicians has often been observed. Some French psychiatrists even believe that behind these figures are persons who are exalted father or mother substitutes.

As early as 1937, Jean Fretet [21] in his Paris thesis refers to the family romance in whose frame we must search for the primary figures of erotomaniac disorders. In the typical fantasy of the "family romance," as Freud calls it, the daydreamer, usually a boy or girl of the prepuberty age, imagines he is not the child of his parents but of socially higher or more prominent fathers, and that the people who took care of him in his childhood only adopted him. His "real parents" will some day come and give him his proper place and rank. Social and personal insecurity and inferiority feelings, as well as pride, contribute to the formation of this typical fantasy.

It cannot be accidental that so many cases of erotomania are seen among persons in a subordinate position or who are poor and dependent. In their delusions they imagine they are loved by persons of high social rank who also want to elevate them and support them and who appreciate their hidden good qualities. The erotomaniac who imagined that Princess Juliana was in love with him also anticipated that she would free him from his poverty and finally make him prince-consort.

It is obvious that the objects of erotomania often represent veiled substitutes of the figures who once appeared in the family romance. Vaguely libidinous and egoistic interests often fuse in the erotomaniac delusions.

As I have already said, Freud, who does not himself consider the significance of the family romance for the erotomaniac, conceives of this disturbance as one form of paranoia. According to this conception he writes that erotomania is unintelligible without an understanding of the projection operating in it.[22] The symptoms of paranoia are characterized by the process of projection in which an internal perception is suppressed and in which its content becomes conscious (after some distortion) in the form of an external perception. The process is similar to that whereby a picture is cast upon a screen.

Erotomania, according to Freud, develops in three phases: the inner perception which goes first of all in the direction of homosexual love. The sentence, *"I love him,"* is contradicted, rejected and replaced by the other, *"I love her."* Under the power of projection this sentence is changed into: *"She loves me."*

Freud emphasized that many cases could make a first impression of exaggerated or distorted heterosexual fixation on an object, yet such an assumption is refuted by the fact that all these infatuations do not begin with the awareness of loving, but of being loved. Freud is certainly correct in considering erotomania as a form of paranoic disturbance. His theory seems to be unsatisfactory to me because it does not recognize sufficiently the importance of narcissism in the genesis and character of erotomania. Narcissism, which could be translated as self-love, is the love which is withdrawn from the external world to the self and is clearly manifested in ideas of grandeur and in the megalomania of paranoics. Freud recognized that such patients usually have a fixation on the narcissistic phase of development, or rather have returned to it; but he does not accentuate the special significance of the regression to narcissism in erotomania.

It is also correct to say that this return to narcissism is facilitated by a rejected homosexual inclination. To be in love disturbs the narcissist's self-love; to be loved confirms and intensifies it. It is remarkable that those who become erotomaniacs are mostly financially poor people or in a subordinate social position and that their ego suffers great mortification when they compare themselves to others. The delusion of being passionately loved restores that self-sufficiency which distinguishes narcissistic self-love from pride.

The modification that I would like to make in Freud's theory considers especially the role of narcissism within erotomania. In this psychiatric disturbance we recognize a distorted striving to regain the original self-esteem and self-admiration of the patient. What appears to us as mental illness is an attempt to rescue the poor self from the depths of contempt and humiliation which threatens the person with insignificance. We must recognize this rescue-attempt in spite of the morbid and delusional impression of erotomania. To be loved means to be important again—more than this: to be all important.

3. *Erotomania in Literature*

> The lunatic, the lover and the poet
> Are of imagination all compact.

says Shakespeare in *A Midsummer-Night's Dream*. Considering these mental and emotional affinities, we are not astonished at meeting erotomaniacs in plays and novels. In the following paragraphs I shall deal chiefly with representative figures of this type— a comic one and a tragic one. Space forbids me to treat these figures of literature in detail and allows me no more than a glance at their creators.

The comic character is, of course, Malvolio in Shakespeare's most delightful comedy *Twelfth Night*. Malvolio's character is "perhaps the most discussed and least understood of any in *Twelfth Night*," as a modern critic wrote.[23] It is even questionable that the steward of Olivia can be conceived as a purely comic character. Charles Lamb, at least, confessed that he never saw Bensley in the part of Malvolio without a kind of tragic interest. There is indeed an undertone of sadness in his situation and we would today call Malvolio rather a tragicomic figure.

While the main plot of Shakespeare's play is concerned with Viola and her brother, the comic subplot is centered around Malvolio and the trick that is played on him. This trick is dismissed in the comedy as a bit of "sportal malice" and is not more than a superstructure to explain the behavior of this presumptuous and conceited upstart who believes that he is a possible match for his mistress. Olivia's comment, "You are sick of self-love, Malvolio," is admirable as the shortest characterization of his mental disorder, especially if one adds the qualifier "unreturned" to self-love. When we examine the superstructure of Maria's intrigue and of the counterfeit letter, it becomes obvious that Malvolio belongs to Shakespeare's "characters who exhibit occasional symptoms of undoubtedly deranged mind." [24] In the opinion of the critic quoted, Malvolio is "surely not wholly sane, since it is difficult to believe that a completely sane man would have been

taken in by the obvious trick of the forged letter." We are therefore psychologically justified in conceiving of the trick played on
him as an artistic device of Shakespeare, and to treat it here as if
it were a projection of mental processes cast on the external
world. It reflects the emotions and thoughts of Malvolio who
suffers from erotomania. If we think of the statements in the forged
letter as externalizations of Malvolio's thoughts and emotions, we
have a remarkably clear picture of erotomania with all its symptoms. Other people in the play characterize Malvolio as an
erotomaniac; not only his mistress by that pronouncement, "Oh, you
are sick of self-love," but also her maid Maria, who calls him an
"affectionate ass" and "the best persuaded of himself, so cramm'd
as he thinks with excellencies, that is this ground of faith that all
look on him love him." Even before the letter, Malvolio imagines
that he heard the countess say "that, should she fancy, it should
be one of my complexion," and is convinced that "she uses me with
a more exalted respect than any one." He remembers that "the
lady of the Strachy married the yeoman of the wardrobe" and
anticipates in his fantasies how he will behave, once married to the
countess. Thus the sentences of the forged letter contain clearly
enough the text of his delusions. "In my stars I am above thee; but
be not afraid of greatness: some are born great, some achieve
greatness, and some have greatness thrust upon 'em. . . . Be
opposite with a kinsman, surly with servants; let thy tongue tang
arguments of state; put thyself into the trick of singularity;
she thus advises thee that sighs for thee. Remember who com-
mended thy yellow stockings, and wisht to see thee ever cross-
garter'd. . . ." He acts then as he was advised; he does nothing
but smile at the countess. He is afraid to remain a steward
and misinterprets every word she says in the framework of his
erotomania, while the countess sees in him a case of "very mid-
summer madness." He argued, for example, that the countess did
not call him by his name or title, but spoke of him as "this fellow,"
and he saw in her wording a proof of her love: "Why, every
thing adheres together, that no dram of a scruple, no scruple of a

scruple, no obstacle, no incredulous or unsafe circumstance."
When then the inevitable disappointment occurs and Malvolio lands
in prison, he is full of accusations against his mistress who has
given him so many unmistakable signs of her love.

We admire the psychological insights of the poet, who presented
such an excellent symptom-picture of erotomania with its delusions
and misinterpretations ("Oh, what a tangled web we weave, when
first we practice to deceive!"). We admire the psychiatrist Shakespeare who wondered about these cases of madness and yet always
gave such a precise clinical description of them and with such
compassion ("Lord, what fools these mortals be!").

It cannot be accidental, and it is certainly psychologically determined, that the erotomaniac personality occupied the imagina-
tions of two of the greatest poets. Malvolio is the funny Don
Quixote of love. The other, the tragic aspect of erotomania, is
represented by Goethe's ill-starred Torquato Tasso, written more
than two hundred years after *Twelfth Night*.

It should help us to look briefly at the historic figure of Torquato Tasso, the much admired author of *Gerusalemme Liberata*
with whom the German poet so vividly identified. There were
certainly many psychological affinities besides a few similarities
in the lives of the two writers. Goethe had studied the biography
of Tasso, written by his contemporary Battista Manse, as well as
the biography of Abbate Serassi, published in 1785. The material for the tragedy is taken from these and other sources. We know
how much the figures of the play can be traced back to the
history of Alfonso II and of the persons at his court at Ferrara,
where Tasso came in 1565. It was said that the Italian poet
became infatuated with Princess Leonore of Este, the sister
of Duke Alfonso. Serassi tells us that Tasso mistook for love the
princess' admiration for his work. Once, in the presence of the
Duke, he kissed her suddenly, carried away by a passion stronger
than a poet's (*"transportato da un estro più che poetico."*). The
Duke said to his courtiers, "Behold the terrible disgrace of a great
man who goes crazy in this instance!" (*"Mirache che fiera dis-*

grazia d'un uomo si grande che in questo punto è diventato matto!") The poet was then taken to the hospital of Santa Anna, where he spent several years.

Goethe's Tasso does not end as a mental wreck after he is rejected by the Princess in that dramatic scene of the fourth act. In Schopenhauer's opinion[25] Tasso in Goethe's presentation is also "doomed to madness" and Richard Wagner, too, foresaw this fate for Goethe's hero.[26] Anyone who has studied the life of Goethe recognizes that he mastered a deeply disturbing experience, similar to the one in which the Italian poet perished. Goethe himself said to Eckerman that the play is "bone of my bone and flesh of my flesh" and confessed that he took the congenial material of Tasso "in order to free myself" in treating it from what struck him as "painful and troublesome from my Weimar impressions and memories."

The great conflict that stirred Goethe to the depths was his relationship with Charlotte von Stein, the wife of the Master of the Horse, Herr von Stein. When the poet came to Weimar and made the acquaintance of this "angel of a woman," she had seven children. Charlotte was seven years older than Goethe. She insisted, as does the Princess in *Torquato Tasso,* that Goethe should contain himself and moderate the expressions of his passion. Relations with her became severely strained even before Goethe left for Italy. Like Tasso, Goethe mistook the lady's admiration for his work for love and was not content with a "marriage of souls." He explains the magic power this woman had over him in terms of metapsychosis:

> *Ach, du warst in abgelebten Zeiten*
> *Meine Schwester oder meine Frau.*

> Ah, thou wert in ages past
> My sister, or, maybe, my wife.

and complains

> *Leb ich noch stets um deretwillen*
> *Um deretwillen ich nicht leben soll.*

I cannot help living for her
For whose sake I am not supposed to live.

It came to the final break. Six weeks after Goethe's return from
Italy to Weimar, Frau von Stein explained that "Goethe parted
from me as from a perfect stranger." When the poet became intimate with Christine Vulpius, his relationship with Mrs. von Stein
was definitely broken.

There can be no doubt that Goethe showed well-marked erotomaniac features in his lovesick relationship with Charlotte von
Stein. He not only misinterpreted her behavior as a manifestation
of her love for him, but his attitudes showed the typical course
of erotomania from hope to flight to withdrawal. The middle-class
citizen of Frankfurt fell in love with this older woman who represented to him a socially elevated mother figure. Goethe "harbored
in his mind this pandemonium of invisible spirits," as his biog-
rapher says.[27] W. Bode emphasized that Goethe remained sexually abstinent until his thirty-ninth year, which is in keeping with
his erotomaniac trends.[28] Werner Meyer, a physician, guessed that
the poet had suffered from psychic impotence from which he
was freed only late in life—in Italy by Faustina. The platonic
character of his love life indirectly speaks in favor of erotomania.

What, then, saved Goethe from the fate of Tasso, whom he
gives these lines in his play:

Und wenn der Mensch in seiner Qual verstummt,
Gab mir ein Gott zu sagen was ich leide.

While man by misery is rendered dumb,
A god gave me the gift to tell my woes.

The artist neutralized, as a critic says,[29] the tormenting problem
"by giving it objectivity in a tragic figure and thus bringing it to a
close." In the play as in the novel *Werther,* Goethe saved himself "by making his poetic image pay the fatal prize," while the
historic Torquato Tasso drives on to the catastrophe. Enough of
the pathological has, however, penetrated Torquato Tasso so that
the psychiatrist can, with the help of the case history, diagnose it

as a "persecutory paranoia," [30] but until now the erotomania of Tasso had eluded the observation of the psychiatrists.

As I write this, I cannot remember a case of erotomania in contemporary literature. Only Arthur Schnitzler's short story, "The Diary of Redegonda," comes to mind.[31] The story, dated 1909, deals strictly speaking not with erotomania but with some symptoms typical of that disturbance, especially with telepathic communication between lovers. The essence of the story, put into the frame of an experience of the writer, is as follows: A young lawyer in government service was transferred from Vienna to a small Austrian town. There he saw the beautiful wife of a cavalry captain. Since the officers garrisoned in the town associated with each other almost exclusively, he had no opportunity to meet the lady socially and admired her from a distance when she was in the company of her husband or of other officers. Once, she passed him in a park and it seemed to him that she smiled at him, but he did not dare to greet her. He did not regret this omission since he could not expect any success from such an attempt. The young man was compelled to imagine what would have happened if he had been courageous enough to speak to her on that occasion. In his fantasy they would have had a lively conversation during which she would have complained about the emptiness of her life and expressed her pleasure at having met him. In his imagination, she gave him such a promising glance on leaving, as if a precious secret existed between them, when he saw her in the theatre on the evening of the same day. The power of his fantasy led him to imagine that this meeting was followed by many others until the adored creature visited him in his apartment. There were some dangers connected with their imagined affair and an expectancy of impending calamity emerged in the young lawyer. The news came that the captain's regiment was to be transferred to Galicia. The lover decided in his despair that flight with his mistress was the only recourse. Under the compulsion of his delusion, he made all preparations for their journey, packed his trunks, and wrote farewell letters. On the last evening, in expectation of

Redegonda, he looked up and down the street, listened for her steps, but could not awaken her shadow-image as before. He had the impression that something terrible had happened to keep her from him. Near midnight, the bell rang. For a moment he hoped to find Redegonda, compelled by his fantasy, appear on the threshold. But here his delusion ended when reality broke in. It was actually the colonel who stood at the door and said, with a mocking expression: "You expect Redegonda. She has been prevented from coming; she is dead."

He reported that she had died perhaps from shock when he unexpectedly entered her room where she sat writing in a little book. The captain presented this diary to the lawyer, who read in it the last lines she had written: "Now I am leaving my home forever; my lover waits." Asked to read, the ghost lover discovers in the diary the entire story of their love, from the first meeting to their plans for flight. All is there that he had not experienced in reality, but in his aroused imagination. He is not astonished; he guessed that Redegonda had the mysterious power to live all the experiences of his fantasy with him. Any attempt to deny their affair had no chance of success. The captain could accept only the natural explanation. The lover considered himself responsible for the consequences of an adventure he had wanted to experience and which he was only too cowardly to live in reality. In the morning a duel took place near the spot in the woods where he had met Redegonda the first time. The captain shot the ghost-lover through the heart.

In his erotomaniac delusion, the lover had imagined that Redegonda shared with him their wonderful experiences and was convinced that she loved him. The character of erotomania is proved also by the telepathic experience in the inscription in Redegonda's diary. A feature of erotomania, met with in many clinical cases, namely, the conviction of a thought-communication between the lovers, appears here in isolation. It jibes with the erotomaniac character of the experience that the two persons involved had never spoken to each other. Their love is only romantic and platonic; it is shadow-love; they embrace each other only in imagination. Both are ghost-lovers.

A psychoanalytic investigation into Schnitzler's plays and novels would lead to the impression that the writer, as a mature man, had paranoic ideas of various kind. Just now I recall some memories of Schnitzler, whom I had known for many years. We often took walks on the Sommerheidenweg near Vienna and I vividly remember that our conversations moved from general topics to personal things, and that he sometimes revealed suspicious thoughts and paranoic tendencies.

FROM THE PATHOLOGICAL
TO THE NORMAL

Our point of departure was the pathology of erotomania. But the pathological presents only an exaggerated and distorted picture of the normal. Our point of arrival should be a recognition of the normal counterpart of erotomania, and we must find traces of it in the life of all of us. The way to this normal erotomaniac pattern is paved for us by the psychological understanding of erotomaniac characters in literature. If there were no echo is us, how could we enjoy the comic figure of Malvolio in *Twelfth Night* and the tragic character of Torquato Tasso in Goethe's play?

Our own responses lead us to the insights that erotomania presents a pathological form of that primary need to be loved. We can understand these erotomaniac strivings to regain that self-love which is the other side of autoerotism, the phase we call secondary narcissism. This narcissistic development is a later structure built above the foundation of an original and primal narcissism which a baby enjoys in the all-encompassing love of a mother, in a phase of symbiosis when there is not yet the later differentiation between the self and the object. In this earliest phase there are no demarcation lines between mother and baby. Erotomania is the delusive and delusional attempt to be loved as in the past.

8 : *The Collective Form*

THE CHOSEN PEOPLE

1. *Introduction*

Professor G. E. Wright wrote that "there can be no real under-standing of the meaning of the Old Testament nor of the course of Israel's history without paying close attention to the doctrine of election." [32] H. Rowley similarly conceived of it as "fundamental to the thought of the Bible in both the Old and the New Testament." [33] According to the writers of the Old Testament, Israel is chosen by God, whereas to the writers of the New Testament the church is the heir of that divine election.

To the superficial reader it may seem as if that doctrine had been there in its present form from the beginning of Israel's history. Nothing could be more mistaken. It began as another concept, was subjected to many changes, and is still flexible except in the view of embittered fundamentalists.

Another superficial view may point to the fact that many nations have made the claim that they were chosen to save the world. There is a direct line leading from H. St. Chamberlain's theory of German superiority and Emanuel Geibel's prediction (1871) that *"am deutschen Wesen wird die Welt genesen"* (the world will recover through German entity) to Hitler's "master race." There is another popular line from Dostoëvsky's and Tolstoy's Pan-Slavism to the present Soviet leaders who are convinced that the future of mankind will be determined by the Russians. The British once claimed that they were the remnants of the lost tribes of Israel and their heirs. Are we Americans entirely free from a similar notion? Do we not speak of the United States as "God's country?"

As a matter of historical or, rather, prehistorical fact the belief that one's nation or group is especially favored by God has very humble origins. The evolution of that conviction can be traced to primitive society in which there were yet no highly complex groups such as nations or states. There were only small tribes with more or less fixed territories. Each tribe had its totem, generally an animal, that was supposed to be the common ancestor of its members and which was the object of veneration. This totem animal, an early predecessor of the gods, gave the tribe special protection and forbearance. The members of the tribe are, so to speak, his special favorites.

This is not the place to follow the social and religious tribal system of totemism from primitive society to advanced stages of civilization. It would certainly be highly rewarding for the study of religion and ethics to pursue this development until it reaches the state of monotheism and its moral correlates.

We shall restrict ourselves, however, to a very brief survey of the evolution of the conviction of the Hebrews that they are "the chosen people." How did that loose conglomorate of individual, primitive shepherd tribes arrive at this belief so energetically and obstinately maintained over three millennia? Seen from the other side, why should a god have elected those tribes? What was their merit and what were the qualities that make the claim of their election plausible?

Other peoples have had abundant reasons to wonder why God

bestowed upon Israel that exceptional and glorious privilege of election. They still wonder, as is testified in the lines of William Norman Ewer:

> How odd
> Of God
> To choose
> The Jews!

2. *The Doctrine*

The prophetic vision that Yahweh will reveal himself to all peoples and that all nations will call on the name of Yahweh was not known to the books of the Torah. The outlook there, as Kaufman described it,[34] is cosmic, but God who governs the earth reveals His name and His law only to Israel and shows special favor to the people of Israel. This outlook is monotheistic, but national, and can still be traced to primitive tribal organization.

The change this concept underwent is best shown by a survey of the biblical passages referring to election. God is loyal to the oath He made to the patriarchs. "But because the Lord loved you, and because he would keep the oath which he had sworn unto your fathers hath the Lord brought you out with a mighty hand, and redeemed you out of the house of bondmen, from the hand of Pharaoh king of Egypt" (Deut. 7:8.). The Lord Himself says that this love originates in Israel's infancy:

> When Israel was a child,
> I came to love him
> And out of Egypt, I called my son. (Hosea 11:1.)

Amos (3:2) speaks in Yahweh's name: "You alone have I chosen from all the families of the earth and therefore I will visit upon you all iniquitous deeds." Ezekiel (20:5) proclaims "Thus saith the Lord Yahweh: In the day when I chose Israel, and lifted up mine hand unto the seed of the house of Jacob, and made myself known unto them in the land of Egypt, when I lifted up my hand unto them, saying, 'I am Yahweh, your God.' "

The election is an act of grace on the part of Yahweh: "The Lord did not set his love upon you, nor chose you because ye were more in number than any people; for ye were the fewest of people." . . . Here must be a hidden key to that closed door.

Just a glance at the heirs of this election-concept is in this context necessary: Jesus Himself preached only to the Jews, and only once did He go beyond the borders of His own country during His ministry. He declared that He was sent to the lost sheep of the house of Israel (Matt. 15:24). When He sent forth his disciples He commanded them to go only the length and breadth of their land. Paul thought of the Church in terms of the remnants. He conceives of the election beyond the bounds of the nation, to those among the Gentiles who should share the faith and task of Israel. As H. H. Rowley especially emphasized,[35] the term "elect" is found in the New Testament many times for the Church, "testifying to the belief that the Church is the elect of God" and as a confirmation of the belief. The Church not only accepted the obligation of Israel's mission but claims to be "the spiritual Israel." The Remnant could claim that Israel's promises were reinforced by those of the Gentiles.

In a later work [36] Rowley pointed out that Yahweh did not chose Israel "because she was strong or cultured or good, but precisely because she was weak and helpless and downtrodden." There was nothing in the doctrine of election "to foster self-esteem in the elect though there were many in Israel who have shown a spirit of pride and superiority to others." Rowley emphasized that it is "need rather than worth" that calls forth the election and that election is not something that merely confers a favor, but demands a response from the elect.

Indeed, Israel could not claim any great political or national achievements. She is the smallest of nations and the weakest, as the Bible often states. The Scripture speaks of the "worm Jacob."

Israel took the obligation that election conferred upon her. Yet there were countervoices. One of them is uttered by Jacob who, in the grandiose vision of Beer-Hofmann's drama,[37] speaks up: "He chooses us and asks not if we want it."

3. *Contribution to the Psychological Interpretation*

Tracing the doctrine of election back to the primitive system in which the tribal god conferred special favors on the group presents only a general historical background and does not explain the peculiar belief of the chosen people. Such a simplification is certainly not permissible, and the transfer of psychological explanation to a nation does not explain the evolution of that doctrine. Setting aside for the moment the possible objections to a transfer from individual to collective psychology, must not particular reasons be present, must not unusual conditions operate to make possible the emergence of such indefeasible and unshaken conviction?

I do not pretend to have arrived at an ultimate solution to that problem. It seems to me a significant contribution to a psychological explanation can be inferred from examining the situation of the Hebrew tribes compared with that of their neighbors. When Israel entered upon the stage of history, she was a conglomoration of poor tribes in search of pasture on the fringes of the desert. The nations in whose midst the Hebrew tribes dwelled were superior in civilization and two thousand years ahead of the Hebrews. When God chose them, it was just because they were few, poor, and needed His favor, in the way a father prefers the son who is delicate and small while the others have grown to vigorous maturity.

But these considerations are to be found or can be inferred from the Biblical texts; chapter and verse can be quoted.

We have to deal with the doctrine of the election as with an emotional and mental product. Here is, if anything, the most obvious example of wishful thinking, of a pathological idea, born of the envious comparison of one's own miserable or pitiful state with the privileged and rich condition of others—a comparison of the powerful Egyptian and Babylonians "haves" with the Hebrew "have-nots."

It often happens that pathological notions, psychotic ideas, or syndromes later become realities to some extent. Two hundred years ago a person who asserted that he was being observed by people in foreign countries, that conversations he was having with friends were being eavesdropped, was considered insane. Today we know that those morbid notions can become realized with the help of technical devices. Nothing prevents us from assuming that the grandiose vision of the Hebrew prophets will also some day and in some form become realities. The presumptuousness contained in the claim of being the chosen people became to some extent justified by the infatigable and stupendous efforts of the Jews to disseminate and to propagate the teaching of an ethical monotheism among the nations of the earth. *"Noblesse oblige."*

To transpose Shakespeare's words, "Though this be method, yet there is madness in it," to which psychotic delusion of the individual can that collective idea be compared? In the preceeding chapter, we paved the way for its psychological understanding by our exploration of erotomania. We showed that the victims of this kind of insanity belong to the underprivileged classes. They are in the grip of the delusion that a very socially elevated person—for instance, a king or a queen—has fallen in love with them and gives them signs of favor. Quite frequently we encounter the idea that this important person is ready to bestow upon the patient a significant part of his power, selects and appoints him authoritatively as his delegate, entrusts him with a mission. Why that great and distinguished person chooses precisely the patient remains an enigma. We penetrate the core of the psychological problem when we refer to the narcissistic character of that delusion and to the unconscious consolation and supreme support it offers to the poor, unloved and lonely patient.

The psychological understanding of the evolution of the idea of the chosen people is thus facilitated by the psychoanalytic insights acquired in the exploration of erotomania. We need only put a people, an underprivileged group of tribes, in the place of the individual and substitute Yahweh for the important personality who mysteriously falls in love with the patient.

The doctrine of the chosen people is thus the collective expression of erotomania, formulated as religious teaching. Yet in following that idea, that people endured untold suffering that could not have been vain and fruitless. Perhaps even that sublime vision of the prophets of the future will not always remain a phantom and a delusive chimera. There will be perhaps a day when people "shall beat their swords into plowshares, and their spears into pruning hooks; nation shall not lift up sword against nation, neither shall they learn war any more." (Isaiah 2:4)

4. *The Appearance of Self-sufficiency*[38]

The need to be loved, we have said, must be discovered by psychology as a powerful and pervasive factor in the emotional life of men and women. Discovered? Yes, because it is often so cleverly disguised and concealed that it has to be found, or it is taken for granted and therefore not acknowledged. There are, furthermore, strong defenses built up against its revelation. These defenses protect that weak point of the ego as a hidden fortress blocks the approach to a vulnerable place. To tell the truth, we are all in a way ashamed to admit that we need to be loved, as if it were the confession of a hidden weakness or an expression of emotional immaturity.

How do we protect ourselves against indiscreet intruders into this secret area? We surround ourselves with a kind of emotional insulation. We assume before others—and sometimes even before ourselves—an appearance of self-sufficiency while we are actually deeply insufficient in our emotional isolation. "No man is an island, entire of itself"—why do we pretend that we are such an independent and self-reliant territory? In doing this, we wrap ourselves in a *cache-misère,* as the French call a cloak covering poor or shabby clothes. We hide the loneliness of the individual who needs social contact of many kinds.

This appearance of self-sufficiency assumes different forms in men and women. Take an everyday situation: look at the passengers on a train or a bus. They are either occupied in thoughts or engaged with something else and they display the often deceptive appearance of self-sufficiency. It is as if they were not paying the slightest attention to anyone around them.

There are mixed attitudes or compromise attitudes between those two possibilities. Look at that man over there who opens his portfolio and attentively reads a brief. As he does this, he sometimes furtively glances at the pretty girl sitting opposite him. The young woman is busy searching for something in her bag, but while doing this she knows very well that she is being looked at. She pulls her skirt down, but in making this movement she draws attention to her well-shaped legs. According to her sex-role and her education the woman is better trained than the man in awakening the impression of self-sufficiency or self-reliance. She is a better pretender and seems not at all aware of the admiring glance of her *vis-à-vis*. It is not difficult for her to assume the appearance of self-sufficiency and she is good at it.

The most interesting aspect of that pretense is not its purpose, but its effect, or better put, the impression that real and assumed self-sufficiency makes on the other person. It works in the manner of an attraction or a lure. It awakens in us a kind of envy. Freud once pointed out that small children and animals at play make us thus envious of their narcissistic self-sufficiency: they seem not to need us. The woman in our example similarly appears to be sufficient to herself. This means in the last analysis she does not need the attention, affection or tenderness of the man. He, on the other hand, seems not to need the sexual gratification he really desires. Yet she longs to be admired and wooed, and he wants to be sexually united with her. Beneath that first and superficial level is another one, mostly denied or disavowed: her sexual need, of which she is perhaps not aware at all, and which would be aroused by his courting and his submerged need to be liked, appreciated and loved.

The funny or strange aspect is that for the time being the other person is tempted to believe in the self-sufficiency. He or she shares, so to speak, that illusion. The woman accepts the appearance that the man does not need her or her affection. So far as she can see, he is mostly interested in his work and is self-contained. The man, even more willingly—or more easily deceived—would be astonished if he could quickly discover that she would like to be admired and desired.

A woman, seventy-two years old, with grown-up grandchildren, told me in a consultation the other day that in her many years of married life her husband had never told her that he admired or loved her. She knew he did, yet she suffered from his unwillingness or inability to verbalize what he felt.

The woman, a better actor than the man, certainly gives no sign that she too wants sexual satisfaction and the man does not betray in the least that he wants to be treated with affection. She would be indignant if a question in that direction were posed to her and he would be ashamed to admit that he too needs tenderness. Yet both sexes take those needs silently for granted; the man that the woman wants to be treated tenderly, and the woman that every man wishes sexual gratification. Sometimes she is inclined to believe that he wants only the latter.

But those are the hidden psychological sides of the situation. The other one, clearly to be perceived by every practiced observer, is the fact I have already mentioned, that the real or assumed self-sufficiency is mystifying, intriguing, and alluring to the other sex. There is a difference in the way we look at playing children and animals whose self-sufficiency we envy. There is no temptation to break in, to disturb, to make our presence known; no itch to be acknowledged, and no regret that we are passed by.

Yet the man would like to break through the apparent self-sufficiency of the woman, to become Pygmalion to this unconcerned Galatea. She often wishes that he would turn his attention away from his work to herself. He envies her because she seems to be at ease and reposeful within herself. He would like to change that, to disturb her apparent inner peacefulness. She would like to be the object of his attention and the aim of his activities. I remember seeing a cartoon in which two young girls look at a young man who is attentively reading a horse racing sheet. The caption renders the thoughts young girls might have of the man who pays no attention to them. It reads: "Bookworm!"

Many a woman wishes her husband or lover would give less attention to the form and shape of his car and more to her own. But she would rather bite her tongue than tell him so. Very few women are ready to admit that they are often jealous of their husband's work, or rather of the zeal he shows when he is intensively occupied with it. Many men, on the other hand, would confess that they sometimes are secretly envious of the fact that their wives or sweethearts have the center of gravity in themselves.

There is really a kind of shame or fear that a person of the opposite sex could "find out" that secret of one's own. A kind of pride is maintained in order not to give oneself away. Women are, of course, much more sensitive and vulnerable in this direction than men, not only for reasons of self-protection but also because they hate to show a man the interest he has awakened in them. Yet Homer's sirens did not want to let any man pass and tried to divert Ulysses, eager for home, from his serious and urgent task.

5

What is that melody that has occurred to me before, and now recurs while I am thinking of the higher defense built by woman's pride and pretense? I have not heard the tune for many years and I can't say why it emerges nor where it is from. Then I seem to see the pale face of Bruno Walter with his hands raised in conducting. The tune emerges again, a tender minuet, and then, suddenly, roaring march rhythms. After the middle part, again that delicate minuet, *dolcissimo*. . . . And now the words come back with the melody—the poem by Li Po, the greatest Chinese poet. The masculine and the feminine element are here put side by side and contrasted.

A scene by the riverside; girls plucking flowers, teasing each other; and then boys on horseback riding swiftly by. The clattering of hoofs is heard in that *allegro*. Only after the boys have passed—

> *Sendet die schoenste von den Jungfrau'n*
> *Lange Blicke ihm der Sehnsucht nach.*
> *Ihre stolze Haltung ist nur Verstellung.*
> *In dem Funklen ihrer grossen Augen,*
> *In dem Dunkel ihres heissen Blicks*
> *Schwingt klagend noch die Erregung ihres Herzens nach.*

> The fairest of those lovely maidens
> Sends long looks of desire after him.
> Her haughty pose is mere pretense.
> In the sparkle of her lustrous eyes,
> In the darkness of her ardent glance
> There trembles still the dolorous vibration of her agitated heart.

When Gustav Mahler composed *The Song of the Earth* in 1908, he knew that he would die soon. Perhaps such a reminiscent and retrospective glance at youth and romance, such a penetrating and all-embracing understanding of life is allowed only at leavetaking.

Part II : *Contrast and Complements*

CONTRAST AND COMPLEMENTS

1. *Male-Female Contrast*

A young man and a young woman had declared their love for each other. Both were married and were hesitant to go beyond the platonic relationship. The man asked during a pause in their conversation: "What would you do if I should never make physical love to you?" The woman answered: "I would still want you to be always with me." Rarely would a man feel this way. The same woman said to a friend: "That he loves me so much, makes me love him even more." This feeling is characteristically feminine.

2. *On Feminine Sexuality*

It is difficult to describe the nature of feminine sexuality in non-technical language and to grasp the essence of its dynamic processes. Take for instance the difference between clitoral orgasm and vaginal orgasm, a difference not only of theoretical interest, but of the greatest psychological significance, and one which has a vital bearing on marital life. I have often tried to make that difference understandable to women patients (it is astonishing how little many women know about their own sexuality) and I have had to use comparisons to make my meaning clear. I have compared, for instance, the nature of clitoris sensations to the ticking of clocks and the spasm of the vaginal orgasm to the opening and closing of a fist.

The reason I am discussing this now is that I recently found myself envying gifted and perceptive writers who have a marked advantage over us poor psychologists in describing such sensations. In a novel by Colette, Claudine,[39] the first-person narrator, now married, speaks of certain kisses that are "sesames" (what a wonderful comparison!) and says that afterward "I want to be conscious of nothing but darkness, nakedness, and the vain, silent struggle to hold myself back one minute, just one minute, on the edge of delight."

This is not only a marvelous description of the sensations before orgasm, but also a source of psychological insight into a phase of the process. The "silent struggle" to hold oneself back on the edge of delight: here is a factor I have never seen described in sexological literature and which opens a new aspect of the process of sexual arousal and the orgasm of women. In describing the sensation "on the edge of delight" the writer characterizes a struggle between two opposite emotional powers, the one that urgently wants to let go and the contrary one of wishing to hold on and to hold out. It is not sufficient to explain this moment simply as an attempt to prolong the sensual pleasure. It is more than this. First of all, it has the character of subtle self-torture, it has a masochistic tone. It must also be the result of interference by a psychological agent. It is as if an old prohibiting factor makes the woman still hesitate at the last moment to surrender unconditionally to the man. Yet she knows she will. Her body says "yes" even while she says "No, no!" Therefore "the vain, silent struggle."

Another situation comes to my mind, a situation far from the sexual process. A man is sitting on a ledge high up in a building and wondering whether he should jump or not. Should he not end all misery by an action lasting only a minute and then have peace forever? He is "on the edge."

This situation is apparently remote from that of sexual intercourse, but there are concealed threads running from the one to the other. Freud let us understand that the fear of jumping or falling from a height, often found in neurotic patients, has a feminine character. And did not the Victorian era speak of a "fallen woman"?

These situations are, of course, opposites seen from the point of view of pleasure and pain. Yet their common and most significant element is their suspense factor, that they are localized "on the edge"—either of despair or delight.

Regular and routine love-making bores most women, but improvisations also rub them the wrong way although it comes closer to the unforeseen and adventurous. What they really want is a kind of prepared and daring venture, love-making on the spur of the moment, but anticipated with desire. It must be protected against the danger of disturbance and interruption, under comfortable circumstances and unhurried, yet should be an exciting and unusual experience, should have a somewhat forbidden or dangerous character simultaneously with a legitimate and homey atmosphere. The experience should combine familiarity with newness. Women take it for granted that the experience must oscillate between torture and delight, must be safe but risky, sometimes even risqué. Then she would be willing to throw her lot in with the man, but of course with some reservation.

Here is a biological as well as a psychological problem.

3. *Psychological Experiment in Thought*

If one has enough perceptiveness and imagination, it is easy to indulge in thought experiments of a decisive nature. Suppose one imagines a certain situation alternately with a woman and a man as the main or only person acting or feeling. In such thought experiments the profound and deep-seated psychological differences between the sexes become easily recognizable.

Imagine, for instance, a woman in her late forties or early fifties thinking of her son who has just gone away on his honeymoon. The mother imagines him now sleeping with his bride for the first time. The mother's jealousy, her hatred of the young woman who will now have her boy forever and who will even bear his child, while she, his mother, remains alone. Change the situation in your thoughts: it is now the father thinking of his daughter on such an occasion; ask yourself if he experiences the same or similar emotions.

A young girl feels deeply hurt by her lover and is tempted to burst into unrestrained sobbing. She knows that her nose will turn red when she weeps and she will look ugly. She therefore restrains herself from crying. Imagine the same situation for a man.

The husband kisses his wife and says, "Your hair smells wonderful." She is worried that he might have seen some gray strands on her head. Imagine the same situation for a man. . . .

Who has ever seen a man smooth over a soft material on which he had been sitting so that the imprint of his behind will not be visible when he rises? But almost any woman would do this or feel like doing it.

A woman who was enjoying herself at a garden party suddenly discovers that she looks bad or that her dress is not appropriate. At that moment the whole environment changes as if transformed by the curse of a witch. All pleasures become shallow, all people meaningless shadows, nature arid and ugly. What was charming a few minutes ago is changed as if by black magic. Has the awareness of one's own image the same effect on a man?

4. Sexual Initiative of the Woman

We are so accustomed to thinking of the woman as passive in sexual intercourse that we are almost astonished at the idea of her taking the sexual initiative. Yet there are cases in which the psychological situation drives the woman to the active role. Such a situation is when the man is shy, clumsy or inexperienced sexually, compared with her. Another is that of the woman in an advanced stage of pregnancy. She is well aware that in this situation she has lost a great deal of attractiveness, and so takes the initiative when she is sexually aroused.

5. *Little Girls*

I do not understand why we psychoanalysts do not gather sayings of little boys and girls instead of leaving this privilege to the writers. Mind you, not the remarks and utterances of neurotic patients of children's psychoanalysts, but sayings of average children who spontaneously speak about the world around them and within them. Jotting down such sayings would help us to understand the mental and emotional processes of little girls and boys in whose thoughts and feelings we all are interested.

Here are two instances, one from the stories of Anatole France, the other from life, concerning my daughter Miriam when she was small.

Jessy in Anatole France's story[40] was six years old when her mother died and when she was taken to her old uncle Bogus. During the first week there the little girl cried and did not say anything. Then one morning she said to her uncle, "I have seen Mommy; she was dressed in white and had flowers in a fold of her robe. She threw all flowers on my bed, but I did not find them again this morning. Give me them, please, the flowers of Mommy." Is this not a charming example of the psychology of a child's dream?

When my daughter Miriam (now getting her Ph.D. at Columbia University) was a child we often played a little game when we took a walk together. It was called "I dare you" and had mostly the character of a challenge to be met. She must have been very small at the time because I remember that I stood with her before a window where children's dresses were displayed and said "I dare you

—if you are insolent I'll buy you that dress." Miriam, wanting the dress very much, looked up at me and asked, "How is one insolent?" On another occasion, on a very warm summer day as we were walking down Fifty-ninth Street near Fifth Avenue, I saw two men, old acquaintances of mine, strolling together a few steps ahead of us. I said to Miriam, "Do you dare me to go to those two men and ask them to buy us an ice cream?" Of course, she doubted very much that I would do such an outrageous and unheard of thing, but I went up to them and asked them to take us to the St. Moritz nearby for the ice cream. They greeted me with pleasure and were quite willing to do what I had asked. While we were having coffee and ice cream, we chatted; Miriam, eating her ice cream too, did not say a word. After we left and continued our walk alone, she seemed deeply embarrassed and was plainly groping for the right expression. Finally she said reproachfully: "That is not a proper thing to do." She supposed, of course, that I had addressed two strange men on the street and had asked them to buy us ice cream, and she considered such a behavior quite unsuitable. She must have felt very ashamed of me. I explained to her the following day that the men were old acquaintances of mine.

6. *A Little Girl*

When my younger sister Margaret and I were children, we used to visit an old aunt every Saturday. Auntie promised Margaret that she would inherit a beautiful watch on a golden chain. Every Saturday the little girl heard Auntie's promise of the gold watch after her death. Finally, Margaret asked impatiently: "When will you die?"

7. *Reactions to Success*

A patient saw an article on which he had worked a long time published at last in a scholarly magazine. He recognized that he had now reached a crucial point in his professional life and was, as he said, "in." He reacted to the event with a mixture of triumph and modesty: "Now that I have been acknowledged as an expert, I feel that I have to jump seriously into the material and must learn about it."

8. *Fire*

They saw each other only a few times, but the man fell in love with the girl immediately. He was like a house on fire. Yet he did not know that it was she who had set it ablaze. She seemed to calm him down and to control his fire, while actually she was the incendiary who revived it. When my son Arthur was a little boy it was his notion that the fire brigade was setting fire to a house, and could not believe that its function was to extinguish the conflagration.

9. *Mirror*

It is possible, as historians assert, that Phoenician men first discovered the mirror, but it is certain that Phoenician women found out how best to use it to their advantage. Their need to be admired created that silent but eloquent witness who too willingly attested to their beauty. "Mirror, mirror, on the wall, who is the fairest of them all?"

10. *Dresses*

"You talk of dresses as a blind person talks of colors. You men don't understand anything about them."

"You can't generalize in such a way. There are prominent male couturiers and fashion designers."

"Perhaps they are men, but only in an anatomical sense."

11. *Women's Professions*

As far as I know, nobody has ever recommended the profession of detective for women. Yet there is no doubt that most women have a native talent of this kind. Every husband will pay tribute to this ability, brought to light in married life. It only needs to be channeled in another direction. We shall thus perhaps see a great number of brilliant sleuths who know very well how to investigate, probe, interrogate, grill, deduce, and expose! Some women have developed and employed an amazing technique of their own in their domestic life.

12. *Psychologist*

Every woman who is emotionally involved with a man is a psychologist, whatever occupation she may have, whether she is a salesgirl or a kitchen helper. No man who is emotionally involved with a woman is a psychologist, even though professionally he may be the most prominent psychologist or expert in human relations.

The psychological mistakes a woman makes are mostly due to wrong analogies from herself. She might assume, for instance, that the man is aware of his infatuation with her long before this feeling dawns upon him, because men are usually dull in this respect. Or, she may think that the man has affectionate feelings for her whereas he experiences only sexual desire. In sexual relations, she will often be mistaken about timing, because she often measures his rhythm in relation to her own, which is usually slower than that of the man. Yet it sometimes happens that the woman, in an attempt to judge the man's behavior, will overestimate his speed. Besides these errors, there are many others on the woman's part, wrong deductions based on insufficient intuitive premises, and other mistakes that have their roots in the individual personality. In the area of applied psychology, as in astronomical observation, there is also the factor of the "personal equation" as a source of mistaken judgments.

13. *Paradox*

A woman who is so terrified that her knees tremble can still encourage a man. She who talks so much more and so much easier than a man, wants to be wooed with words, and never tires of hearing those three words said repeatedly to her. She who always looks at the man—except when she casts down her eyes—hopes that he will be conquered by looking at her.

14. *Magician*

A woman who for many years had led a very unsatisfactory sexual life with her husband had an affair with a younger man and experienced her first ecstatic orgasm. Although she clearly realized the moral and intellectual shortcomings of her lover, she fell under his spell and succumbed again and again to his sexual technique. She thought of him as a kind of magician, and did not doubt that no other man could make her as "happy" as he. Even though she occasionally caught him in a shameless lie, and was struck by his utter stupidity, she yielded to him nevertheless. Her mind said "no," but her body cried "yes," so great is the power of complete sexual satisfaction over women. Her body seemed to lead a life of its own, entirely separated from that of her mind, and her body ruled her. When she felt the man's hands on her flesh, she felt her blood bounding and singing, and was hungry to be in his arms. In the beginning it was merely a kind of innocent flirtation and she did not recognize the depths of passion into which she would be driven. It was as if she was wading in a shallow though passable body of water, and was suddenly and irresistibly swept away and forcibly submerged by successive and overpowering waves.

15. *Lips*

She looked at his lips and blushed, because she felt ashamed at her wish to be kissed by them. No man I know would think in these terms, and he certainly would not blush because of such a wish.

16. *Dedication*

A man must have a dedication toward and concentration upon something outside of himself, whether it is a cause or a task; it must be some impersonal interest. Such a psychological necessity does not exist for a woman.

17. *Poor Fish*

The woman stood beside me, looking at the man preparing his fishing tackle, and said: "Poor fish." "Why is it," I asked her, "that there are so many fishermen and so few fisherwomen?" "Well," she replied, "it's a man's sport." And then she added: "Women perhaps don't like to touch live fish." I thought that in this distaste there was perhaps a connection with the male genitals. Walking along, it occurred to me that we use the phrase regarding women that they "fish for compliments." Do they not throw out alluring and tempting bait for us men to swallow? And then they keep us helplessly and deliciously dangling. Then, after a long time, we poor fish are taken off the hook and put into the safe box of married life, no longer to enjoy adventures or freedom. Why are there so few fisherwomen? Is it because fishing is a silent and lonely sport? Women like to be in company and like to talk. When that woman said "Poor fish" it was perhaps not because she felt sorry for the fish, but for us men, who are ensnared by the bait.

Women, of course, do their fishing in society, and have no need of the sport itself. A Bikini swimsuit worn by a young girl is much more seductive bait than a worm.

Two hours later, I sat in the dining room of the hotel near the lake and observed how the young women scanned the men entering the hall. It was as if these young girls were looking through the glass walls of an aquarium. "Poor fish," I thought again.

18. *The Boy, the Girl*

"That's the boy to watch!" said a man pointing to the fellow who appeared at the tennis court. "And that's the girl to look at," said the other man, pointing to the woman just passing by.

19. *Unfair*

It is obviously unfair to expect that a woman who chooses the chair that blends best with the color of her dress should follow your political views with great interest and attention. It is unfair to expect that while she smoothes her skirt and sits down prettily, she should decide how to vote in the next elections.

20. *Acting*

There are professional actresses. But most women are actresses in their private and social lives. There is, for instance, a certain occasion on which it may occur to a woman that it would be a good idea to start crying, although there is not the slightest reason for an emotional outbreak. She might even cry at the funeral of her mother-in-law. When she does, it will be a Grade A performance. Yet "What's Hecuba to her or she to Hecuba that she should weep for her?"

21. *The Difference*

The wife looked indignantly at the clumsiness with which her husband handled the pots and pans in the kitchen. She turned to me and said, "Look at him, just look!" and she added in a low voice:

"The damnable thing is that we women love it." It is also true that men like the weakness, the ineptitude, and the inexperience of women, but one can never know if these shortcomings are not simply pretended and acted, which is very rare with men.

22. Unsexed Woman

Lady Macbeth is unsexed in more than one respect. She is not, in contrast to her husband and to most women, superstitious. She is excited by the thought of murder, which very few women, and only very masculine women, would be; and she never asks her lord and master what the witches were wearing.

23. Sexual Symbolism

The patient, a man in his late thirties, had told me about his affair with a girl and the many conflicts he had had with her during its course. "I finally decided to break with her and to return to my wife. I went home early, had dinner with my wife, and went to bed with her. . . ." He paused and continued: "It was like an old shoe after you've been walking around in new ones that don't fit."

The sexual symbol of the shoe is known to psychoanalysis since the interpretation of the Cinderella fairy tale in which the symbol is turned around to make it unrecognizable. The patient who compared life with his wife—really his wife herself—with an old shoe, certainly had no conscious knowledge of this symbolism. Its universality is also shown in the nursery rhyme, "There was an old woman who lived in a shoe . . . ," which means her body is unconsciously compared to a shoe.

Another example of sexual symbolism from analytic practice: A young woman told me in a psychoanalytic session that a man with whom she had a date had come too early to pick her up. She had dressed, but had not yet put on her lipstick. "He sat there," she continued, "and looked at me. He stared at my lips and it was distinctly indecent. I was so embarrassed that I could have shrieked."

The symbolism of the lips as representative of the female genitals was certainly not known to this patient, who nevertheless felt embarrassed.

24. *Men and Boys*

"Boys will be boys," women say, and shrug their shoulders. Men pretend to have grown up beyond boyhood. Yet they remain essentially grown-up boys.

The playing of little boys is continued in various forms in the adult life of men. The most astonishing form is the ritual of professional meetings, the pomp and circumstance, the ceremony and the formality on certain occasions. Men endure these rites to such a degree that they become, so to speak, enslaved by them. Women are much more free in this respect. Their sense of formality encompasses only the kind of dresses they should wear. To be dressed a certain way or not to be dressed that way—that is the question.

Boys' games have certain premises or rules. For instance, the attainment of a desired, ultimate goal and a series of actions required to reach it. Such actions are mostly of a competitive and violent character. Think of football, for instance, or of other sports. The continuation of these games in adulthood is seen particularly in the arts of war and politics. A certain kind of political activity combines theory and terror. Theory without action is powerless; terror without theory is blind. The union of theory and terror gives birth to a child that resembles both parents. Its name is fanaticism.

There is even a continuation in adult life of the play activity of very young boys. It entails riding a particular hobby horse. Every man has such an animal and rides it in a certain direction. Thus passionately occupied, he excludes every other interest in the world. It is as if not the horse but the rider had blinders. Have you ever observed women as they listen to their men discussing their dominant hobby? Did the situation not remind you of patient mothers looking at their young sons untiringly riding their hobby-horses?

I shall not discuss militarism and soldiering since their character as play is too transparent. Moreover, the Viennese writer Karl Kraus has said the last word on the subject. "Children play soldiers; that makes sense. But why do soldiers play children?" There is even an institution called Military Intelligence, which is the perfect example of a contradiction *in adjecto*.

25. *Status of Women*

A very pretty girl of thirty had many suitors, but could not make up her mind to accept a marriage proposal. None of the men fulfilled her high requirements. She was waiting for the "dream man," yet she also set herself a deadline for the time when she should be married. In her arguments with herself she finally arrived at the horrifying possibility that she would be laughed at as a bachelor girl. For the man, such a reason for marriage is nonexistent, because his social status does not depend upon the condition of being married or single.

A certain divorced woman feels acutely that she is handicapped compared with her married friends. She states that she cannot go to certain places alone without an escort, and is dependent on the invitations of married couples for occasions to spend weekends with them and be taken out by them. After a conversation with one of her women friends who lived in the suburbs and who visited her, she thought of the argument that woman had had with her husband. However, the patient knew that John, her friend's husband, had driven his wife to the station when she went to New York, and would meet his wife at the station when she arrived home in the evening. The patient reflected with sadness that she would have to go to the station alone, and that no one would meet her upon her return.

26. *Flowers*

Women love flowers, not only because they are beautiful, but also because they remind them of themselves. Both bloom, mature, and grow only a short time, quickly fading when they are not taken care of. Both the beauty of flowers and of women lasts but a day, and fades forever as if it had never delighted the eyes of many.

27. *Still*

Men may sometimes ask women, "Do you love me?" Women often ask men, "Do you still love me?" What is the meaning of this difference? Whoever solves this problem makes decisive progress in our psychological understanding of the variations between male and female emotions.

28. *Sweet Poison*

An unknown correspondent sent me two instances of compliments a woman paid to another woman. The correspondent, who kindly collected the examples for me, added that she is sure neither speaker would ever admit having intended to include a barb in her compliment.

"Oh, what an attractive rug you have, Jane! I always say there is nothing like a rug for tying old sticks and pieces of furniture together."

"Dorothy, you always look so nice and I am always so sloppy. I just wonder how old one has to be to take such good care of oneself."

In each instance the technique is the same: flattery that contains barbed hooks.

29. *Babes*

Shaved eyebrows and mascara give many women of today the appearance of permanent wide-eyed astonishment. This is the more remarkable since women in general know their way around better than men. From their appearance, however, one would think they are all babes in the wood, including those in their late fifties.

30. *Minimum Response*

There are blank greetings that indicate that one did not recognize the other person or that one has not the faintest idea who he or she might be. Such blank greetings, in which some women indulge, are offensive to those so greeted.

Demonstrative casualness is often the sign that a woman is in a state of high tension. She can be on tenterhooks and yet behave nonchalantly and casually. Women are much more skillful dissemblers than men.

On some occasions women are so demonstrably not paying attention to a man that it would be conspicuous if men were not so stupid in this respect. Women then are so preoccupied with not noticing the man so that he should become aware of their lack of interest. They look so purposely away from him that he is startled. The trouble is that a man can never tell whether this behavior shows that the woman is not interested, or wants to conceal that she is too interested in him.

31. *How Retain Him?*

One has to admit in all fairness that woman, in her relations with man, is at a serious disadvantage. She will try to hold a man by showing him affection and by treating him lovingly. But by so doing, she acts according to a mistaken projection, since this would be the way to retain her; because only women are held by tenderness and consideration. If she then tried to keep him by sexuality, she is often just as much frustrated, because male sexuality wants variety and she can offer him only homely fare.

32. *Moment of Truth*

Women are generally more reticent in expressing their feelings toward men than men are regarding women. This is, of course, associated with their modesty and other psychological factors, but their reserve also has other purposes: it puzzles and mystifies the man and it protects the woman from danger. Moments of truth are therefore often against her interest. The other day a woman said to her lover: "You can't do anything that would deeply hurt me except to leave me." Was she merely being frank at that moment? Or was the sentence ill-considered and imprudent?

33. *Fragment of Conversation*

A young woman said to the man who had wooed her for a long time: "I can't fall in love with you because your behavior does not correspond to the picture I had built up of you." She then told him that she always had thought of him as a serious, scholarly man, devoted to his studies, and that the role of lover was incompatible with this image. She nevertheless must have sometimes thought of him in this disavowed role because after they had kissed the first time she said: "My feeling was much stronger than my mind realized." Saying goodbye that evening, she said: "I shall not forget you—ever," as if that had sometimes happened before.

34. *Mutual Effect*

It is impossible to reach a profound understanding of the psychological relations between the sexes without considering the proverbial unconscious communication between them. The allusive and half-concealing, half-revealing garb of women is more attractive and seductive to men than nudity. How did women first find out about this? How did she learn this secret and when did she make first use of it?

35. *Stage Fright*

In our day the anxiety of brides is perhaps different from that experienced by their grandmothers, who were often uninformed or only partially informed of what awaited them on their wedding night. In this age of complete sexual knowledge this kind of anxiety is rarely encountered. The apprehension of young brides of today involves questions of this sort: Will my husband be happy and satisfied with what I have to offer him in my body? Will he enjoy my physical endowments when he sees me naked? But these thoughts must have been common to brides of all times, in addition to the other forms of stage fright.

36. *The Other Purpose*

Women are not created for the same purpose as men, and therefore their outlook on life is different from that of males. Women always have to think of the other life dormant within them. Eugene Field once said in regard to boys, "They never had been mothers and never could hope to be." The strange thing is that some neurotic boys still hope for just this in their early fantasies, while the majority of boys choose work instead of motherhood.

37. *Understanding*

Men are not supposed to understand women but to feel with them, to have empathy with them. Yet women would often be terrified if men could intuitively grasp their motives, and some women would not be caught dead with their intimate feelings exposed.

Reasons are lost and wasted on women except when they would

like to be persuaded by reasons, for what they had already decided in the first place is the best and only possible approach.

38. *Love and Sex*

Psychology and biology are still occupied with solving the problem of love. It seems to me that the problem of sexual attraction, which is independent from that of love, is more urgent and deserves more of our attention. Those electric affinities of which Goethe speaks in his novel are much more intimately connected with sensuality than with affection and tenderness. We psychoanalysts should be more interested in the question of what makes a person desire a member of the opposite sex than in what makes him love her. This desired individual is often not loved at all, but often even detested and despised. Nevertheless he or she is sexually irresistible and his or her power over the other person is all-consuming and imperative.

Desire, not tender affection, often governs the vicissitudes of male and female relationships. The ruling force is not that which according to the poet moves the sun and the planets, but the much more profane passion that causes the blood to coalesce in the genitals.

Indeed, here is one of the still inexplicable and flagrant contradictions of human nature. What is it that gives the desired person that power, that awakens his or her image even during sexual intercourse with another person? Is it something biochemical, is it some quality of the skin, or is it a memory of some movement or attitude? What is responsible for the awakening of the memory, which, after many years, is still much more capable of arousing sexually than that of another woman with whom the man has had sexual intercourse a few hours ago. It can happen that this actual sexual intercourse whets the appetite for the other person—if it does this at all—but it never satisfies this longing. Once aroused, such desire can be appeased and gratified only by this one person. The *"femme fatale"* is not the woman who is loved, but the one who is sexually desired.

It is as if the flesh has memories as well as the mind, and as if those carnal desires push every other consideration into the background. Here, perhaps, is the decisive reason for the (relative) fidelity of women. The man who first gratified her sexual desires left an indelible imprint in her heart. In her heart, did I say? No, in her blood.

39. *Return*

Women who are unhappy in married life often return to their mother, who was their first love-object. Men never do; they search for a mother-representative figure in another woman.

40. *Men Joking*

"You are now together for twenty-three years?"

"Yes, married. But the two years before that when we lived in sin were the best."

A man said that "there is a tide in the affairs of men that, taken at the flood, leads to fortune." "I doubt," said the other man, "that Shakespeare meant this with regard to stock exchange speculations. It is quite possible that he was urging a man to have an affair with a very rich heiress, leading to a fortune in this way."

"You say that a woman drives you crazy? That's because you are in love with her. A woman can drive you sane, too."

"How so?"

"Well, marry her and sometime you will not only feel sane, but, more than this, you will feel extremely sober."

"I agree with you. Lucy is very attractive and has sex appeal. But Jane—she is a clothes horse of a different color."

My glance followed the two men who crossed the spacious hall together. One stopped at the fireplace and took the heavy iron poker into his hand, swinging it around playfully as if it were a weapon. "No," said his friend, "don't use that on your wife!" The other man, thus admonished, only grinned.

"You are blindly mistaken, my dear fellow," I heard a man say to another sitting beside him. "How can you say such a stupid thing as that women are good for only one thing? Have you forgotten that they cook for you, prepare your bath, mend your socks and a hundred such things more? I hate such simplifications!"

41. *The Room*

It is not accidental that rooms are representative of the female body in dream symbolisms and other productions of the unconscious mind. Not the slightest change or irregularity, not a bit of ash on the carpet eludes a woman looking at her room. Not only housewives, but also other women, less fussy, pay a great deal of attention to their room. When visitors are expected, most women wish their room to be spick and span and beautiful, even when they have to cram things in disorderly fashion into drawers. The appearance of the room must be neat and attractive.

The displacement from her body to the room reveals itself in the meticulous attention women bestow upon their living quarters which are, so to speak, a part of themselves. The beautifying and care devoted to the room reflects their effort to make themselves attractive. The indirect confirmation of the psychoanalytic theory that the room unconsciously signifies the extension of her own body for a woman is also exemplified by their regard for the slightest damage to the furniture. A merest scratch on a table surface, an almost invisible sign of wear on the couch or a drawer, are unconsciously treated as if they were tragedies. The analytic experience shows that this kind of feeling is explainable only when the woman conceives of these small damages as if they were damages inflicted on the surface of her body.

Men are in general much less concerned about the appearance

of their room because they are not as aware of their looks nor as vain as women.

This is the dream of a young man in whose symbolism the room appears in the meaning of the female body: "I am entering a new apartment. It is much wider than I had thought. There were several men in it and a few women." The day remnants for the dream are the following: On the evening before, the young man made the acquaintance of an attractive girl with whom he had a long and vivid conversation. Before falling asleep he thought of her and imagined the possibility of having sexual relations with her. He considered whether she had many sexual affairs with men and, perhaps, even with some women.

42. *In Musical Terms*

Life with women sometimes delights us with wonderful times, with exquisite harmonies, comparable to the music of the spheres, but it sometimes produces excruciating and striking discords. Yet, when one imagines what life would be without women, you can think of it only as deadly monotony.

"A pretty girl is like a melody." It will depend on the individual temperament whether the melody is an *allegro, andante* or *adagio*. Sometimes it is a *furioso*.

43. *Saying And Doing*

"When all is said and done, more is said than done." This is, of course, true about women, but whoever attends committee meetings and similar occasions will get the impression that it is at least equally, if not more, valid for men.

44. *Lonely*

No man can imagine how lonely a woman feels after being deserted by the man she loves. On the other hand, no man can imagine that a woman who is pregnant will never be lonely because she lives with the child within her.

45. *Smiles*

There are the smiles of a woman that do not vanish when she leaves the room. Those smiles are separated from her. Some of them warm and illuminate the room; others are similar to the grin of the Cheshire cat "which remained after the rest of it had gone."

46. *Rejection*

Situations occur in the life of lonely women when they offer themselves to a man and want to be made love to—with love and without love. It sometimes happens that the man is not at all interested and cannot be sexually aroused. The situation that confronts the woman then is like that of a beggar asking for alms from a passer-by who walks on without paying the slightest attention to him.

47. *Sexuality Seen from an Economic Viewpoint*

An extraterrestial observer would be mystified and intrigued by what these outlandish human beings call their love-making. What strange, absorbing and irresistable passion, what violent frenzy toward a goal lasting only a few minutes and then forgotten! What a waste of time and energy for pleasure of such short duration! Such an observer would sometimes be moved to tears and sometimes roar with laughter at the spectacle of love-making. He would not understand the method in this madness. He hears on a radio-wave that reaches his planet a song, "A woman is a Sometime Thing," announced as being composed by one Gershwin and is staggered at the contrast of this line and the behavior of the human male who is so persistently and so incessantly preoccupied with a woman, especially when he is frustrated by her.

Considered from the economic point of view, sexual intercourse seems an unproductive and tragicomic waste. A different view occurs when sexual intercourse is considered not as an act of two isolated individuals but in the interest of the species. I have read somewhere the lines:

> *Es gibt im Menschenleben Augenblicke,*
> *In denen es im Augenblicke Menschenleben gibt.*

> There are moments in human life
> In which human lives are created in a moment.

Let us return to the observer who follows the behavior of men from another planet. He will be astonished to see that for the human male who is mostly occupied with business, money, politics, and so on, the body of a woman becomes sometimes the only and most important thing of all. That observer, seeing daily the same performance millions of times repeated, must ask himself what extraordinary force compels a man to forget all his other interests for the sake of a satisfaction so brief. Is it curiosity? It cannot be, he will answer himself. There are, for instance, gynecologists who know the bodies of women and examine them daily and who behave sexually exactly like other men. Indeed, cooks too get hungry and eat with great appetite.

I remember a meeting of the Vienna Psychoanalytic Society at which one of us (if memory does not fail me, Otto Rank) reported the case of a young man who was occupied and preoccupied with sexuality. He had sexual intercourse several times every night over a period of many months. In the discussion of the case Freud predicted that the patient would become impotent in a short time. After a few weeks Rank (or the psychoanalyst who treated this patient) reported that the prediction had proved correct. The patient became incapable of functioning sexually, losing his erection in every attempt at sexual intercourse. His overpotency had been merely the other side of the coin.

47. *Promiscuity*

Whatever the deeper motives are for a woman's promiscuity, her behavior is inevitably accompanied by a loss of self-esteem and results in contempt for herself as an individual and for her sex. It corrupts her self-image when she is degraded to the position of a sexual object of the male. No woman with a high opinion of herself as a person and as a member of her sex will drift into promiscuity except in utter despair or under the pressure of dire need of money. The demoralizing effect of promiscuity is akin to that of a man who sells himself into slavery.

48. *In the Shadow of Previous Experiences*

A woman had been courted a long time, until at last she became infatuated with her lover and was almost ready to yield by going to bed with him. Moreover, she was aware that she felt desire for him as she wished to be desired by him. The evening before the decisive date, she remained at home alone, anticipating with delight the occasion of the tryst. Thinking of him and the future, she could not fall asleep. Suddenly she felt sad. In the morning, so eagerly awaited, she sent him a telegram saying that she could not come.

The man was greatly disappointed and brooded over the possible reasons for her sudden change of heart. He could find no explanation for her behavior. Wasn't she ready—after being wooed so long? More than this, was she unwilling to enter into a sexual affair with him?

He could not have guessed what went on in the girl's mind during the previous evening. Indulging in wonderful daydreams, she had considered her future with this man, and suddenly felt sad because the memory of a previous love experience emerged. In that past experience, the man who had finally overcome her resistance seemed to have been happy and satisfied; but slowly, by and by, their relationship cooled. He seemed to have become tired of her and finally left her for another girl. She became lonely and unhappy. Her hope of a permanent relationship with a man had been frustrated.

Recalling that sad and disappointing experience, she foresaw that the relationship with this man would take the same course. After a brief happiness she would again have to face loneliness and hopelessness. And so when dawn arrived, she cancelled the date. The shadow of the earlier affair had fallen on her expectations. A burnt child dreads the fire of passion.

49. *Another Anticipation*

A young girl who was infatuated with a man ten years older than she, was taken out by him several times. Then followed an interval of some weeks when she did not hear from him. She thought of calling him up and considered all possible and absurd pretexts. The thing that prevented her was that he might consider her forward. She finally decided against calling him because she anticipated that she would do so only half-heartedly, which would be at once apparent to him. She concluded in the end that it was the man's function to take the initiative, not the woman's.

50. *Looking and Being Looked At*

Many experiences prove that a woman observes much more keenly than a man the people she passes by, for instance, on the street. By just a sidelong glance she detects many things that escape a man.

A man may occasionally become aware that he is being observed by a person sitting or walking behind him. A woman always knows it.

A woman, aware that a person behind her is watching, often pats her hair. Men never do.

It frequently happens that women—very rarely men—become

aware first that they are being looked at and only later of the person looking. The best analogy to this is in animals for whom being looked at means danger.

Men who are vain look into a mirror to see their figure, but they are almost never concerned with their appearance from the rear. Women always are; when they have a full-length mirror before them, they turn around to see their backside. There is only one comparable thing in man's vanity: when a man looks at the back of his head, it is to see if he is getting bald.

51. *Rehearsal*

In a woman's thoughts, what she and a young man would say to each other in an anticipated love scene is often rehearsed. A man almost never does this; he sometimes hasn't yet realized that he is in love with the woman, whereas she can already predict how he will behave when he declares his love for her. "He will say. . . ." and "I shall then say. . . ." is prepared and rehearsed by her long before he has any idea of voicing his feelings toward her.

52. *The Not Excluded Third*

Men, in general, believe that a thing cannot be its opposite at the same time. Women have no difficulty assuming that something can be its opposite. They are able to keep away the disturbing factor of a canceling logic; or rather, they can develop a logic of their own. For them, there is no either/or.

53. *Dresses*

Men will discard a suit that is worn out or looks shabby. Women will sometimes get rid of dresses that are quite good and well suited to them because they are fed up with them and cannot stand looking at themselves in them. They sometimes abruptly dislike the color or style. A woman in another dress is another woman.

54. *Women's Ways*

The expression "connoisseur of women" is paradoxical. It is as if someone were called an expert in undiscovered territories, or a specialist in unfathomable mysteries. There are, of course, many theories about women, but they are comparable to maps of unknown countries. Those theories give precise information about something unknowable. The best they have to offer is guesses and plausible conjectures from the borderland, inferred from superficial contacts with stray natives. The following remarks and observations have nothing more to offer than this. Only a fool can promise more than he has got.

Women's ways are as dark as those of the Lord; on the other hand, they can be observed to a great extent. Yet the most accurate observation does not help us much in understanding their mystery. The essential nature of femininity is unknown except to women, who are neither interested in it nor willing to enlighten us men about it.

Shakespeare, the actor, who saw the world as a stage and men and women as merely players, enumerated the many parts one man plays in his lifetime. Among them is the lover,

> Sighing like furnace, with a woeful ballad
> Made to his mistress' eyebrow.

Under the heading of lover, Shakespeare certainly included the insincere lover, a part every man plays in his time. He pretends to love a woman in order to sleep with her. Shakespeare does not enumerate the parts played by women, perhaps because he knew that women are also actresses in life, even when they are wives and mothers and grandmothers.

55. *Question and Answer*

"Who is the most talked at person?" "The man who shows himself eagerly attentive to what a woman tells him about herself."

"Which man is most liked by women?" "The one who knows how to make them feel exactly as glamorous and interesting as they wish to be thought."

56. *Indirectness*

"You need not be catty toward another woman who is objectionable," said Mrs. M.; "you can be oversweet, which hurts her even more." How cleverly and perplexingly devious women sometimes are! They suggest, hint, and allude instead of speaking their mind. But when some of them are direct, we men think they are not feminine.

57. *Observation*

A girl in her puberty speaking to another about a young woman at a summer resort: "Do you know that she went to the lake in her bathing suit in high heels! That's ultrafeminine. She is a hard, masculine woman."

58. *Other People's Children*

We take it for granted that women talk with each other of their children. But you occasionally see two middle-aged women on a street passing another woman who is leading a little girl by her hand. Both women look after the child and smilingly discuss her. You will never see such a thing between two men.

59. *Father of a Teenager*

A father had to mail an important letter at the post office twenty minutes away. Since he was expecting a long-distance call, he hesitated to leave. Just then he heard his teenage daughter talking to a girl friend on the phone. "Well," he thought, "I can leave now. When I return after an hour the girls will perhaps just be beginning to say goodbye to each other."

60. *Almost*

A woman whom a man passionately courted for a long time said to him: "I passed your apartment yesterday evening and I almost went up and rang the bell." "Why didn't you?" "I was afraid." "Afraid of what?" asked the man. "I was afraid I would yield and then I would become emotionally so deeply involved that I would not ever want to leave you."

61. *Equalization of the Sexes*

The masculinization of women in this country makes such rapid progress that it is sometimes difficult to differentiate the mores of the sexes. A contemporary novel, in which conversations are set down without identifying the sex of the characters, would be a puzzle to a reader trying to differentiate the men from the women, since both speak and act alike. One is often inclined to utter a complaint that is in contrast to Professor Higgins': "Why can't a woman not be like a woman?"

62. *Parents of a Teenager*

The father: "I remember that only a few years ago my daughter clung to me in such a way that I could not get rid of her. She is now sixteen years old and, believe it or not, she is rarely willing to go with me even to a movie and considers it a favor when she doesn't go instead with the girls and boys."

The mother: "Jane is very perceptive. The other day we were at a party and one of the women had a very low décolleté. We talked about it later on and Jane said that the woman was not very feminine. 'Where is the element of hunting for a man?' said Jane, 'if she exhibits herself so freely?' "

63. Beyond Sexuality

Seen from the viewpoint of biology and from the interest in preserving the species, sexuality is only a means and not a goal. The male functions as producer of progeny and is bribed by the woman's attractiveness to plunge into the task nature has imposed on him. He, unaware of his role, wants to produce a child by the woman who pleases him best. The woman wants to bear a child who most resembles him. She is comparable to a goddess who creates man in *his* image.

64. Wrong Account

We blame women for things that are not their fault, for example, their moodiness, their mood fluctuations. These changes surely have mainly biological causes, are manifestations of what is taking place in their bodies. We often take them severely to account, but it is the wrong account.

65. The Sex Roles

A couple in love had a rather serious quarrel, after which the young man neither saw nor phoned the girl. Finally he called her up. In his psychoanalytic session he told me part of the ensuing dialogue. He said: "I thought you did not want to see me any more." She replied: "It is not that I don't want to see you, but I wished that you would want to see me." In this dialogue fragment the contrast in the sex roles of man and woman is psychologically reflected.

66. *Preoccupation*

An intelligent, twenty-nine-year-old-man came to me for psychoanalytic treatment. Among many other neurotic symptoms, he complained about a conspicuous change which he had observed in himself during recent months. He seemed, he told me, preoccupied to an extraordinary degree with sexual topics in his thoughts. Previously he had always treated sexuality casually, meaning he had not been tormented by sexual fantasies and had had several casual affairs in the city and overseas during the war. He had not been deeply involved emotionally. He had always functioned normally in sexual intercourse with the women he met. Several new things he now observed in himself disturbed him. The first was an odd preoccupation with the question of whether he was sexually as potent as other men. That question now occurred frequently when he saw other men. He often asked himself if his penis was as big as theirs. He also had similar obsessional thoughts. Recently, for instance, seeing the hand of a man in a car making a sign to the cab driver, he had asked himself whether the hand of that unknown person was more virile than his own.

During the first weeks of treatment the origin and the onset of those disturbing trains of thought became clearly recognizable. The influx of latent homosexual tendencies was of course too obvious to be elaborated. The question was: Why had they emerged from the emotional netherworld just now?

He had made the acquaintance of an extremely pretty girl and had soon entered into a sexual affair with her. Jane was no more intelligent or beautiful than some other young women with whom he had had casual affairs. Yet she was different from the others in one way. She had been promiscuous before she met him—as had been some of the other women—but in contrast with them she spoke often and at length about those past lovers. In fact, she had started to discuss John, a friend of the young man, who had enjoyed her favors before him. Those disturbing thoughts of my patient first occurred during, or rather, soon after that discussion. Jane had not only mentioned John, but had spoken of his sexual potency and of how often they had sexual intercourse. She had praised John's indefatigable accomplishments in this respect. My patient was surprised at himself, because shortly afterward he demanded sexual intercourse from Jane more often than had been usual before. It was as if he had to prove to himself that he could be as potent as John and like other lovers of whose potency Jane had spoken. The girl also discussed the length of the penis of her previous lovers. She had, she told my patient, sometimes measured the size of the erect penis of those men, and she had made an attempt to do the same with him.

It was in this context that the first obsessional thoughts—comparing his sexual potency with that of other men—emerged. They had at first been concerned only with John, the previous lover, but had then been displaced and generalized regarding other young men. At the same time he began to suffer from jealousy, a passion that had been alien to him before. He caught himself, for instance, suspecting that she was being unfaithful when she went out shopping; yes, once even when she was a long time in the ladies' room. In her absence he inspected the telephone pad on her table, because he thought she had jotted down dates. It was obvious that those obsessional thoughts had entered his mind only after the girl had discussed exhaustively the potency of her previous lovers. This unusual behavior on the girl's past had, so to speak, opened a concealed door for those disavowed or repressed thoughts. She held him in bondage from which he could not escape on account of the concealed homosexual connection. She had become a mental and emotional bridge between him and other men.

67. *As Others See Us*

Is there a mature female being who does not become self-conscious when a man looks at her closely? Much more and much oftener than men, women see themselves as others see them.

This gift or curse of seeing themselves with the eyes of others is not restricted to appearance. In sexual relations the faintest suspicion of an undesirable smell on her body or a dirty spot on her underwear is enough to sober a woman even if she was at first sexually aroused. In identifying with the man, she anticipates his disgust, which is fatal to her own desire. She not only sees, but smells and hears herself; yes, even touches herself as this other person, the man, might do.

In projecting her own tentative feeling onto the man, she often cannot understand that the man is not disturbed by such self-perception. A woman whose husband does not take a bath frequently complained about him: "I can't understand how he can become sexually aroused, knowing he has not bathed."

68. *The Forgotten Language*

Sexual intercourse is the most primitive and common preverbal communication. Yet it can be best compared to a language spoken between two people, to an attempt at understanding each other. This attempt can fail when the language each speaks is very different from the other, and can succeed even when they do not speak the same but similar dialects. Yes, it may succeed when each partner in the communication speaks out loud to himself as if the other person were not present. (This is the case in sexual arousal by fantasies.) Sexual intercourse is the most primitive, yet the universally understood language, an Esperanto created by nature. It has achieved more in the interest of communication between nations than the efforts of diplomats.

69. *Between Two Women*

A patient, a man in his late thirties, vacillates between his wife, with whom he has had a child, and a divorced woman who has, as he says, the "charm of newness." He is not ready to give up either one nor can he give himself to either of the two. "The shadow of my life with Joan (his wife) falls on Anne and vice versa," he says. "I can't have two cakes and eat them." Once, his wife told him how important it is to have one person to whom you could turn in any emergency. He replied: "Leave me alone! Take a lover!" He was torn between the two women, and the kindness and affection both showed him increased his guilt feelings. Being American, he shied away from the idea of a *"maitresse légitime"* customary in many circles of French society.

70. *A Mother Figure*

"These things have to be renewed from time to time," said Mrs. L, our middle-aged housekeeper, pointing to an object in my room, and added humorously: "If only *we* could be renewed occasionally!" This exclamation came to mind the same evening when my young hostess at the dinner table complained about her difficulty in finding a reliable and efficient housekeeper. I then told her about Mrs. L, a doctor's widow with two grown daughters, who came to America as a Jewish refugee from Hitler's Germany. I praised Mrs. L, who not only is a good cook, but takes excellent domestic care of us, and I expressed the hope that my hostess would shortly find a housekeeper as good as ours.

"Oh," she said, "I could never take one like her, so much older than I, and Jewish. I couldn't tell her what to do and what not to do in the household. It would be like ordering my mother around."

71. *Mother and Daughter*

A girl, thirty-two years old and unmarried, in her psychoanalytic session spoke of the previous evening spent with her parents. Her mother had, as often before, been urging her to accept one of the men who was courting her, meaning especially a young man who was eager to marry her.

"But I don't love him; I don't even like him," protested the girl.

"You make too high demands on the man you should marry. You expect too much of a man, and I am afraid you will be an old maid because no man could meet all your requirements."

"You want me to live through a loveless marriage, Ma?" asked the girl.

"If you can't get what you love, you will love what you get," said the worldly-wise mother.

72. *Selectivity*

The girl whose conversation with her mother I reported above told me that she, still a virgin at thirty-two, during her teens objected to petting with boys. "I remember that we had parties and kissing games in which the partners were decided by lot. I just did not like it. Why should I kiss a certain boy with whom I had nothing in common and whose acne repelled me? My sister tried to persuade me that a kiss did not mean so much. 'It is,' she said, 'no more important than shaking hands with a person you know.' She was five years younger than I and went out with boys much earlier than I. She petted a lot then, and now she is married and has two children. I just could not see things the same way she does. You also have to be selective about whom you kiss. I cannot bring myself to respond to a man who makes a pass at me, for instance, in his car. Once you consent to a good-night kiss on parting, where will it end?"

During the analytic treatment it became clear that the patient was yielding to her younger sister, for whom she relinquished the middle of the road without competing with her in relations with the opposite sex. To avoid competition she did everything different from her sister and later from her own younger girl friends. In contrast to her sister, whom she considered "wild" in her teens, she was controlled, well-behaved and highly idealistic. In another case in which competition with a younger and prettier sister was shunned in a similar way, the patient traced its origin to an experience in her teens. She had liked a boy in their neighborhood. On one occasion the sisters were together in the walled-in garden of their home when the boy came along the street and threw a rose over the wall. As she bent down to pick it up the boy called out, "It's for Anne!" —the younger sister. From that moment on she always stepped aside for Anne.

73. Toilet-Training of Infant Girls

Men sometimes observe that a single piece of toilet paper remains floating after a woman has left the bathroom. It seems to me that this toilet paper is a remnant of the early toilet-training of girls. Mothers accustomed them to wiping off the last drops after urinating, and toilet paper is an unconscious token of the girl's obedience to mother's admonition.

There are two other traits of behavior worth noticing in this connection: women much more than men are intolerant of cigars or cigarettes left burning in ash trays and feel almost compelled to extinguish them. This, of course, has good reasons: women are made aware of the danger of such burning objects, but the psychoanalytic theory of symbolic presentation has made us aware that fire is related in the unconscious thoughts to urine.[41] It seems also that taking special precautionary measures means an unconscious protection against soiling oneself, externalized and displaced to the outside world. At the same time, the burning cigarette or cigar perhaps reminds women of the dangerous penis in heat.

74. Contrast of the Sexes

Certain emotions and thoughts are characteristic of one sex and alien to the other. There are, for instance, relations between men and women in which the man—in spite of his desire—has his farewell letter already in mind before going to bed with the women for the first time. Women almost never anticipate such letters because of their wish for permanence, or at least for a longer lasting relationship.

On the other hand, there is a certain behavior to be met with only in women: a kind of make-believe naïveté, a fake feeling of modesty, even a pretended embarrassment, sexually. This particular behavior can sometimes be observed in girls in their teens as well as in old ladies. It is entirely alien to men.

75. Words

The patient told me that her husband, a writer, has a wonderful gift for words, along with a facility to formulate thoughts and emotions. She then reported some conversations they had had during their last marital conflict. It was obvious that she was far superior to her husband in speed and volume of words. She may have had a limited vocabulary, but what ample use she made of it! I am sure that while her husband still groped for the right expression she was well ahead of him.

As I listened to her, I had the feeling that I was in danger of drowning in the overflow of words. It was impossible to stop her.

76. Can't Understand

We take it for granted that many women, listening to a man, pretend they understand what he is talking about. It is, however, a particular attitude of femininity that enables some women to pretend they do not understand what the man is saying although they know perhaps better than he. I once had occasion to listen to a man who was explaining the nature of love to a young woman. It was as if Einstein were eager to learn the most elementary physics from a six-year-old grammar school pupil. No man could have followed that dissertation with so much unself-conscious attention as she gave it—and all because she wanted him to feel superior in an area where she could think and feel rings around him. It is on such occasions when deception is practiced in order to flatter the man, that the nature of femininity becomes fully recognizable.

77. *Conceit*

Evelyn refuses to go into competition with other girls, especially with regard to men. She says, "I am no threat to any girl," because she is convinced that she is superior to any other.

78. *Illusions about the Opposite Sex*

Each sex has certain vague illusions about the central purpose in the life of the other. Men entertain the misconception that they represent the fulfillment of a woman's life. Women cherish the idea that they are the most essential part of a man's life. The fulfillment of woman's life is in reality the child, not the man, even if he were the more loved one. The misconception of the woman is that she sees herself as the center of a man's existence whereas it is really his work that matters most to him.

Sometimes, especially in an emotional crisis, the essential aim clearly emerges to the surface of consciousness. A woman who was divorced from her husband after some years of unhappy married life drifted into several affairs. After breaking off with her lover she cried a long time. She became aware that she was really not grieving over losing him, but was mourning for a child she might have had but lost by an abortion.

A man who vacillated among a number of women suddenly thought that the choice was not the most essential thing in his life—

not the main battle but only a skirmish. Before that idea struck him, he saw himself at a crossroads, but decided that he could not be rescued by women but only by himself. He understood that he had unconsciously substituted an important decision in his work for the area of relations with women. He pushed aside the decision about women and returned with renewed determination and energy to his work.

79. *Ostrichlike*

They say that the ostrich puts its head in the sand so as not to be seen. It is not the only creature that behaves in this strange manner. Women who do not want to be observed closely put on dark glasses.

80. *Pleonasm*

At a party, a man called a certain woman known to most of the gathering a "mystery woman." A psychologist said, "That's the pleonasm of the century." A pleonasm is the using of more words than necessary to express an idea. Only after a lawyer among the guests clarified the word "pleonasm" as meaning "redundancy" ("It would be as if you said 'black Negro' "), did the other understand what he meant, namely, that the word "woman" includes the idea of mystery. Women are mysteries to us men and sometimes even to themselves.

81. *The Cartoon*

I saw recently somewhere a cartoon showing a young woman about to go on her honeymoon, embracing her mother at the door. The caption conveys the admonition the mother gives to the daughter at leave-taking: "Now promise you will be a good wife, dear . . . industrious, thrifty, domineering. . . ." The interesting aspect of the cartoon is that not the mother's words but the behavior of the woman whom the daughter had observed since childhood and who will serve as a model to the bride. It is not accidental that the adjective "domineering" follows the conventional ones in the mother's advice. It is the most important one.

82. *The Meaning*

Women sometimes say things they don't mean or mean only at one moment and not the next. Some of the things they say are mysterious or elusive. Men, on the other hand, for instance when discussing philosophical or political problems, sometimes say things that are utterly meaningless.

83. *Psychological Resemblance*

Women resemble one another more than men do. The psychoanalyst who has had many years of experience will often detect striking similarities in the psychology of women who are different in social position, education, and so on. The biological restrictions imposed on them—menstration, pregnancy, motherhood, and menopause—form a pattern of life to which they must conform.

Men are much more dissimilar in psychological direction than their mothers, spouses, and daughters.

84. *Subterfuge*

"One can't keep anything secret from you," said the woman to the man in make-believe humility and shame. She pretended that he had found out something she had wanted to conceal. But she had tricked him, hiding behind that "secret" one much less harmless, of which he has not the slightest notion. She acted surprised, confused and taken aback by his discovery, and had then said to herself, looking at him with a mixture of malice, contempt and triumph, "How stupid men are and how easy it is to deceive them!"

A man can pretend to a woman that he feels something which

actually he doesn't, but he cannot hide what he really feels. A woman can do both successfully.

85. *Change of Personality*

A woman in her forties who had been married some ten years and had had several extramarital affairs, experienced for the first time an intensive vaginal orgasm. Several minutes later, she said: I'll never be the same person again."

In spite of its emotional intensity, few men would feel that complete sexual satisfaction had changed their personality to such an extent.

86. *Motives for Suicide*

Men nowadays almost never commit suicide on account of unhappiness in love; women still sometimes do. Men often commit suicide on account of financial failure; for women, the question of money almost never becomes the question of "to be or not to be. . . ."

87. *On Sexuality*

In making love we return to primitive phases of evolution. The skin regains its importance and the sense of touch achieves the priority it once had in the protozoan phase. The hand of the man who caresses her intimately becomes personified in the woman's thoughts and sensations. It is experienced as impatient or too hesitant, as gentle or brutal, as knowing or inexperienced—as though the hand were not only an instrument but the very person.

There is also a return to the power of the male's words. Women who know the whole arsenal of seduction sometimes suddenly yield to a man because they wish to be desired and even more because they want to hear him pronounce words of love. Yes, sometimes it does not matter who says those words, only that they hear them and that they are addressed to them.

"Words, words, words!" says Hamlet contemptuously. Never underestimate the power of words over women.

A woman who did not yield to the passionate sexual wooing of a man suddenly surrendered when he showed her the powerful erection of his penis and plaintively accused her: "See what you do to me!" He had convinced her by this demonstration whereby he aroused her compassion.

88. *Sexual Symbolism*

It is remarkable that Freud's discovery of sexual symbols in dreams once aroused total incredulousness because some symbolism was to be found in sexual colloquialisms and jokes. Here are examples of both. The word "box" in England and America is colloquially used as a synonym for the vagina. A joke: a woman who sometimes caught her husband in infidelities threatened to get even with him. Alluding to her genitals, she said: "Before I was married it was a hope chest; during my marriage it has become a tool chest. But you will drive me so far that it will become a community chest."

89. *Moment of Clarity*

A woman who was neglected sexually by her husband said to him in bed: "Come over; nestle up to me." Then, when he made a pass at her, she said, "I feel amorous, but not passionate." A few minutes later she told him: "What I want, is to be raped every fortnight."

90. *Why Women Understand Men Better Than Men Do Women*

A highly intelligent married man told me in the initial interview that for two years he had been having an affair with another woman whom he visited every Thursday evening. "Your wife does not know of it?" I asked him. "No," he answered quite positively. "Even though you stay away from home until very late every Thursday?" I was skeptical, but he assured me that he did not neglect his wife and that she believed he went to an important professional meeting each Thursday. "She believes that?" I asked, and added, "If she really has not the slightest idea of it, she must be a kind of freak as a woman." A few weeks later, the patient told me that his wife had said to him during dinner: "Today is Thursday. That's your bum night."

I was, of course, not surprised, but the confirmation of my preconceived notion made me think of the psychological difference between the sexes in a specific way. We assume from the start that women understand men better than men do women, and we explain this by asserting that women are more mysterious than men. The truth is quite different. First of all, women are much more childlike than men and "understand" men in the same way children understand grownups, that is, for the most part intuitively. A woman who does not "understand" men in this way, who cannot see through their subterfuges and pretexts, is less feminine than her sisters. Closer to earth than the man, who has withdrawn further than she from the instinctive and perceptive soil, she still can guess and feel what goes on within him. Although she has no intellectual "understanding" of his professional or technical problems, she is capable of knowing, or at least divining his hidden motives and what makes him tick. To say it in another way, a woman who hasn't this kind of perceptiveness and psychological insight is less of a woman, but—and this is what I am driving at—

a man who "understands" women in this intuitive manner is less of a man.

Here arises another thought that had occurred to me before but had been pigeonholed for later examination. Since Freud, we know that the terms "feminine" and "masculine" are, in a psychological sense, arbitrary. Freud wrote that to distinguish between male and female in mental life is "clearly insufficient, empirical and conventional" [42] and he points to the bisexuality of the individual, who is "neither man nor woman, but both at the same time, only rather more the one than the other." [43] The ratio of mixture is, of course, individually different. There are, in the conventional sense, very masculine women and very feminine men. Extreme development of those tertiary sex characteristics is perhaps not even desirable for the evolution of civilization. To use a comparison: an entirely masculine man would perhaps behave like a bull in a china shop, and a purely feminine woman would be like a cow peacefully chewing the cud in the pasture. We meet such extreme types only rarely in psychoanalytic practice, but approximations of them can well be observed in our society.

To return to our original subject: a woman who is very masculine and lacks that peculiarity of intuitive psychological understanding is—in the sense of conventional evalutations—less feminine. Men, on the other hand, who show a high degree of intuitive understanding of women are—again in the conventional sense—less masculine; in other words, they have strong feminine characterological traits in their character structure.

To present and contrast two types of poets: Friedrich von Schiller's female characters are not very convincing or lifelike; they speak and act as if they were men in disguise. The women in Goethe's dramas (for instance, Gretchen in *Faust*) are real representatives of their sex. Schiller did not understand the emotional and mental processes of women very well. He was an extremely masculine man, also as a poet. Goethe shows a penetrating and acute understanding of women's psychology. The biographers discover some distinct feminine features in Goethe's life patterns.

To conclude these remarks, I quote a maxim of Goethe: "If the eye had nothing sunlike in it, it never could see the sun."

91. *The Always-Never Syndrome*

The patient was a writer in his late thirties. He had married early and his conflict with his wife was for the most part kept under control by him, but was rarely absent from his thoughts when he was at home. In his analytic sessions he often complained about his wife's "always-never syndrome." A syndrome is a concourse or combination of symptoms characteristic of a known disease. As examples of this "always-never syndrome" he quoted his wife: "You always throw ashes around although the ash tray is at your desk," or "You never bring me flowers as other husbands do to their wives," or, "You never pay me a compliment when I have a new hat or a new dress."

Continuing his complaints, he pointed out that these remarks were utterly absurd, but that it was invariably futile to challenge them. What would be the use if he were to say that he was usually cautious; he put his cigarettes and ashes in the ash tray, and only rarely or accidentally beside it? How would it help him if he reminded her that he had said some nice things about her spring costume and only did not like a certain winter hat of hers? She would, nevertheless, belligerently insist that he always threw ashes around and never praised a hat or a dress. "Women are funny, aren't they?" he added.

I confess that at that moment it was the patient who appeared funny to me, his psychoanalyst. Did he, who was in general quite imaginative, not know that his complaints showed a lamentable lack of understanding of women's psychology? He was, of course, correct when he rejected his wife's allegations as wrong from a logical or grammatical point of view, but what man would do that in a discussion with women? Logical or grammatical arguments are inappropriate and inadequate in the war between the sexes. Even if she yielded to such arguments, "a woman convinced against her will, is of the same opinion still."

He should know better and understand the psychological foundations of that "always-never syndrome." The utterly subjective and grossly exaggerated character of the allegations is not the point. When she says that he always throws ashes around she did not mean it literally, but that his carelessness showed lack of consideration for her and her work in cleaning his desk. When she said he "never" brings her flowers, she could also have phrased it "It is an eternity since you brought me flowers as other husbands do. . . ."

Granted he sometimes expressed his approval of a new dress, but did he not also say that he did not like her winter hat? While he defended himself against the allegations of her "always-never syndrome" during his psychoanalytic session, I remembered a cartoon I once saw (was it in an old *New Yorker?*) in which a woman comes home with a new hat which the husband regards somewhat disapprovingly. The caption: "When I want your honest opinion, I'll ask for it."

No, the patient was psychologically wrong. His mistake was that of Professor Higgins, who complains: "Why can't a woman not be like a man?"

92. *Sleep*

It seems that only strong homosexual tendencies caused the Greek mythmaker to conceive of sleep as a beautiful young man. It is otherwise not easily explained why they did not imagine sleep as a tender woman, as a mother. Only mothers take you as gently and affectionately into their arms, rock you, and fulfill your wishes —even those you are unaware of as in the dreams you have during sleep.

93. *Flight*

She runs away screaming from him who wants to kiss her almost as much as she wants to be kissed by him.

94. *More Pleasures*

In general women enjoy life much more than men because they have pleasures very few men experience. Women enjoy the change of clothes, and they look forward to taking a bath and dressing for the evening—an exhilarating anticipation that cheers and buoys them—a sense of pleasurable expectation rarely experienced by men.

95. *Trends of Violence*

The cruel impulses and the trends that drive men to violence have many rationalizations. Men in the seat of high authority are still convinced that people can be made better by means of salutary punishment.

Especially within the family, those dark drives have free rein because men can hide behind the sacred purpose of education. Parents and teachers sometimes imitate the God in whose image they are made also by chastising the ones they love.

I know the wife of a seventy-eight-year-old-man whom she still attempts to educate and to reform. She daily preaches to him and nags him in the belief that the old man will and can give up some bad habits. This, in the words of Talleyrand, is worse than a crime, *"c'est une stupidité."*

96. *Self-Deception*

It is often said that a woman cannot fool another woman nor pretend to be different in character from what she really is without being detected. However, there is at least one woman whom she can deceive about her nature and whose pretense she cannot pierce, namely, herself.

97. *Reasons*

It would be futile to ask a woman what her reasons are for this or that opinion about a man. She could answer as Lucetta did in speaking of Proteus in *The Two Gentlemen of Verona:* "I have no other but a woman's reason; I think him so, because I think him so."

98. *Women's Appearance*

I don't like those fashionable ironing-board figures of many women of our time. They remind me of a story in which a man introduces his wife to his friend and whispers: "Where the pin is, is the right side."

The loss of a single secondary sex characteristic can cause the disappearance of all charm in women. Imagine a group of old ladies; there will be some who are still attractive to men. Then imagine a group of beautiful young women who are all bald—and all charm disappears.

99. *Consistency*

Many women abuse the privilege of their sex to change their minds—to such an extent that they change it with every passing whim, which means every hour (and not on the hour). They resemble those weathervanes that are moved by the slightest breeze in a new direction.

Many men, on the other hand, are overconsistent at any price, to the extent of absurdity. In their obstinacy and arbitrariness they resemble mules that cannot be managed and cannot be veered from their path, however dangerous or senseless it may be.

100. *Death of the Husband*

A fortnight after her husband's death Mrs. Meyer is still disconsolate when she talks about him to her friend Phyllis. "He was so considerate of me and he always thought of providing for me and making my future financially secure. Two years ago he decided to buy those shares of Alhambra. I told him not to buy them, that they were not a good investment; I did not trust the company. I argued with him, but he refused to listen to reason. We lost fifteen thousand dollars. He should have a stroke. . . . Oh, poor Charlie!" she mournfully wailed and bitterly wept.

101. *Make-up*

How far back are the times when women made a secret of beautifying themselves, when they retired to put on lipstick and powder. Our grandmothers would, if they could see women using all these cosmetics publicly before men in drawing rooms and on buses, call them "shameless." Such lack of secretiveness is certainly a sign of the times and shows that a good deal of hypocrisy has disappeared. There remain still enough secrets in this domain.

102. *Secretary*

The president of a large corporation declared that he wouldn't have a male secretary. "Sooner or later a man would inevitably compete with me, an annoyance I wouldn't have with a woman secretary."

103. *For the Birds*

The female bird listens with absorbed attention to the male singing. Is she an expert in music? No more than the human female who listens to a man. What both want to hear is the wooing voice.

It isn't what those voices sing or say that is important. "Heard melodies are sweet, but those unheard are sweeter."

104. *Dresses*

Few women think of themselves as beautiful unclothed. They imagine that they are better-looking when dressed and that they are irresistibly attractive when half-dressed.

105. *Women's Consistency*

The following dialogue was reported by a patient during a psychoanalytic session. He had phoned his girl friend.

"Darling, I have work to finish. Do you mind if I come an hour later?"

"No I don't. Perhaps you should not come today at all. I don't want to rush you."

"As a matter of fact, I really don't know how long it will take me to finish this article. Would it perhaps be better if I came tomorrow evening instead of today?"

"If you don't come today I don't want to see you anymore."

106. *Fragment of a Conversation*

A young man took a young woman out to dinner and a new French movie. After a short walk in the park they returned to the woman's apartment for a drink. They had a pleasant chat. At a certain point in the conversation the woman asked, "What would you wish to do if you knew you were going to die in the next half hour?" The man said: "I would wish to kiss you." Some minutes later he said, "You know, I feel as if I might die in the next half hour." She laughed, and he kissed her.

107. *The Incestuous Taboo*

A patient of mine, a man in his late thirties who was rarely sexually potent, had not approached his wife, slightly older than himself, ever since she gave birth to their child. It was clear that he had unconsciously re-created the incestuous taboo of mother, displaced now to his wife.

One day, about four years later, he had sexual intercourse with his wife. He recognized that this signified a breakthrough of the incest barrier. The morning after, he felt that he had grown up and was mature.

During the time before this occasion he had entered into a kind of platonic relationship with a divorced woman who had a daughter. He had never dared to make advances to the woman although he was very much attracted to her and had many sexual fantasies in which she was the central figure. Sexual intercourse with his wife had a surprising psychological effect; he was now determined to go to bed with that other woman. He said: "If I can function sexually with my wife whom I always considered a mother-figure, I can do so with any woman."

108. *Battle of the Sexes*

We do not question that all is fair in love and war. We have now to learn that all is fair in the war between the sexes.

The various situations on the international scene have their prototype in the domestic life of married couples. There also are secret weapons and cold wars.

I know a married couple whose behavior astonishes me. The wife feels inclined to have sexual intercourse only when there is a serious marital conflict. Her attitude reminds me of the double-faced Roman god Janus. The gates of his temple were closed in time of peace.

109. *Fathers and Daughters*

Fathers walking with their daughters are reluctant to recognize that young men passing by look at the girls with libidinous thoughts. When fathers finally recognize the nature of those glances, it comes as a shock to them. It is as though they have forgotten that they were once young men who looked exactly the same way at the daughters of other men.

A young college girl with whom I discussed this subject said: "I would feel insulted if the men did not look at me with desire." Which proves that we also neglect to consider the attitude of the daughters.

110. *Vanity*

Mystery writers say that criminals in general are vain. Are detectives less so? Think of Hercule Poirot in Agatha Christie's stories and of Inspector Maigret in Simenon's mysteries. The master criminal is vain after he has committed the crime or in the phase of planning it. What distinguishes him from other men —for instance, from artists—is not his vanity but his occupation.

When does a woman give up being vain about her appearance? A Viennese writer remarked that a certain lady dressed for a party self-complacently and looked in the mirror at her shoulders whose beauty had been admired for more than forty years.

111. *Women Once and Now*

A young girl who looked forward to her wedding in a few weeks was, when she consulted me, full of questions about the first night with her husband, especially about her behavior in sexual intercourse. She asked, for instance, "What should I *do* in the situation?"

Such questions are scarcely imaginable in the time of our grandmothers. Women were not supposed to do anything; they were supposed to remain passive throughout the procedure. The man, on the other hand, was bent upon his pleasure (*"Il prend son plaisir"*).

I remember that as a boy I heard of a certain woman who, before going to bed, asked her husband: "Do you want to use me tonight?"

112. *On the Origin of Shame*

A husband wondered that his young wife had no hesitation about taking her panties off in his presence, but never her brassière. It did not occur to him that she was so "paradoxically modest" because she was not proud of her breasts.

113. *The Dullness of Men*

Here are two examples of the strange dullness of an otherwise very intelligent patient in his relationship with women.

On a night flight to Mexico he sat beside a young, attractive girl with whom he chatted. When she finally fell asleep, she leaned upon his shoulder and remained in this position until she woke. A few weeks later she rang him up; he did not recognize her voice or her name. She said: "I called you yesterday. It was a kind of anniversary. Don't you remember, we flew to Mexico together in the night, a month ago?" He did not understand that her call amounted to an approach.

The same man got into an argument with his wife when they returned in a taxi from a performance of Ibsen's *Rosmersholm*. The discussion was about Rebecca West and his wife became angry and embittered. The next day she asked him not to consider the argument "too personal." It still did not occur to him that she had felt hurt because he had not noticed that she wore a new dress for the theatre. He continued to argue in his psychoanalytic session against her reasoning which he took *"au grand serieux."* The incredible dullness and lack of psychological understanding in the relations with women is all the more apparent when you consider that in other areas such men are often very intelligent and perceptive.

114. *You Made Your Bed*

The following bits are, so to speak, vignettes in the picture that I wish to present—a picture whose main subject is the need to be loved, so much more vividly experienced by women than by men. The German poet Adelbert von Chamisso wrote a cycle of lyrics he called *Frauenliebe und-leben,* in 1831. Robert Schumann set some of those poems to beautiful music. Here are a few psychological variations on the theme of *Women's Love and Life*.

A married woman in her forties felt restless and almost unhappy as she tried to get some sleep beside her husband, who slumbered peacefully. At the end of her sad train of thought she arrived at the proverbial saying: "You have made your bed and you must lie in it." Far from giving her peace of mind, that old saying made her all the more restless and disturbed. It occurred to her then that she had made also her husband's bed on this evening as on every night.

Strangely enough, this thought quieted her. Thinking of that part of her daily routine work, she felt at peace. It was as though this reminder aroused her affection for her sleeping husband, an emotion akin to what a mother feels for a child she cares for.

Half smiling, the woman fell asleep thinking of something she had read just recently. It was the inscription engraved on brides' wedding rings long ago—"To his virtues be kind, to his faults a little blind."

115. *A Man's Paraphrase*

Freud has described a certain type of man who is impotent or nearly so with women whom they consider as belonging to the mother or sister group. Such men achieve their full sexual potency only in intercourse with women whom they consider akin to prostitutes. In psychoanalytic practice one often meets this kind of division in the love life of some men, but it is often disguised or displaced. One patient was rarely potent with his wife, of whom he said she was "too much of a lady." What he meant became clearer when he mentioned that he had never seen her in her underwear. Furthermore, he said, "I wish she were more of a whore." It was easy to guess that the expression "too much of a lady" concerned her sexual behavior or, rather, brought her akin to his mother and thus made her sexually taboo.

116. *Parents of the Bride*

A thirty-year-old patient told me why his marriage went on the rocks. Among other reasons, he said that the parents of his wife had a strange concept of sexual life. His mother-in-law told her daughter that sexual intercourse is wished by men when they feel nervous and that they sleep better afterward. A friend of his father-in-law explained that this man would feel much happier if the bridegroom slept with his mother-in-law rather than with the daughter.

117. *Love*

Love is not blind. It sees the qualities and virtues of its object in a glaring light. Love only has blinders which prevent the lover from seeing the other's faults and weaknesses.

A historian of customs will recognize that in France during the eighteenth century love was not treated as tragic. Scarcely even as a serious matter. Valmont told his mistress whom he no longer loved, "One tires of all, my angel." And the angel understood, resigned herself to the fact, or found consolation elsewhere. Men were easygoing, almost libertines. Only after Goethe's *Werther* became fashionable was love considered a tragic theme, something for which one committed suicide or killed. But Goethe the writer was himself far from putting a pistol to his head on account of an unhappy love.

A certain type of man lives according to the tenet, "Love them and leave them." No doubt the second part is correctly defined but it is doubtful that the first is properly named. Should it not be better put: Desire them and leave them?

Young men consider it difficult to be alone with a woman they love for a long time without making love. They think that it is easy only for a eunuch. It is hard for young women to understand that there is such a thing as making love without loving. They imagine that this is possible only for prostitutes.

The well-known actor and singer Ives Montand recently wrote an article titled "Dictionary of Love." [44] He states there that a man "traditionally is pressing for immediate privilege, a woman for long-range advantage"—a sentence charmingly coined in the French manner.

A comparison much less delicately worded than this characterization occurred to me: A man is like a dealer who wants to dispose of his wares quickly in order to sell his goods also to other customers. The slightest criticism of her merchandise offends a woman and makes her disinclined to do business with the purchaser. There are, it is true, among women some who, in their relations with men, are comparable to shopgirls who know the inferior quality of their goods and are eager to sell to whoever asks for them.

A poem by William Morris is titled "Love is Enough." A reviewer reacted to it briefly commenting, "It isn't." He is right: love is not enough for young men with eager sexual appetites, and it is not enough for old men in whom the desire remains without the possibility of satisfying it.

Even the wisest men make fools of themselves about women and even the most foolish women are wise about men.

118. *Periphrastic Delicacy*

Among the many modifications which psychoanalytic technique has undergone in recent decades is a remarkable change in the first interview of the patient before treatment begins. A greater freedom of discussion is allowed the psychoanalyst of today than his predecessor. He is at liberty to ask certain pertinent, or even impertinent, questions from which the psychoanalyst of forty or even thirty years ago would have shied away. Nowadays the psychoanalyst, for instance, feels free to ask about the sexual life of the patient in order to acquire necessary information for basic orientation. In this change of technique, the transformation of our mores is of course reflected. In a majority of cases that *"pénetration pacifique"* for the fundamental insights of psychoanalysis that Freud predicted has already come into effect. Not only the content, but also the manner of expression of information the patient offers in that first interview, may be very instructive. It allow the analyst to draw certain psychological conclusions.

An illuminating example of this kind is from a first interview. The patient was a young, somewhat shy woman in her early thirties who had numerous neurotic symptoms which she described with some hesitancy. Several difficulties had occurred in her married life which had led to open conflict with her husband. For psychological reasons, easily discovered, I asked about their sexual life. After a pause she said that her sexual life was unsatisfactory. Asked why that was so, she became embarrassed and evasive. She played nervously with her handbag, and when I insisted that upon knowing the source of her dissatisfaction, she was obviously at a loss for words. Finally she hesitatingly said that her husband had "paid only lip service" to her for some years. I understood this merely as a way of saying that he did not approach her sexually. When I then asked her if I had understood her correctly, she looked at me with that mixture of pity and contempt women sometimes have toward the lack of male understanding. There was a kind of reluctance or impatience with men's stupidity in her ensuing efforts to clarify what she meant. From her subtle allusions, which became later more intelligible, I at last understood her phrase.

It was simple enough: she meant that her husband restricted his sexual activities to cunnilingus, to kissing or licking her genitals. She did not like this; she even detested it. Her husband's lovemaking left her unsatisfied not only sexually but also emotionally, since she conceived of it as humiliating.

What I wish to point out is the periphrastic delicacy of her statement, the clever and subtle manner of circumlocution or verbal circumvention of the information she had to give me about her sexual life. This is a good example of feminine modesty in speaking of a delicate subject, a masterpiece of subtle allusion to a sexual perversion.

It would be erroneous to assume that only women succeed in such subtle hints. I forget in what scholarly book on sexuality, written by a man, I found cunnilingus described as "displaced osculation." This is certainly correct as a periphrastic definition, but one can't help wondering about such farfetched modesty. Why not call a spade a spade in discussing sexual matters?

119. *Sexual Desires*

Sexual desire for a certain object may sometimes re-emerge long after it is considered dead. Memories of certain scenes or situations that one thinks are long forgotten are suddenly revivified. These memories, which unexpectedly emerged, stir up old sexual desires that had seemed to be dead long ago. Men experience such revivals of old experiences they thought buried long ago and find themselves burning in a fire they had imagined extinguished for many years. The erections they have are resurrections.

120. *New York Legend*

Lucy put the newspaper on the table near the couch on which she spread the sheets. "It will not be as comfortable," she thought, "but it serves him right. He can't treat me this way any longer." While she made the bed for her husband she cried, not only in grief but in anger. She remembered his sarcastic remark of an hour ago, before he went out to the meeting. "No," she thought, "I can't take it any longer. Let him sleep alone. There should be a judge to decide who is right or wrong. Perhaps only God can judge between us."

She went to the bedroom and shut the door; then she undressed and tried to sleep. Her last impression before falling asleep was the sound of cars along Park Avenue. Her last thought was: "O God, be our judge!"

She dreamed that she stood before God to whom she complained of the mistreatment she endured from her husband; she spoke of their last violent quarrel. God's countenance reminded her of Michelangelo's picture of Him. At the same time she recognized the features of the Supreme Court Judge whose photograph she had glimpsed in putting the evening paper on the table. Her knees trembled. She stumbled forward. She heard herself finally stammer: "He wants to live with me but he does not want to live together with me." The Judge looked puzzled and frowned at her: "You don't make sense," He slowly said. "You speak as if you were insane. What do you mean?"

She became terrified and said incoherently: "He does not speak to me, and when he goes to bed he reads the paper. Then he suddenly reaches out for me. . . ." "Well?" said the Divine Judge encouragingly. "I cannot stand this kind of existence any longer. He humiliates me. I am good only for one thing." "Namely?" she was urged. "Just to live with him," she replied. "But you have just said that he does not want to live with you," said the Judge.

She blushed and hastened to explain: "I mean he wants only to sleep with me, but not to share anything else with me." "So you decided that you do not want to live with him. Is that what you mean?" "It's not as simple as that," she hastened to say. "It is difficult to understand you," said the Judge. "You don't want to live with him if he does not live with you. Is that it?"

She felt helpless. How could she explain? "O God!" she said with a deep groan. As the features of the Divine Judge became blurred, she remembered that he was also a man and would not understand.

121. *Showing Off*

Besides modesty there are two factors that determine whether a woman shows certain parts of her body in the company of men. It will depend on whether that part is beautiful and whether it is suitably and attractively dressed. No woman will put her best foot forward, if it is not well stockinged and shoed. Dior in Paris said a dress is beautiful if it awakens in the man the desire to disrobe the woman. She must be well dressed when he wishes to see her nude.

122. *A Showpiece*

A jewel put into a window for display is keenly aware of the impression it makes on passers-by: this is the most appropriate and accurate comparison suggested by a woman coming into a room where, for instance, a cocktail party is in progress.

123. *Skirts and Trousers*

The shape and cut of men's trousers will not interest a woman in the same manner or to the same extent that the skirts of women arouse a man's attention—this is also an indication of the difference in sexual curiosity between men and women.

124. *The Reversed Case*

The book of Proverbs says, "The wicked flee when no man pursueth." Some women pretend to flee in the hope that a man will pursue them. There is a story of the governess who tells little Hans of her experience yesterday evening. "When I left you, a man was waiting at the door outside. I walked away and he followed me. I began to run and he ran after me. . . ." Impatiently the little boy asked: "And did you get him?"

125. *Gracefulness*

" 'She walks in beauty,' " Albert quoted Byron, "but what does this mean? How does the observer become aware of it? I'll tell you: by the movement of her skirts. Your Schiller defined *Anmut* (gracefulness) as beauty in movement. I would dare to claim that a woman's skirt fluttering in the breeze can be given as an example of beauty in movement."

126. *An Important Difference*

Psychologists neglect, it seems to me, a very important difference in the mental and emotional life of men and women. Not only in their sexual behavior, but also in other ways. Women, much more than men, are motivated by the thought of others' opinion of them. This is especially valid in the case of the man a woman likes or loves. ("What will he think of me?") This psychological variation has to be taken into account when men consider how a woman behaves in a certain situation.

127. *Pains*

Women tolerate physical pain better than men and are more able to ease and to assuage pain. They learn this task of softening and easing when they treat little children. When they ease the pain of men, they treat them as if they were babies; that is, cry-babies.

128. *Gallantry*

There are several consolations and compensations for congenital weaknesses and handicaps. One of these, applied to women, bears the noble name of gallantry.

129. *Mother and Daughter*

A man who looks at his prospective mother-in-law will perhaps think: This is how my future wife will look or behave some day. No woman thinks that of her husband when she looks at her prospective father-in-law.

130. *Generalizations*

When one makes a general statement about men, they will agree with it or contradict it. Women dislike generalizations about women because they feel included in them and each woman feels she is an individual entity. If there is a rule, each woman is the exception. Women, therefore, do not like to be compared to other women, not even with respect to a praiseworthy quality. Do not praise a woman in the presence of another woman; she will think you might prefer that woman. Each comparison with another woman, regardless whether it refers to dress or to the preparation of food, is offensive.

131. *The Importance of Sexual Response*

In his *Three Contributions to the Theory of Sex,*[45] Freud pointed out that there is a remarkable difference in the attitude to sexuality between the ancient and the modern world. In antiquity sexual satisfaction was highly appreciated without paying much attention to the partner, while we moderns have a low estimate of sexual gratification as such and evaluate it only as it relates to a certain partner.

If one takes these contrasting attitudes seriously—and I do not think that the difference has often been properly evaluated—one is tempted to follow the line farther back into prehistory, about whose sexual customs we know nothing. It is certainly harmless to indulge in speculations of this kind which might be fruitful and could perhaps be ascertained by new discoveries.

Nothing hinders us from believing—and much could be said for the probability of the assumption—that to the man of the early Stone Age sexual intercourse had the character of rape. We would guess that the Neanderthal man and his predecessor approached the woman from behind. His "courtship" had the character of an attack. To the subhuman male animal the sexual response of the partner was a matter of complete indifference. When a body met a body, it was much more in the manner of animals, *more ferarum:* the man took the woman from behind and what remained of this experience in her memory was perhaps only the sensation of his hands on her and of his sharp teeth in her shoulder. There must have been some sexual gratification for her even in this act—a satisfaction traces of which we sometimes find in the fantasies of our neurotic women patients. In some of them the dark urge to be raped is unconsciously still strong, as Ludwig Eidelberg showed in a recent book.[46]

We need not think of this situation as altogether nightmarish and horrible to the prehistoric woman. Even in those days a woman was perhaps chased by a man until she caught him. It is likely that during the transition from animal-like creatures to *homines sapientes,* sexuality was still tied more closely to periodicity and the ardor experienced was closer to heat in its character and timing. The expression "love-making" is utterly inappropriate for what took place. Foreplay was probably restricted to the behavior we observe in the courtship of animals.

It is also important that the copulative position many primitive

Australian tribes prefer is the sexual entry from behind, as B. Malinowsky, Victor Robinson,[47] and other anthropologists have said.

What I mean to say is that originally sexual intercourse had no personal character and gained it only in the course of man's evolution. Face-to-face intimacy in the sexual position preferred by Western man is a manifestation of the personalization of sexuality.

As I have said before, primitive man was not interested in the sexual response of the female. Possibly he was not even aware of its existence, since for him the removal of his sexual tension was the only important thing. With the individualization and personalization of sexual life the importance of the response of the female partner increased more and more, until it has reached the highest significance in our own time. All psychoanalysts know many cases in which marriages and love affairs have failed because of the woman's frigidity. Often enough we see cases in which the sexual potency of the man disappears when the woman displays coldness and indifference. Some men even expect that a woman should encourage their sexual approach and even take the initiative. Without such obvious or subtle "invitation to the dance" these men can hardly function sexually. In pathological cases of this kind we recognize in distortion and exaggeration how important the sexual response of the woman has become for the man.

In contrast to such extreme behavior there are many cases in which the absence of response is hardly noticed and in which the man does not need the sexual participation or interest of the woman in order to reach his gratification. Sometimes these cases give the impression of relapses into the behavior patterns of primitive man for whom the sexual response of the woman was immaterial.

In the stage of personalization and differentiation of love life we have arrived at in our time, responsiveness has become very important to the man, who often cannot reach full gratification without it. Sexual intercourse has become a two-way street. Very rarely in our world today would a cynic like Bernard Shaw say that sexual relations need not be personal.

Anatole France wrote in *Le Jardin d'Epicure* that Christianity did much for love in presenting it as a sin. The church regarded beautiful women as demons. He reminds women that in the time of the cavemen they did not have as much power as they have over men today, that in those past times they resembled men and men resembled animals. Speaking to them directly, he says: "To change you into the terrible wonders you are today, to become the cause of sacrifices and crimes, two things were needed: civilization, that gave you the veil; and religion, that awakens scruples in us. With all this done you became a secret and a sin." One of Anatole France's most attractive characters, the Abbe Jerome Coignard,[48] who remained devoted to the church, looks admiringly at Catherine, the lacemaker, who sits beside him on a bench. He is inclined to praise God in all His works, including beautiful women. He tells her that if one must sin—and no one is allowed to consider himself infallible—he wishes that the divine Grace would now desert him. Her charms would certainly be an excuse in the eyes of the Lord and would wonderfully reduce his own guilt. "All," he says, "that I see of you, Catherine, speaks to my senses, and what I don't see, even more."

It is obvious that the attribute of sinfulness favored the selectivity of sexual relations and increased with it the value of the sexual response of women. It is strange that the consequences of the transition from impersonal sexuality to a personalized stage are almost never discussed in sexological and psychoanalytical literature. I shall illustrate what I mean by a single feature: at one time, the woman who wanted to escape the male had only one possibility: flight. She had to run away. Modern woman (according to a clever remark by Oscar Wilde) "advances by retreating"—of course, retreating only far enough so that she is still within reach. If we restrict our consideration to the male, the natural and most conspicuous change is, of course, the giving up of promiscuity in favor of a choice of the sex-object. There are, however, other far-reaching transformations of male sexuality. In that age of brute force, when women were attacked rather than wooed, doubts of virility did not exist.

To use a comparison: A man knows whether he is hungry or not. If he is not hungry he will not reach for food. If he is ravenous, it will also not matter much what kind of food it is. Selection and preference of food come only at higher levels of civilization. Only on this level will the question of potency also emerge. Sexual intercourse then became a kind of test for the man. When confronted with this test he was forced to prove that he was potent.

Added to this kind of trial there was, later on, another. A new problem, unknown to our ancestors of the Stone Age, was posed to modern man: to awaken the sexual response of the woman. In this aspect every man is put to the test in sexual intercourse, since success or failure affects his gratification. He is thus in almost every attempt at sexual intercourse put into the situation of Pygmalion, whose task it was to transform a statue into a living and passionate woman. But this new test makes courting and wooing necessary, and is only possible if a prelude precedes intrusion. At this point we reach a stage of evolution when the madness of love sets in and enters a wide area that was originally alien to man's sexuality.

132. *The Ages, the Sexes, and Speed*

"You must slow down," said the physician to me during the long recovery period after my heart attack a few years ago. He demonstrated what he meant by showing me how I should get up from a chair or move from my desk to the door. "You must not jump up now as you used to, nor hurry. Go slowly, move slowly!"

After he left me I wondered about his advice. I was not aware that I had been moving too quickly or hurrying most of the time. Is slowing down not a natural consequence of becoming old? Don't we all check and curb our speed in old age? That is, of course, true, but you must not consider the biological age alone, but also the individual temperament of the person.

Later on, when I was able to stand at the window of our apartment and look at the street below, I observed children as they played or went to school. They all move very quickly. They rarely walk; they almost always run. When you get older, you learn to walk, and the older you get the slower becomes your walk. That old man there moves almost at a snail's pace compared to those playing children. We know, of course, that his slowness is determined by his physical state—for instance, by the fact that he gets short-winded when he walks too quickly. We almost feel that he has not far to go, that his destination is just a little distance away, literally and figuratively speaking.

There must also be another, psychological factor: when we were young we were impatient, we were in a hurry to arrive at our destination. The intensity of our drives did not allow us to move slowly or to linger. Our drives propelled us onward; we were their slaves. When we become old, our drives lose their intensity and immediacy; we are less driven, pulled and pushed by them. Our final and inevitable destination is in sight.

It seems that women are much more patient than men, constitutionally or by education. You have to be patient or, rather, you cannot become impatient when you carry a child within you. You have to learn to wait the full nine months until it arrives. Then, as a mother, you will have to be patient with the child. Yet also here the intensity and force of the drives in women have to be compared with those of men. They are less driven by their drives and do not stand so much under their power.

Thus patience and impatience are not only a question of individual temperament. They depend also on the two sexes and the seven ages of man.

133. *Pregnancy*

In general, a woman who is in love with a man often thinks of him as the father of her child, but a man rarely imagines his sweetheart as the mother of their baby. The imagination of women goes beyond the point of seeing the baby and in the baby its father. They anticipate even the future possibilities of the yet unborn child. In this sense the baby is not only conceived but preconceived. The announcement of the future of yet unborn children, so often met with in legends and the tales of many religions, are perhaps projections of such daydreams of the mothers-to-be.

134. *Old Women, Old Men*

Old women can still mother men, and thus fulfill their functions late in life, while men cannot father their work, and rarely produce something worth while. Yet there are wonderful exceptions: Michelangelo (eighty-nine years old), Franz Hals (eighty-six), Goya (eighty-two), Tintoretto (seventy-six), Rodin (seventy-seven), Renoir (seventy-eight); in literature Goethe (eighty-three), Shaw (ninety-four), Maeterlinck (eighty-seven), Tolstoi (eighty-two), Voltaire (eighty-four), Tennyson (eighty-three), Gide (eighty-two); in music Verdi (eighty-eight), Richard Strauss (eighty-five), Handel (seventy-four), Bruckner (seventy-two), Wagner (seventy); in science Freud (eighty-three), Einstein (seventy-nine) and so on.

135. *Body Movements*

One does not find any good comparisons between the two sexes with regard to body movements. Such comparative observations would show that the body movements of women are much more frequent and vivid than those of men, at least in Western civilization (sport, of course, excluded). In this respect also women are psychologically so much closer to the child than men.

136. *Speech and Silence of the Sexes*

A full bus is an excellent place for psychological observation, especially for comparing the psychology of the sexes. Who has not, for instance, observed that most women wear gloves—even the cheapest cotton gloves—when riding a bus? Do we not get the impression from this that women in general are daintier than men? And who would not notice that a woman for whom another makes room in the seat responds with a smile, which no man in this situation bestows upon his neighbor? It is not difficult to conclude that women have friendlier manners than men.

Certain observations must be re-examined in order to exclude their subjective character. Is it, for instance, correct to assume that women are tardier and more cautious in getting off or on the bus than men? Do more men have their fares ready than women, who often stand beside the coin box or sit behind the conductor to open their bags and search in their purses? To ascertain the facts, for instance by statistical methods, would of course be the first task before attempting a psychological interpretation.

The most fruitful field of comparative observation is perhaps in the different behavior patterns of the sexes in talking and in silence. Observe a man who chances upon an acquaintance in a bus. They sit down beside one another and, after the amenities, discuss business or politics, and so on. You will notice that there are pauses in their conversation and that silences occur after each has said what he wanted to say. Men can sit side by side without talking. For women, this isn't impossible, though difficult. Yet the talk of women is not uninhibited; they avoid certain subjects in their conversations. These subjects might be different from those which women in general steer clear of, but they are there.

Other psychological factors must be responsible for that difference of behavior patterns; what are they? First, examine our basic impression. Men avoid talking when they have nothing to say or do not want to say certain things. Women avoid silence. We will perhaps come closer to the psychological difference when we approach the problem from another side. The Viennese have a proverbial saying, *"Durch Reden kommen die Leut' zusammen,"* which means that in talking with one another, people come together, find a common ground, and become friendly. Should we thus conclude from the evidence that women are more sociable and amiable creatures than men? That is certainly so, but the psychological situation becomes clearer when phrased otherwise. There exists more undiluted hostility between men than between women, who have, despite their rivalry, a kind of sister-feeling. Relations between men are somewhat like between hostile brothers. They will, of course, be occasionally friendly and helpful to one another, but they must first break through the "sound barrier." They must first talk together, and even then there is more often the danger that their conversation will degenerate into a dispute or argument than the dialogue of two women.

We have then, first, the factor of a relatively greater aggressiveness among men responsible for that behavior difference. Even when we assume that there is a great deal of concealed hostility among women, their way of avoiding the risk of expressing it is different from the manner of men. It is not by silence but by talk. Only diplomats among men are convinced that speech is given to mankind not only to express thoughts but also to conceal them.

There are perhaps other factors to be considered in that psychological difference. Women are, in the area we are discussing, more childlike—not childish—than men, which means that they have not withdrawn as much from childhood psychology as men. Observe, for instance, little girls and boys in a bus with their parents. The children say everything they think; yes, thinking and speaking are almost simultaneous. We smile as we listen to their chatter, not only because of their naïveté, spontaneity and uninhibitedness, but also because they verbalize the essential just as they do the trivial. They are not selective in what they say; everything is treated with equal attention. It seems to me that, relatively speaking, women are in this respect, that is, in the simultaneity of thought and speech, closer to the child then men.

Women are enthusiastic talkers or conversationalists. Pursuing our observations of behavior on the bus, don't we notice that women often do not interrupt their conversation while boarding the vehicle together and continue when leaving together? It often happens that the one leaving the bus goes on talking to the one remaining, even while other passengers are being taken on. Is there such a thing as a woman left speechless? At times women continue talking when they are on the step of the bus, turning toward their companion on the curb.

Will the wonder of speaking women never cease? True, woman may be silent, but is a laconic woman imaginable?

When men have said what they wanted to say or wish to avoid a subject, they stop. The rest is silence. Women in the same situation change the subject or the direction of their topic. The rest for them is conversation.

It is not true that women annoy men by talking too much. Rather, women talk when we men wish them to be silent, and they wrap themselves into impenetrable silence when we men wish them to talk. They seem to know the answer to all questions, but when we ask certain questions they don't answer at all.

137. *To Wait and to Keep Them Waiting*

Women's privilege of letting men wait for them is matched by their impatience and annoyance when they themselves are kept waiting by a man. They behave in this situation as if the man had committed *lèse-majesté*. However unmindful they are of their own unpunctuality, the man who is tardy on a date is treated as if he had committed an unpardonable crime, as if he had sinned against the dignity of the waiting woman.

It came to pass, as the Bible has it, that a woman took a cab to the place where she was to meet a certain man. Since the traffic was light, she arrived three minutes early. She had to wait on the street just two minutes. One minute ahead of time, the man appeared. To his astonishment she greeted him coolly, even in a somewhat unfriendly manner. She let him feel guilty, although he was not aware of having done anything wrong. Unconsciously she punished him because he had come "too late," or rather that he had "made her wait" for him, although he had been punctual. She did not, of course, tell him that, but he soon guessed that this must have been why she had seemed cool during the first minutes after his arrival.

There is an analogous psychological situation in the anecdote the historians tell about Louis XIV before whom a nobleman appeared two minutes early. The King received him with the words: "I almost had to wait" (*"J'ai presque fallu attendre"*). So sensitive and vulnerable is the pride of women and kings.

138. *Peculiar Phrases*

A man is supposed not to take insults lying down; a wife is sometimes compelled to do that, but she takes her secret and spiteful revenge on the husband in this very position.

"She uses him as a meal ticket," someone says of a woman, but the listener thought that the meal ticket included the Diners' Club card and iced champagne.

139. *War of the Sexes*

When his wife was more than the usual half hour late, he was about to offer a mild reproach. Before he had even begun to speak, she said, "I know I am a few minutes late. After all, I am not a soldier who must be punctual." He wanted to say that she was not a soldier but a warrior. As if anticipating these words, she bitterly condemned him because he was inconsiderate and failed to realize that a woman going out to dinner needs time to dress suitably and carefully. He remained silent because he knew that anything he might say would change the tiff into fierce encounter. The question in his mind was: is she a clothes horse or a war horse?

140. *Crisis*

The worst crisis in a man's life is not characterized by inertia or inability to work, because such phases occur in everybody's life. The most critical point arrives when he is utterly unwilling to accept responsibilities and feels like becoming a hobo.

141. *Four-Letter Words*

The frequent and casual use of four-letter words by some women, especially of expressions denoting sexual and excretory functions, is rarely characteristic of a low level of upbringing and education. In most cases it is an unconscious travesty or parody of men and their manners and reveals a concealed and often repressed hostility to the male. As such it is comparable to the unconscious mockery contained in the manner in which homosexual men imitate and parody women's speech. Unconscious abuse, rather than use, is in the repetition of these words.

142. *Inscrutable*

We often hear that women are altogether inscrutable and unpredictable; but boys, even when very young, know exactly what they can expect or fear from their mothers. These boys are often terrified of their fathers, who seem to them mysterious and overpowering—no one can tell what goes on in their minds.

143. *The Differences Between the Sexual Curiosity of Men and Women*

While I am trying to formulate some emotional and intellectual differences between men and women, my glance slides from the sheet of paper to the picture before my desk. It is a reproduction of Ingres' famous painting *Oedipus and the Sphinx* that hangs in the Louvre. In the light of the electric lamp the sphinx who poses her well-known riddle to young Oedipus seems to acquire a new significance. The new meaning is contained rather in the contrast of the two figures in the foreground. The sphinx as the mythological representative of woman does not pose a riddle but is herself the enigma for the man. The man she looks at might sometimes appear to her as a funny creature but he is not puzzling to her.

With this digression I return to the problem which was my point of departure.[49] The contrast of the figures conveys the fact that woman is and remains a mystery to man, while he holds no mysteries for her. The psychological distinction originates in the difference of the sexual curiosity of the two sexes—a subject scarcely dealt with in the psychological research of our time. Psychology has taught us that all curiosity has its roots in the sexual inquisitiveness of the child about the anatomical differences of the sexes. This kind of infantile curiosity is originally shared by boys and girls and is directed to the genitals of the other sex. It precedes the curiosity about where babies come from.

Clinical experience in psychoanalytic practice as well as direct observation of children show that the initial curiosity common to both sexes is much sooner and much more easily satisfied in little girls than in boys. The different future vicissitudes of that curiosity of the sexes is determined by the first observation of the anatomical differences.

We have good psychological reasons to assume that the detection of the anatomical differences of the sexes leads to the first manifestations of feminine vanity.

Another result of such early knowledge is the development of shame. The main part of this development comes, however, from external sources and will be later internalized. An old tradition, conveyed from one generation of women to the next, provides for the education of girls to feel shame. A patient of mine remembered from her early childhood how her mother often admonished her "to hide the flesh" when the child exposed herself accidentally.

The interest in where babies come from sets in when curiosity about the anatomical differences of the sexes is almost satisfied and survives the other kind of inquisitiveness. The psychoanalyst Margaret Krafft told her daughter the facts of life early; for instance, the secret of where babies come from. Shortly afterward the mother observed that Lotte built a house with blocks and put a little doll in the middle of it. As soon as that was done the little girl threw all the blocks down. After watching this several times the mother correctly concluded that the child was acting out the delivery of a baby which she conceived as a kind of violent explosion. The mother then built a house with the blocks, put the doll into it and added a door, from which the baby came out peacefully. The little girl understood this application of play technique and repeated this new kind of play.

In contrast to the girl, the little boy who sees the female genitals remains "mystified" for a long time. He assumes at first that everyone, inanimate objects also, are built like him, with a penis. My son Arthur as a little boy thought that a table or chair also had genitals. How is the boy affected when he first observes, for instance, when his little sister is bathed, that girls have different genitals? He denies or disavows his observation and maintains his original view. He assumes, for instance, that a girl's penis is smaller or that it will grow. He might later on think that girls at first had genitals like his but were deprived of them when they were naughty. In other words, he resists at first with all the power of his imagination and with the intensity of rationalization that the anatomy of women is different from that of men. When, later, he hesitatingly accepts this fact, he often develops castration-fear and other symptomatic manifestations of his reluctance to acknowledge the basic difference.

His sexual curiosity remains essentially unsatisfied. This frustration is heightened by the fact that the female genitals are located in a secret place of the anatomy. The aim and direction of the little boy's sexual curiosity is thus determined by the failure of his inquisitiveness in this direction. In reality the man retains curiosity with regard to the secrets of the female body although he has been consciously familiar with them for a long time. This unconscious curiosity is revived with every young woman he sees and enhances her attractiveness. He will be sexually aroused by fantasies of nude or near nude female bodies, whereas most women are not sexually excited by imagining a nude man.

The original curiosity directed to the female genitals is extended to the dresses and underwear of women. In August Strindberg's play *The Creditors* a character speaks of the "mystery of the skirt." It is as if that mystification by the concealed location of the woman's genitals is transferred to the garment that has become sexualized. Strindberg, that monomaniac playwright, is for us no longer a tragic figure but rather a pathetic one. Yet any man who reads Strindberg's biography in which he is presented as moaning, "The skirts, the skirts," is aware of a faint echo of that emotion in himself. Men's garments do not acquire that kind of sexualization in women's thoughts and are thus not objects of sexual curiosity.

It is perhaps advantageous to approach the problem of curiosity from another angle. We acknowledge that inquisitiveness has its roots in infantile sexuality—but is that curiosity indissolubly tied to the area of sexual drives? Is it not later transferred to the region of affectionate feelings and directed to the object of love? Did not Casanova once say that love is three-quarters curiosity? Without being clearly aware of it we understand that love is here conceived in the sense of the French *"amour,"* which means sexuality. Don't we call sexual intercourse "making love," although frequently love during this activity is conspicuous by its absence. This is a misnomer since the process is often no more than a "scrotal frenzy," as it was once characterized, and its essence is not to make love but *"faire l'animal avec deux dos,"* as the French say—to present the animal with two backs.

It seems to me that curiosity might be transferred from its sexual origin to other areas, yet it is alien to love. Love presupposes familiarity and intimate understanding of the object and excludes such an indiscreet and often rude emotion as curiosity.

Is it not significant that women are rarely inclined to sexual curiosity about men? The French language has no feminine form of the word *voyeur*. There is no female type corresponding to the peeping Tom. There are, of course, fleeting moments of sexual curiosity also in women, especially in neurotic or prepsychotic ones. In my own psychoanalytic practice I have observed only one case in which repressed sexual curiosity produced a compulsive symptom in a neurotic woman. The patient was compelled to search immediately for the door latch in a room whenever she was in it with a man or with many men. This originally vague and incomprehensible compulsive symptom became clearer when I understood that the patient had forbidden herself to look at something that was lower than the door latch. The origin of this strange prohibition became transparent later. The patient had been tempted to look at a man's fly on a certain occasion and fought against that temptation. By a process of generalization she developed a counter-compulsion and protected herself against the re-emergence of this kind of impulse by always searching for the door-latch or another object at that level in the room. Such pathological cases are, however, rare with women. In general their original sexual curiosity loses its sexual component and is not even revived in puberty, as it is with the adolescent boy. Besides the psychotic and neurotic cases of women in which the original sexual curiosity emerges from childhood, there is a singular occasion when it returns for a moment. I mean just before sexual intercourse. Experienced men have observed that women in this situation sometimes cast a sidelong, furtive glance at the body of the naked man. A woman told me that when she saw the erect penis of her husband on their wedding night she thought: "How will I ever get that big thing inside me?" What appeared as a renewal of childhood's sexual curiosity of women is in reality a wish to see how much the man desires her. The size of the erection is, so to speak, a measure of her desirability.

Anatol France once remarked in *Le Jardin d'Epicure* that men

need forms and colors in love, while the women strive for sensations. They love better than we men, says France, because they
are "blind." He refers to the beautiful allegorical fable of Psyche
who is forbidden to look at Cupid, her lover, and raises her lamp to
see him in the night. But Psyche is not the woman but the soul.
Psyche wanted to see and women want only to feel. Psyche was
searching for the unknown and what women search for is not the
unknown. It is mostly men who insist on "making love" when there
is light, never women.

The original curiosity of the child does not remain restricted to
the genitals and body of the opposite sex. It is significant that in the
fantasies of men the sexual response of the woman plays a considerable role, whereas the fantasies of women begin with the
courting of the man and slowly move to the sphere of sexuality.
While women in general imagine first how the man woos them,
calls them sweet names, admires and desires them, men anticipate
in his imagination how the woman will sexually surrender to him.
I assume that Casanova's remark that love is three-quarters curiosity refers to the man's eagerness to know his object in the sexual
situation. It cannot be accidental that the language of the Bible uses
the expression "to know" a woman (Hebrew *yadda*) in the sense
of having sexual intercourse with her, as if in this most intimate
situation the curiosity of the male is finally satisfied. Nothing in the
psychology of women can be compared to this kind of sexual inquisitiveness in the male.

We anticipate that the character and the direction of men's and
women's curiosity will be different. They are, in the last analysis,
also determined by the anatomical differences on which the curiosity of male and female child was at first focused and by the kind
of satisfaction that early inquisitiveness achieved.

No one will claim that women are less curious than men. The cat
that was killed by curiosity was certainly female, and it was curiosity that made Bluebeard's eighth wife open the door of the forbidden room. We see here a new aspect of the problem. Women
are as curious as men—perhaps even more so—but their inquisi-

tiveness is aroused by other things and their interests go into different directions from those of men.

Even women's curiosity about people has a different character. Above all, it is personal and often competitive. My daughter-in-law, Mignon, said the other day: "Men sometimes look at each other, but women size each other up." Impersonal inquisitiveness is rarely to be found in women. Yet, as a British historian wrote some years ago, "Disinterested intellectual curiosity is the life blood of real civilization." [50] There is certainly a significant difference between that personal inquisitiveness and the "holy curiosity" of which Einstein often spoke.

Very few women are interested in the nature and laws of the planets—except the moon, which is important to them because of their monthly cycle. Very few women feel the urgent wish to explore unknown territories of even our little planet.

Curiosity is mostly mixed with many aggressive and sadistic impulses which are not as developed in women as in men and which are energetically suppressed in the course of a girls' education.

When the original sexual curiosity loses its sexual component, becomes "desexualized" in later development, it will be applied to the solution of other problems. The infantile sexual curiosity of the boy is, as Nunberg pointed out, often sublimated to interest in business and scientific investigation. In the earliest stages curiosity is "amalgamated with sexuality" [51] and its energy is later used to master the external world and is directed to other kinds of reality. The infantile search for the genitals can even become research.

To return to the beginning of this discussion—the solving of the sexual problem, the answer as to the nature of the genitals of the opposite sex leaves indelible traces in the evolution of the sexes.

To illustrate the direct connection between infantile sexual curiosity concerning the female genitals and the man's later interests, here are two instances. A comparative study of the sexes proves that boys and men (because men will remain boys) are much more interested in machinery than are women, who take the forms and functions of machinery for granted. A few years ago I presented an excellent example of such a contrast in the analysis of a little story by Louise Field Cooper in *The New Yorker*.[52] The unconscious meaning of a subterranean pump is there clearly understood as representing the vagina with all its mysteries of form and function.

A second example is men's great interest in cars. You hear a taxi driver speaking of his car and saying: "Today she's moody again," calling it "she." In dreams cars also represent symbols for the female body. And why not? Is not a person sitting inside like the embryo in the mother's womb? Even the joke unconsciously acknowledges this concealed meaning. A cartoon comes to mind: a man is saying to his friend who is desperately trying to catch a bus: "Never run after a bus or a woman! In one or two minutes another one will come."

144. *Why Women Smile More Often Than Men*

More than thirty years ago I published a theory according to which our first reaction upon hearing an aggressive witticism is unconscious fright.[53] This emotion is awakened by the attack on persons or institutions that are highly esteemed or tabooed. That fear at the emergence of forbidden thoughts is immediately recognized as superfluous. The facial effect of this sudden removal of fright is a momentary relaxation of the facial muscles, the expression we see when we look at someone laughing or smiling. The transition from heightened and frightened attention to a sudden relaxed attitude is the simplest analogy to this process.

I should like to follow this theory just a few steps further before I come to my subject. The psychological preposition for it is the presence and efficiency of a certain kind of free-floating anxiety which is intensified when we hear a joke directed, for instance, against marriage, religion, and other highly valued social institutions, or against respected persons. The transition from thought-fright to laughter is the extreme case, but the same process of sudden relaxation also takes place in a diluted or weaker form when we smile. Also, the conditions for the facial change are the same.

It is at this point that the question arises: why do women smile more often and more easily than men? The superficial answer is, of course, that they are friendlier or more sociable than men, but this shallow reply does not satisfy us and we go on searching for a deeper psychological explanation. If the theory presented here is correct, we are confronted with the following alternative: either women are more anxious, whatever the reasons might be, or it is easier for them to make the transition from an anxious or concerned state to a relaxed one. A combination of the two factors could well explain the greater frequency of female smiles.

If my theory is correct, that initial anxiety is aroused by the attack on highly esteemed institutions or persons by the temptation to attack those things or people, oneself; by temptation-anxiety. Well, are women generally more aggressive or inclined to violent attack and do they therefore experience more anxiety? All the findings of biology and psychology contradict such an assumption. We must therefore exclude any attempt to explain the frequency of feminine smiles by presuming a more intensive aggressiveness of women. The other attempt at explanation, namely, the easier transition to a relaxed state, is perhaps more realistic. It takes into account the fact that women are psychologically closer to the attitude of children whose changes of mood are so swift and numerous. We shall thus consider the changeability of mood as a contributing factor.

Yet it is certainly not sufficient to explain why women smile so much more often and so much easier than men. We have perhaps overlooked something in our first assumption or dismissed it too soon. We return to it by a detour. Without doubt women in general are less aggressive than men, but when we come back to the theory of the relaxation of the facial muscles, a theory explaining the emergence of smiles, we must ask: is intensive anxiety really the only underlying emotion that is suddenly diminished and loosened in smiles? We know from the papers of Anna Freud that children react with loud laughter when they recognize that a strong anxiety they had felt was superfluous; for instance, when they realize that mother had merely put on a mask which she quickly removes.

However, this is not laughter but smiling—something much less intense, although the relaxation is basically the same.

We guess thus that the underlying anxiety that is relaxed is either much less intensive or comes from another source. We arrive at the idea that women are much more concerned than men about the impression they make upon persons around them. They are much more concerned with the effect of their appearance and with how they seem to others. This interest is in some sense anxiety-producing. This means that they allow themselves the emotional relaxation whenever they feel that they are liked or accepted. The smile expressed in the muscle relaxation of the face is thus the manifestation of a loosening or diminishing of that anxiety or attention directed to the impression upon persons around them; their smiles indicate that this impression was pleasant, the previous slight anxiety superfluous.

Since a smile usually beautifies a face, the sequence here sketched can be reversed; in order to please or to appear pleasant, a woman may smile. This she does, for instance, in greeting a person.

But with this extension of our theoretical attempt we already enter another problem area, namely, that of the uses of feminine smiles. This territory is wide: it extends from the simple welcoming smile of a salesgirl to the tantalizing and enigmatic smile of Mona Lisa.

145. *A Feminine Notion*

When I was a little boy we had a kind of housekeeper who was a distant relative of my father's. This woman, who spoke in Viennese-Jewish jargon, was once invited to dinner by a neighbor. My mother asked her what food she had been served. She answered: *"Zwetschkenknödel"* (dumplings filled with plum preserve), and added, "You could have sat down on them in a silk dress." I still remember that I was puzzled by that remark. Afterward, I understood that she had meant the dumplings were cooked with so little fat that you could risk sitting on them in a silk dress without getting grease spots.

146. *Male Symbol*

Anatole France, discussing Napoleon with his secretary, Jean Jacques Brousson, asserted that the Emperor was not much of a man. "Napoleon was not, in the strict sense of the word, impotent, but he was not a particularly lusty fellow either. Not much of the Luxor obelisk about him." The witty allusion to the erection of the penis is the same as it appears in dream symbolism.

147. *Mother's Advice*

A mother told her daughter, who complained that not many boys looked at her, "You know, men look at the eyes and the mouth of a girl. You are almost not aware of the expressions of your eyes and mouth; you never do anything about them. The eyes and mouth of a woman must cooperate to arrive at a certain impression."

148. *The Romantics*

Women like the romantic attitude men have toward them and they encourage it. They avoid everything that could minimize it, and even develop a kind of protective coloring to maintain it; but they themselves are uncompromising realists with regard to men.

149. *Rotation*

They say it is love that makes the world go round. I can well believe it, since that rotation has such an erratic and crazy character.

150. *Sexuality of Old Age*

You will find some astonishing statements about the sexuality of old men in sexological and psychological literature, not to mention the popular books, marriage manuals, and the like. There are, for instance, statements that many men preserve their full sexual potency until their late seventies or even eighties. More important than facts and figures, at present, is the presentation of the emotional processes in the sexual activity of these men. To ask the right questions in this regard is almost as revealing as finding the correct answers. How and by which means are those men sexually aroused, and what images enable them to function sexually and to overcome the inertia and the lack of libido concomitant with age?

It seems to me that very old men develop certain feminine characteristics also in their sexual behavior patterns. That is to say, certain psychological preliminary conditions must be fulfilled in order to arouse them and to enable them to function satisfactorily in sexual intercourse, and that some of those conditions are similar to those met with in the realm of feminine sexuality. It is, for instance, favorable if the woman initially shows some affectionate and then some sexual interest—yes, even that she takes the initiative in the arousal process. It is as if man and woman exchange their pattern of sexual behavior, as if the man had taken the feminine role to some extent. Such initiative on the part of the woman is even supposed to be a therapeutic agent. When King David was old "and stricken in years," he felt cold. His servants said, "Let there be brought for my lord the king a young virgin: and let her stand before the king, and let her cherish him, and let her lie in his bosom." They found Abishag, a Shunammite, whom they brought to the king. "And the damsel was very fair, and cherished the king, and ministered to him" (I Kings 1: 2-4). The courtiers no doubt meant well, but the king was too old; he "knew her not," which is to say he could no longer have sexual intercourse.

151. *Old Man, Young Man*

What is the most precious secretion the human body produces? Only old men know what it is. Young men waste it without considering its value. A little story that, if memory does not fail me, was told by Brantôme almost four hundred years ago, presents a vivid and salutary lesson not soon forgotten.

There was once a very old and very learned man who knew all the secrets of magic and all the mutations of metals. He could manufacture the rarest substances and essences, even the elixir of life. Serving him was a young man who looked after the furnaces and containers, helped him to break metals, and similar chores.

On one occasion, the young man, who envied the art of his master, expressed his great admiration for the old man's science. "Oh," he said, "how I would like to be able to make essences like you."

The old alchemist looked sadly around at the many vials and retorts in his laboratory and gently said, "My boy, I would give all my secrets, all my liquid gold, and the elixir of life for the essence you produce in your body."

152. *Patience*

Young people are impatient with themselves and with others. They think they should be nobler and better than other people. In old age one becomes patient and realizes one cannot run away from oneself. It is also true that emotional experiences can stir one so deeply that the individual may mature as a person to the extent that he can accept himself. St. Francis de Sale said, "Be patient with everyone, but above all with yourself."

153. *Frustration*

American psychiatrists and psychologists often speak of a low or high frustration threshold, meaning the individual reactions produced by frustrations. We know that the child reacts to frustration immediately and intensively. The little boy asking for an apple does not even give his mother the time to go and fetch the apple from the kitchen: he shouts: "An apple, an apple!" It is only later on that he learns to wait. The older we get, the more we can stand waiting and the more patient we become. Youth is vehemently impatient; old age is generally patient.

154. *Money and Age*

If you are a poor boy, you will sometimes be worried about whether you will have enough money to eat tomorrow. Later on you will worry if there is not enough money to carry you through your studies. As a mature man you will sometimes be apprehensive about making ends meet for your wife and children. In time, you will be concerned about the means for the children's education. Then follows a time when you are anxious about leaving your family provided for. If you should get seriously ill, you will weigh life expectancy and the savings at your disposal. In the end, your concern is to leave enough so that your family can live without worries and without paying the government too much inheritance taxes.

155. *Complaint*

We just chatted, an old man and I, sitting on a bench in Central Park. "You are about my age, aren't you?" he said. "You know, only the other day I really understood how old age changes us. When I was young, and even in middle age, I used to look at the legs of women walking in front of me or coming my way. I was especially interested in their shoes, and the tapping of high heels intrigued me. No more. . . . That's natural, but there is more to it. Now I look at men's shoes. I'll tell you why: my feet ache; they kill me. I have tried all kinds of footwear and shoes; nothing helps. I now catch myself looking at what kind of shoes men wear, wondering why they walk comfortably and without complaining. To be interested in women, to follow them, you have to be a good walker—'un marcheur,' as the French would say."

156. Old Age and Reading

Men who become old often lose their taste for reading fiction. Novels and romances make them impatient sometimes; they no longer enjoy the ups and downs of the emotional processes of love and hate. As far as I can see, old men still read mystery stories if well written; these are not read for emotional excitement but because they present riddles to be solved and appeal to the intellectual curiosity. The interest in passions which we experienced when we were young and which we vicariously satisfied in reading is after a while replaced by intellectual interest, until this too vanishes.

157. Old Age and Youth

Only people who have things to look forward to are living a full life. Others, who only have memories, live a shadow existence. There is a deep meaning to the story in Genesis, of Lot's wife who looked back and became a pillar of salt. Properly understood, the legend says that a person to whom only memories are left approaches the inorganic state, becomes like stone.

Young people have an eager appetite for mental nourishment, especially for what is new. When one is old the appetite in this respect diminishes. Old men are unable to swallow and digest all the new thoughts that are served to them and they can take only small bites. It is as if they have mental dental plates and cannot bite off big pieces. They are afraid of biting off more than they can chew.

Old ladies acquire a great deal of practical wisdom and they sometimes regret that they can no longer make use of it with respect to their own love life. They can, however, use it in the interests of their daughters and granddaughters. But when they do, their opinions and advice are considered hopelessly obsolete and outdated. The old ladies have forgotten that the mores also change with regard to love. What they consider wisdom might easily be looked upon as foolishness by the new generation.

The facial resemblance between husband and wife who have lived together for many years is undeniable, and is perhaps the result of the conjunction of various biological and psychological factors. Married life is a continual compromise resulting in the mutual adjustment of the two partners. This ultimate adjustment has, of course, left traces in the facial expressions and physiognomy of both partners. There is, furthermore, the biological speculation that with old age women become more masculine and men more feminine in their facial expressions.

When the candle is down to a nub we recognize—too late—that we have led a kind of half-existence. Is this life, or is it mere vegetating? The candle has almost burnt out, and it does not give enough warmth or light to see things clearly. Is that myself I see in the mirror, grown so dim, or is it a stranger? Alas, there is not enough light to recognize even oneself.

158. *To Speak*

When you are young, you feel like talking a lot and you sometimes say what you really think. When you are old, you want to speak your mind—if you want to speak at all.

159. *Flight*

We are all in a race for dear life: that is to say, we are fugitives from death. While we run for our life we know that death will catch up with us. If this is certain, what is still questionable? Only one thing: when this will be.

160. *Impressions*

As long as you are young, you have many and vivid impressions and you welcome and absorb them quickly. When you get old, you are less and less impressed and less impressionable. A comparison comes to mind: first the door of your mind is wide open and everybody and everything arriving at it is welcome. Later, that door is only half-open and still later it is just ajar, until finally it is shut —not with a bang but soundlessly.

161. *Old Men*

Bernard Shaw who reached the age of ninety-four once remarked that old men are dangerous because they have no future. That is correct as far as theory goes: old men are no longer afraid; they can treat all convention with contempt and they can say terrible and terrifying things—if they are able. That means if they are in the mood to say them and still can. But often they don't feel like expressing those daring truths and sometimes they are already unable to formulate them. The last things Shaw wrote are rarely illuminated by his old wit and sometimes sound childish. Old men are dangerous, it is true, and so are old dogs who would attack every intruder—if they were not too tired to jump and if their teeth were intact. The best those old dogs can do is to bark, and since their senses are not what they used to be, that is, as sharp as they once were, they sometimes bark at the wrong tree.

From Goethe's *Maxims and Reflections:* "When one is old, one must do more than when one was young." It is very doubtful if this sentence is psychologically correct. More likely it appears to be more to the old man who is already tired. Besides, it seems to be more because there is an urgency to bring the haywagon home before nightfall.

162. *The Cup and The Wine*

The psychologist will enjoy the witty remark of a British writer that it is not true that we leave our vices behind when we are old, but that the vices leave us behind in old age. Reflecting on this, the psychologist may be inclined to replace the word "vices" by "drives," because the terms vice and virtue are as alien to the way of his thinking as to the zoologist observing the behavior of an animal.

What is, however, correct is that the aging process is accompanied by a lessening of those tensions characteristic of our drives. Our appetite, by and by, diminishes and so does our sexuality. Yet with them also some emotions connected with those drives are reduced in intensity and slowly vanish. Popularly said, we also lose the virtues of our vices. That detachment of the aging process, called "emotional disengagement" by psychologists, diminishes not only our ability to hate but also the power of our love.

It is mistaken to call old age a second childhood, because children are full of impulses and desires, however split up and fleeting. How right was Bernard Shaw when he asserted that youth is wasted on the young! They don't know what precious qualities we old people envy in them. Old Goethe, looking back on his life, spoke to them in words of practical wisdom:

> *Wen's dir's in Kopf und Herzen schwirrt,*
> *Was willst du Bess'res haben?*
> *Wer nicht mehr liebt und nicht mehr irrt,*
> *Der lasse sich begraben.*

Freely translated:

> What better things do you want
> Than to be driven, confused and hurried?
> He who doesn't love nor err any more,
> Is better dead and buried.

With the pressing intensity of the drives, the pleasures also leave us and the *joie de vivre* wanes more and more. The other day a seventy-four-old woman complained to me: "I can remember how I liked to put my apartment in the best order so that everything in it looked nice. I no longer even take pleasure in bestowing care upon my flowers." Young people should be reminded of that, and told, "Enjoy, enjoy!"

A famous German writer, Friedrich Hebbel (1813-1863), said, looking back at his life: "First the cup is missing and later the wine."

163. *Young Men, Old Men*

Young men without an idealistic concept of the world are to be pitied. They are like people who are convinced that the world ends at the boundary of their village. Old men who are idealists are equally to be pitied. They are to be compared to children who imagine that they can travel through the stratosphere at will. Each age has its own suitable concept of the world; youth should be idealistic, old age should be realistic.

164. *The Old and the Young Ones*

Today, June 8, 1962, I gave the commencement address at Sarah Lawrence. Introduced by President Ward, I improvised a chat on "Freud in Our Time." I concluded it with the following words: "My situation today, looking at you young ladies, is comparable to that of a traveler whose train nears its destination and who sees many persons there about to start on a journey. A has-been who has not been much greets the will-be's."

165. *Illusion*

In our youth we cling to many ideas and cherish many illusions which often amount to the same thing. The most gorgeous illusion is, of course, that of love, and it is often the most dangerous one. The older you become, the more illusions are dispelled and destroyed and the more ideals are forsaken. When you are very old, scarcely any illusions are left to you. They are shattered as are the playthings of a child who has outgrown them. Finally, life itself is recognized as an illusion that dissolves itself. It is doubtful if life can be tolerated without illusions. Perhaps we would be as children without any toys.

166. *Early*

Old people cannot sleep long. They wake up early and they sometimes think: "The early bird gets the worm." But the early birds know that their eyesight is not what it used to be, so that they could not even find the worm, and if they did they could not digest it. It is certain that soon the worms will get and digest *them*.

167. *Life*

Youth wants changes, and hopes of course that the changes it foresees and strives for will be for the better. Old age wishes that all should be as it is and wishes nothing better. It is conservative because the change it foresees can only be for the worse: disease and death. In spite of its faults and shortcomings it loves life, or at least it wants to stay alive as long as possible, to remain loyal to "that bitch Life" (the expression *"cette chienne de vie"* is from Madame de Sévigné) because it is the best of its kind we know.

Part III : *From the Notebooks of An Old Psycholanalyst*

ON UNIVERSAL FETISHISM

I

Freud's theory on fetishism was subjected to some modifications in the interval of more than twenty-five years between his first formulations in 1905 and his last paper on the subject in 1927.[54] Yet the core of that theory remains the same, namely, that the fetish is originally the substitute for the penis which the little boy missed in the women he observed. There is enough that is still puzzling in the problem of the genesis and nature of that strange deviation, as Freud himself pointed out.

I would like to turn the attention of psychologists to a special subject within this area because it has been, it seems to me, neglected not only by Freud himself but also by his students afterward. Freud commented that we can speak of fetishism in its precise sense only when the fetish replaces the normal goal of the sexual drive, when it gets disengaged from a certain person and becomes a sexual object as such. He states that a certain degree of "fetishism" belongs to the attributes of the normal state of being in love, especially in those phases of infatuation in which the normal sexual goal is for the time being unattainable. He thus concedes that a certain degree of fetishism is, so to speak, normal in phases of infatuation in which the things connected with the love object are overevaluated.

Let me compare the case of a shoe- or foot-fetishist with the case of a man who admires the shod foot of a certain woman. The fetishist becomes sexually excited when he sees a certain shoe of the woman, even in her absence, an experience which the normal lover does not have. The psychological difference is sharp enough, but we often find cases in psychiatric literature in which the lover expresses his admiration for the foot and shoes of his sweetheart and is called a fetishist. If this were justified, one could suspect the poet who wrote the Song of Solomon of fetishism since there is a line (VII: 1) "How beautiful are thy feet with shoes, O prince's daughter!"

To return to Freud's theory as formulated in that last paper on fetishism in 1927, he stated again and again that the observations of the female genitals awakened in the little boy castration anxiety. If it were possible that women have no penis (or had been castrated) it could also happen to the boy that he loses his highly valued penis. That castration-fear or -fright is, in Freud's opinion, universal, and no male is spared that experience.

We do not know why it is that most men conquer that fear while others become homosexuals or fetishists. This is one of those psychological problems that has remained unsolved. In all events, the denial of the infantile observation, namely, that women have no penis, is unconsciously shared by all men.

Freud also discusses the frequent shoe- and foot-fetishism of men and explains its origin by pointing to the sexual curiosity of the boy. The male child will try to look at the female genitals from below, and his attempt at exploration is arrested on the way by repression. Thus the foot or shoe was, so to speak, a station on the way to the destination and is retained as a fetish. We may perhaps find an indirect confirmation of that gliding of the glance from Alfred de Musset (1810-1857) who wrote: "When one sees the foot, one will guess what the leg is like" (*Que, lorsque on voit le pied, la jambe se devine*).

Freud's theory goes so far but no further, namely, into the area of the "normal" fetishism, the fetishism "de tout le monde" as a writer called it,[55] meaning that universal fetishism of all males. It is in this area that I want to make my point. But have I a point? It seems to me that I have at least two.

II

It is well known that, at least until recent times, the Chinese mutilated the feet of their female children. It is perhaps less well known that a foot that was not deformed was considered a disgrace in China and that only the husband was allowed to see the naked foot of his wife. A Chinese woman would as little show her naked feet to another man as a European woman her breasts. Travelers have said that many Chinese men experience an "indescribably voluptuous feeling" in touching naked female feet.[56] Also, among the Turks of the Volga it is indecent to show a female foot unshod or without stockings.

How far can we follow that strange phenomenon of bashful feet? Clement of Alexandria, who wrote his book around 200 A.D., recommended that the women of his time wear shoes as it was not fitting for their feet to be shown naked.

We owe to Salomon Reinach much information about the subject contained in a paper he called *"Pieds pudiques."* [57] Many writers of the sixteenth and seventeenth centuries comment on the special shame the ladies of Spain and Italy experienced at the possibility that men might see their feet. Countess d'Aulnoy gave many instances of that shame-characterizing taboo of the feet in her letters from Spain. She described, for instance, a luxurious carriage in Madrid that had an extra curtain reaching to the ground and preventing men from seeing the feet of the ladies when they descended.

To show a man one's foot was *"la dernière faveur"* a lady bestowed on him. P. de Brantôme, early in the seventeenth century, described similar attitudes of the Italian ladies. Roman woman often wore such long robes that it was impossible to see their feet. Brantôme states that a beautiful foot has a special voluptuousness in itself (*"portait une telle lascivité en soy"*).[58]

In her *Memoires* Madame d'Aulnoy reports the arrival of Marie-Anne of Austria, the second wife of Philip IV, at a Spanish City. Among other gifts, the citizens also offered silk stockings to the queen. The majordomo threw those packages back to the deputies of the city and shouted, "Learn that the queens of Spain have no legs." The poor young queen took this literally and cried, wishing to return to Vienna because she thought that there was a plot to cut her legs off. Indeed, the taboo of feet was maintained for a long time. A well-known anecdote tells how Kaiser Franz Joseph once warned his young wife Elisabeth descending from a carriage that people could see her feet (*"Madame, on voit vos pieds"*).

III

It would seem likely that the partiality for high heels in women's shoes was something modern in an age when the ladies wore long skirts covering their legs. High heels are, so to speak, the substitute for the penis, missed by the little boy who had an opportunity to observe the female body. It was considered indecent to look at the feet of women. Yet women have to walk, and it could not be entirely avoided that some part of their shoe was visible. They walked cautiously, of course, always aware of the taboo of feet. In his "Ballad upon a Wedding" Sir John Suckling (1609-1642) described that way of walking:

> Her feet beneath her petticoat
> Like little mice, stole in and out,
> As if they feared the light. . . .

During such occasional observations when the shoes were visible, it was seen that the ladies wore high heels as if they wanted to alleviate the unconscious castration-fear of the male. Again, in transferring the picture of the female genitals down to the feet, high heels provided, so to speak, the illusion of the penis' presence.

High heels on ladies' shoes were already well known in the eighteenth century. As an eloquent witness to their attractiveness was Réstif de la Bretonne (1734-1806), of whom a French writer says that he spent his life at the feet of women (*"on peut dire qu'il a passé sa vie aux pieds de femme"*).[59] In his autobiographical writings, de la Bretonne reports that at the age of four he was already attracted to girls' feet and shoes. When he was a young man he wrote a novel, *Le pied de Fanchett*e (1769), whose central interest is the beautiful foot and the high heels of the Duchess of Choiseul. De la Bretonne praised high heels, asserting that they gave to the gait of a woman something undecided, hesitant and afraid that aroused the appetite of the man. In spite of some defenders,[60] there is no doubt that de la Bretonne was a foot fetishist. Descriptions of his own experiences confirm that impression.

It is, however, noticeable that he had along with *"ce goût singulier"* a good deal of what we would call "normal fetishism." It is not important to us whether his characterization of the gait determined by high heels is correct or not. What matters is that he turned our attention to high heels as an attraction to men.

Continuing our literary researches in this direction (we restrict ourselves to French literature), I recall an episode in Anatole France's *Penguin Island,* written more than a hundred years after de la Bretonne's death. In this novel, a Professor Huddock is described as the *enfant terrible* of the Parisian salons. This savant makes himself objectionable by his daring and paradoxical statements. He asserts, for instance, that the virtue of provincial ladies is solely due to the fact that they wear low-heeled shoes. In a learned paper, published in the *Anthropological Review,* he states that a woman "attracts a civilized man in proportion as her feet make a certain angle with the ground. If this angle is as much as thirty-five degrees, the attraction becomes acute." The position of the feet upon the ground determines the whole carriage of the body, he asserts, and concludes that provincial women, since they wear low heels, are not very attractive and preserve their virtue with ease.

So much for the conclusions of Professor Huddock, which have not been generally accepted. At all events, they bring us back to the topic of "normal fetishism." Before going into the discussion, it will be helpful to remind the reader that Salomon Reinach, in his article on *Pieds pudiques,* found a surviving trace of that taboo of feet in our country sixty years ago.[61] The word "leg" was at that time avoided by polite ladies; instead, "limb" was considered proper. Well, times have greatly changed that taboo of feet—in words and deeds.

IV

In a recent article on fetishism,[62] it is defined as a "psychosexual aberration or complex in which the person's sex impulse or libido becomes attached to or fixated on something that constitutes a sexual symbol of the love-object." It is, of course, a far cry from this kind of aberration to what we called a "normal fetishism" that is to be found in phases of male amorousness. In this case, the fetish is not adored in isolation from the love- or sex-object, but is admired or imagined always in connection with the woman. Many cases of so-called hand- and shoe-fetishism belong to this group. But also in these cases, the "fetishes" represent penis-symbols and their genesis can be traced back to specific experiences in childhood.

We have already mentioned La Bretonne's view that high heels gave a certain character to the gait of women, and the cynical views of Professor Huddock, who related the attractiveness of a woman to the angle her foot makes with the ground. In these and numerous other cases, the "foot fetishism" is not isolated from the person and approaches, so to speak, the area of the normal over-evaluation the average male shows. I would even assert that most men in our time prefer high heels on women's shoes to low heels, and I remind the reader in this connection of Freud's comment that no male was spared the experience of castration-fear in his childhood.

There are, however, cases of "normal fetishism" in which the alternative high- or low-heeled shoes plays no role. Freud himself described such a case of foot-fetishism in his book *Delusion and Dream in Jensen's Gradiva*.[63] True, the case is not that of a living person but of a figure in fiction, but the analysis is vivid and lifelike. You will remember the young archeologist Norbert Hanold, who falls in love with a piece of sculpture found in a Roman museum. The girl presented, called "Gradiva," pulls her flowing dress a little up so as to reveal her sandaled feet. In walking, one foot is on the ground, the other touches it with just the tips of the toes, while the sole and heel rise almost perpendicularly. The young archeologist is not satisfied with buying a plaster cast of the sculpture; his quest for reality leads him to his own observations. He is compelled to look eagerly at women's and girls' feet as they come into view.

The reader is advised to follow the development and the cure of the archeologist's delusion in Freud's analytical study. We are interested here in Freud's characterization of Norbert Hanold's disturbance.

Freud diagnosed the case as "hysterical delusion," but assumed that some psychiatrists would perhaps put the disturbance in the category of paranoia, and describe it as "fetishistic erotomania," "because the most striking thing about it was his being in love with a piece of sculpture" and in the view of those psychiatrists "with the tendency to coarsen everything" Norbert Hanold's "interest in feet and the postures of feet would be bound to suggest fetishism."

That interest is, of course, an important part of the young archeologist's delusion, but we can easily imagine that it could have existed without that emotional disturbance. That means it could have existed in every young man who observed the gait of women. In the "pedestrian researches" of the young explorer upon women and girls, the erotic character of that interest becomes transparent. Such "pedestrian researches" or observations of women's gait are not unusual with young men in our cities.

We may as well bear in mind that all kinds of garments and parts of the female body can become fetishes. Besides, much of this sort of fetishism is "normal," as we observe it during periods of deep infatuation.

The character of pathological fetishism is not always admiring and adoring. It can even be sadistic, as in the case of those perverted men who cut women's dresses, or go on panty raids at girls' colleges.

Sometimes fetishists are eager to observe women's underwear. There is more on a woman than meets the eye and many men are intrigued just by those hidden things. Parts of feminine garments thus sometimes become fetishes. All the intimate things that flatter a woman can become objects of sexual excitement for a man.

AFTER US THE DELUGE

A view of the contemporary world situation shifts for a moment to the recent past and leads to an odd comparison. It is only two hundred years ago that Madame de Pompadour, the beautiful mistress of Louis XV, scandalized the world when she said, *"Aprés nous le déluge."* Stretching her imagination, she anticipated the future catastrophe of the world as a kind of repetition of the Flood in the Scriptures. But Noah took into the ark his own family and two of each kind of birds and beasts of the world. From his family the earth was again peopled. How harmless was even the most somber imagination of people two hundred years ago compared with what confronts us in the foreseeable future! The super H-bomb can annihilate everything on earth—no living being would survive. Compared with the end of the world—perhaps not even after us, but in our time—the deluge shrinks to the dimension of a local disaster.

1. *Apportionment of Love*

It seems to me that the wrong word is emphasized in the admonition to love thy neighbor. The emphasis should be upon the word "neighbor," because it means love first those who are near to you, the members of your family. Love, like charity, begins at home and might spread from there to others admitted into the widening circle. A general love of mankind, or brotherly love, is a later abstraction and has a hazy secondary character. Love in this most general sense can only be thin and diluted. It is not natural that I should "love" a few million Chinese men and women. The clerical and mundane preachers who demand such general love of mankind are supposed to be idealists. We would rather say that they lack a sense of psychological reality.

The idea of "neighbor" need not be taken in its narrowest immediate sense. Absence makes the heart grow fonder, but only for those one has loved when they were present.

2. *Emotion*

The writer and the psychoanalyst have a common ground or shared interest. To both it is emotion that matters. An American patient of Freud, who returned home to New York for the summer vacation after many months of psychoanalytic treatment, was asked by her sister and friends upon her arrival: "What did you learn from psychoanalysis in Vienna?" She answered: "I learned that feeling is the most important thing in life."

3. *Treatment of Masochism*

The treatment of the masochistic attitude of many patients is made especially difficult because they are firmly convinced that they are already on the threshold where unheard of happiness, even bliss, awaits them. Imagine a person rescued from hell and back to earth a split second before being admitted to paradise. What can the therapist offer that could be compared not with that hope but with that certainty? The masochisic pervert knows that the worst humiliation and pain will be followed immediately by delight and sexual fulfillment never experienced before. The social masochist knows that from the most terrible disgrace, glory will emerge, rarely bestowed upon mortals. In anticipation of such bliss the masochist enjoys his suffering, is happy only when unhappy.

4. *Psychoanalytic Treatment*

The repressed is, in psychoanalysis, recognized by its derivatives or consequences, and its original and essential character has to be found by a complicated process. As long as its source and primal nature is not found, the neurotic disturbance continues to exist and to develop its emotional effects. Only after its origin is discovered and exposed is the way to mental health paved.

The best comparison here is the treatment of tapeworm, the parasite that lives in the intestines of human beings and animals. Evidence of its existence is the appearance of segments of the worm. As long as the head survives, it will produce a chain of segments, often a great number of them. Only after the head of the tapeworm is expelled can the patient be cured.

5. *Failure of an Experiment*

Here are two cases in which patients in psychoanalytic treatment used insights they had obtained during their psychoanalysis in the service of their unconscious resistance.

A divorced woman had recognized that her sexual life was determined almost entirely by clitoral excitement. She wanted to prove to herself and to her psychoanalyst that she could experience a vaginal orgasm. When a man with whom she once had sexual relations called her and took her to dinner, she decided to go to bed with him in order to make the test. She became excited, but her excitement during sexual intercourse was localized at the clitoris and was short-lived. She kept thinking, "I am not plugged in," and was entirely without any sensation during sexual intercourse. It will be easily guessed that the purpose of an experiment or of a test of this kind did not create favorable conditions for her sexual arousal and relief.

The other case which comes to mind in this context concerns a thirty-year-old patient who was very shy with women. After several months in psychoanalytic treatment he decided to change his tactics in his approach and to conquer his shyness by daringly propositioning a woman. He made a date with a young girl he knew. As they walked along together he suddenly asked her, "Shall we have some coffee before we go to bed?" She slapped his face and left him.

It is clear in this case also that he undertook the experiment with the unconscious foreknowledge that it was bound to fail.

6. *Without Guilt*

One can feel sorry about something without feeling guilty. Feeling guilty is as useless as crying over spilled milk. One may regret having done something wrong without being emotionally crushed by it. Too deep grief would dishearten and humiliate the individual. A clear understanding of the significance of our misdeeds or wrongdoings is emotionally healthier than hopeless misery afterward. "I have done this; it was wrong; it is done with," is perhaps the better attitude.

7. *Conscience*

Children assume that their parents are omniscient about what children do and think. In the place of the parents their conscience examines their deeds and thoughts later on. The word conscience itself is derived from the Latin *con* and *scire,* to know with. It is remarkable that another characteristic of the child's concept of the complete knowledge of the parents is transmitted to conscience. The child believes the parents know everything without their presence. Conscience is also often unconscious, intangible and insubstantial, but is experienced as effective.

8. *The Bridge*

A man in his late thirties had a beautiful mistress with whom he had a long sexual relationship. He tried in every possible way to persuade a friend of his to seduce the girl. His conscious motive was that he wanted to convince himself that perhaps she would be unfaithful to him. The choice of his devices left no doubt that behind this conscious purpose was the repressed intention of building a bridge between himself and the friend whom he admired and envied. The girl formed, so to speak, the central pillar in this bridge, was the chain coupling the unconscious homosexual joining of the two men together. The attempt was successful and the patient was a hidden witness to the sexual intercourse of his mistress and his friend. The outcome of the experiment is easy to guess: the discovery ended with his breaking off with the girl. The friendship between the men continued until an apparently accidental discussion about an irrelevant sum of money resulted in a cooling of their intimate relationship.

9. *Enjoyment of Embarrassment*

It is strange that while I have many happy memories of childhood, the majority of reminiscences of my late teens and early twenties are not pleasant. There is, for instance, a small collection of experiences whose emotional character can now, in old age, only be faintly recalled but which were once followed by feelings of acute embarrassment. They were mostly of a sort in which I had revealed a deplorable ignorance or lack of tact.

Here are two instances of such unpleasant situations: After the early death of my father, we were left poor and I had to earn some money as a tutor in order to continue my studies. On one occasion I was invited to dinner by the family of a student of mine at a luxuriously furnished suburban villa near Vienna. As I sat at the elegant dinner table, the first dish placed in front of me was oysters. I had never eaten oysters. I glanced furtively at those beside me to see how oysters were eaten and did not know how to react to the invitation of the hostess to help myself. I would have gladly done so, but first others had to help me and tell me how. The memory of that scene at the table followed me, accompanied by embarrassment, for many weeks afterward.

The second situation, remembered with scarcely less painful emotions, confronted me perhaps ten years later when I was a young psychoanalyst. I was invited to dinner by the Princess Maria Bonaparte in the hotel at the Semmering near Vienna where she spent the summer, near the cottage rented by Freud's family. I waited in the hotel lobby for the princess. She came downstairs accompanied by another woman. I hastened toward her and greeted her by kissing her hand. She said a few words (in French) and I understood that she wanted to introduce me to her companion, whose hand I also kissed. I learned later that the other woman was the princess' chambermaid. This situation also recurred in my thoughts in an obsessional manner for a long time.

Such mental preoccupation with embarrassing situations has certainly all the earmarks of masochistic self-torture. Their emotional character is that of a painful satisfaction. It should, however, not be forgotten that such obsessional mental preoccupation has the unconscious effect that those embarrassing experiences are emotionally mastered and conquered.

10. *The Unknown Population Explosion*

The greatest potential population explosion is never discussed by sociologists, by biologists, or by politicians. It takes place daily many million times over all the earth, and the urge from which it is born is not less powerful than the material responsible for the other population explosion. It is contained in the emissions of myriads of human sperms, daily ejected in the masturbation of adolescents and mature men.

11. *Our Concept of Human Nature*

Our psychologists, also our psychoanalysts, have, it seems to me, a too simplified concept of human nature. They conceive of man as if he were made of a similar material, like a marble block, and they present us with a picture comparable to one a marble cutter might give of that stone. In reality human nature is of many kinds and the personality of an individual is composed of many and often contradictory compounds. We make most valuable discoveries in this direction in our psychoanalytic practice where we encounter many apparently irreconcilable and flagrant contradictions and amazing paradoxes in the same person. The woman who is obsessionately tidy and keeps everything in her apartment spick and span has one drawer in which there is an indiscribable disorder because she pushes everything into it she wants to get rid of. The man who is a fanatic supporter of the Society for the Prevention of Cruelty to Animals may be caught occasionally molesting a dog or pulling the wings off a fly. On the other hand, we find that the criminal who commits terrible misdeeds is sometimes sentimental, and that a brutal materialist has a highly idealistic side of which he is not at all aware and which he would be ashamed of if found out.

"There is something of the best in the worst of us and something of the worst in the best of us" presents the situation in moralistic terms, scarcely acceptable to psychologists, who do not evaluate emotional processes morally. It is better to observe and to describe those inconsistencies and contradictions inherent in human nature and to explain them from the point of evolution of the species and of the individual. Freud liked to quote these lines from Konrad Ferdinand Meyer:

> *Das kommt, ich bin kein ausgeklügelt Buch,*
> *Ich bin ein Mensch mit seinem Widerspruch.*

One could perhaps translate it thus:

> That is because I'm not a figure from fiction,
> But a man with his contradiction.

12. *Confirmation in a Joke*

At one of the Wednesday evenings when Freud saw a small circle of his students at his home he pointed out that a bitter emotional animosity exists between nations and other groups that are close to each other and are separated by "little differences." Shortly afterward I saw a cartoon in the German magazine *Simplicissimus* which I showed to him. A Bavarian complains about the irksome peculiarities of the Prussians. His friend patiently listens to his diatribe and says, "Well, there have to be Prussians too in the world." "Yes," says the Bavarian, "but why so many?"

Freud burst out laughing at this confirmation of his theory.

13. *Origin of an Odd Bit of Sexual Behavior*

A patient in his late thirties is compelled to enact the same sexual scene with women, especially young nurses. He undresses before them and has them go so far as to look at his penis and to tell him that he has small genitals. In this scene he especially enjoys the shame of the young women. He differentiates between girls who are embarrassed and those who are not.

The origin of this odd bit of sexual behavior, as traced in the psychoanalytic treatment, was as follows: As a little boy, he was once infected by poison ivy on his genitals. His father put some ointment on the painful rash while his mother looked on from a distance. Mother admonished father: "Be careful; he is so delicate there!" Afterward the boy often repeated mother's words, emphasizing "there," and recalling the half curious, half embarrassed expression on his mother's face. As an adult he was often compelled to re-enact this scene, using all kinds of tricks to make the woman say that he had small genitals compared with other men. In addition to other determining factors which need not be discussed here, the comparison of his small penis with that of the father plays a role in the thoughts of the boy.

14. *Together*

Man is a social animal. This fact was known to the Greeks. The common slogan of today is "togetherness," which covers up a lot of intensive hatred, envy, jealousy, and rivalry. Yet all these negative signposts do not prevent man from feeling that it is better to be together than to be alone. Social existence is even exemplified in hell. There are so many sinners together, and no one is alone. I foresee the formation of a society of enemies of mankind very soon.

15. *Phrases*

The elevator man at the hotel where I spent last summer asked another operator whom he had just relieved, "Well, have you had your ups and downs?" This is, of course, an appropriate pun. Besides and beyond this, it is a question that could have been asked of anyone. Each of us has had his ups and downs.

"Is the pain local or positional?" asked the physician when he examined my elbow. What a strange question, I thought as I left his office. Imagine if the question could be transposed from physical medicine to the area of emotional suffering. For instance, in regard to the problems of unhappy love, of disagreeable situations at the office, of mourning the death of relatives, and other sufferings we experience, it might well be asked: "Is the suffering local or positional? Do you always feel the pain, or only when you make this or that mental movement? Do you feel it when you think certain thoughts, or does it disappear when your thoughts run in another direction?"

16. *Temptation and Law*

It should be possible to evaluate the particular phase through which a society is passing in terms of the various kinds of temptations to which its members are subjected. Those temptations can be defined by the laws that punish and forbid the acts of the transgressors. There are no laws against crimes that are never committed; no laws intended to block nonexistent appetites. There is, for example, no longer a law in our society against cannibalism. Yet as we know from the history of ancient Egypt, there were severe laws against cannibalism. In a short time there will be no specific law against regicide, because there will no longer be kings. Relapses into a vanished or abandoned phase of a civilization are, of course, possible, as the Nazi government proved.

17. *Pronunciation*

"What did you say?" I asked my younger daughter (who was born and bred in New York City) the other day. I really could not understand her. I remembered then that Freud sometimes complained to me that Americans mumbled, spoke from the corner of their mouths, in contrast with his English patients who pronounced words carefully and precisely.

18. *Psychological Interest*

Before I moved my office to West End Avenue, I used to visit a Broadway cafeteria about 4 P.M. for a cup of coffee. I always sat at a certain table whenever possible. A middle-aged truck driver who distributed the afternoon newspapers came to the cafeteria daily. He often sat across from me and said hello. He seemed to like my company. He often opened the conversation with a question such as, "When are you going to retire, Pop?" He certainly did not know what my profession was, or anything else about me. We had no common interest. The man was entirely uneducated and I doubt if he ever read a book other than a prayerbook in his life. Yet when, after some initial conversation, he began to talk about his family, he began to interest me. There was nothing extraordinary in what he said. He complained that his wife took too much of his pay check, that his daughter ran around with some "wild" boys, and that his son went to baseball games instead of doing his homework, and so on. He rarely spoke about his own tiring work. Every thing he said sounded so genuine and human that one could not help taking an interest in him.

Whenever you scratch the surface you will find something psychologically interesting in human beings. Let them only talk freely about themselves and you will discover problems and worries common to all of us, whether the individual is an illiterate truck driver or a highbrow professor. Returning from the cafeteria on one occasion, I had a psychoanalytic session with a young society girl. She talked at length about whether she should go to the Stork Club or to another such place that evening. I was bored, and my thoughts returned for a moment to the truck driver and his ordinary worries that seemed more interesting.

19. *Morals*

Children are not polymorphous perverts, as Freud asserted, because this term is taken from the evaluative language of adults. Children are "innocent" and therefore amoral. Only education, coming as it does from outside, makes them aware of what is "good" and what is "bad." Knowing this, they become like God, as the story in Genesis says.

20. *Wishes*

There is a bit of doggerel from the seventeenth century that goes:

> May I govern my passion with absolute sway
> And grow wiser and better as strength wears away
> Without gout or stone, by a gentle decay.

Time takes care of the wish to govern our passions; they leave us with old age. Thus there remains the second wish; but is it really desirable to wear away "by a gentle decay"? Would not painless death during sleep be better?

For the greater part of our lives we are all fugitives from the fulfillment of our secret wishes. When we finally see them realized, we experience a terrible sense of disappointment, and think: "Was this what I always secretly wished for?" The fulfillment shows that what we wished for was either too little or that it came too late.

21. *Polygamy*

Thomas Jefferson Hogg made a pass at Harriet Shelley. In a letter to Hogg the poet wrote, "I attach little value to the monopoly of exclusive cohabitation." [64] Is the age of communism dawning in the realm of sexual relations also, a reversion to the customs of primitive tribes?

22. *Pejoration of Words*

Everyone interested in the development of language knows the phenomenon of pejorating the significance of words, that means that words lose their original meaning and their significance deteriorates. To give an instance, the English word "maid" originally meant a simple girl or a virgin. It is today used in the sense of servant. The French *"fille"* originally meant "girl" and is now mostly used as a synonym for prostitute; the French say *"jeune fille"* when they mean girl. The German *"schlecht"* originally meant simple or plain, and is now used to mean bad.

While the phenomenon of pejoration of word meanings is generally known, no attention has been paid to the psychological motives of such degradation or deterioration of word meanings. If one may conclude from the effect of a development to its unconscious motives—a conclusion always justified in depth psychology —at least one subterranean motive can be guessed: the destructive, degrading, pulling-down trends that rebel against every elevated word or term. The originally hostile feelings against all authority thus also affect the meaning of words.

23. *Politics*

Authority is a natural attribute of success because it results from a fight in which one party is victorious and is then called government, king, leader, and so on, while the defeated party is called the opposition. It is risky to take the part of the underdog because he can become the upperdog within a few hours. It is all a question of who defeats whom in this dogfight.

A party that wants to bring the country or the nation back to a phase which has been long discarded is sometimes called progressive, while another party that wants to regress to an even earlier phase of evolution is often called reactionary.

24. *The Skeleton*

Society has not one but many skeletons in its closets. Perhaps the most important part of man's history is the story of how and where those skeletons were hidden, and of the courageous and determined men who found and opened wide these closets.

25. *The More Dangerous People*

Those who carry a grudge think of revenge, but the paranoiacs who imagine that they have been wronged and exploited and who never complain are the more dangerous because they brood over those wrongs and make carefully planned designs to take their revenge. They enjoy the humiliations and the sufferings of those they had suspected and who are often entirely innocent people. Hitler's paranoiac fantasies, before he became Germany's dictator, must have been of this kind.

26. *Dream Interpretation*

It is sometimes impossible in psychoanalytic practice fully to analyze a dream and to penetrate its manifest content so that its latent meaning becomes recognizable. In such cases the psychoanalyst has to remain content with understanding a part of the unconscious dream meaning. It is enough to lift, so to speak, one corner of a carpet in order to see what is beneath it. True, only a small area nearby may be seen, but it is better than sweeping the dream under the carpet.

27. *Compliments*

Compliments please and flatter us although we recognize later on that they are not credible. It is like attending a performance of *Hamlet*. You know—you are quite sure—that there are no ghosts. Yet for the duration of the play you believe that Hamlet's father appears to the prince. It is, so to speak, a voluntary delusion, or, to use Coleridge's expression, a "willing suspension of disbelief."

The other day I was invited to a cocktail party that was given for me in the afternoon after a lecture. I was introduced to the amiable hostess, a woman in her forties, with whom I chatted. She told me, among other things, that she expected her daughter, who was coming home from college. I looked at her and said, "You want me to believe that you have a daughter of college age? I see, you are fond of telling fairy tales." She blushed prettily.

Let me add here the story of the finest compliment I received and which I remember with pleasure. It was paid to me in May 1958. The occasion was the dinner given me on my seventieth birthday by the National Psychological Association for Psycho-analysis of which I am president. During the dinner, I sat between my two daughters. One of the guests, a psychologist, came to our table and introduced himself. He said, "I have read your books, Dr. Reik, and I admire some of them," and then added, pointing to my two daughters, "but those two are certainly your most beautiful productions."

To a man, a compliment is a delightful dish he enjoys; to a woman, it is a kind of hors d'oeuvre, whetting her appetite for the following main dishes.

Women are not satisfied with general compliments. They do not like to hear after dinner that they are good cooks, but prefer to be told specifically that the steak was delightful. They do not want to be told that they are beautiful, but rather that their eyes have an expression you have never seen in another woman's.

Compliments paid to women often reverberate in them hours later. Many women listen very carefully to what men say to them so that they can think them over afterward. They resemble in this respect chipmunks who collect nuts for later enjoyment. Very few men would have such delayed reactions to flattering words.

Men who pay a compliment to a woman have various purposes in mind; for instance, to please her, to woo her, and the like. Only women will flatter a person so as to be complimented in turn.

Why does it mean so much more to a woman when her dress is praised than it does to a man regarding a complimentary remark about his suit? Because the compliment about the dress means praising her body beneath it. Women live on compliments as bees on honey.

28. *Dialogue on Values*

"I assert, it is still 'bread and circuses.' It is possible that the circus performance has improved a bit, but—"

"You will not deny that the civilization of the American people has tremendously improved. Only think of the response of the masses when that astronaut returned from the stratosphere recently. . . ."

"I don't deny it, although the cultural level of a people cannot be measured by the reaction of the masses."

"And why not, I should like to know?"

"Well, let's make an experiment in thought. Do you think that Einstein would have been acclaimed as enthusiastically if he rode through the streets of New York?"

"Of course not, but not many people are able to understand the theory of relativity."

"And if Shakespeare were resurrected and walked through Manhattan, would he—"

"Well, a poet. . . ."

"And can you imagine Beethoven in the same situation?"

"The American people are enthusiastic lovers of music. . . ."

"I do not deny it, although there are phonies at symphonies, too. Excuse the bad joke. . . . Now, to prove my point, let's jump in our thought experiment. Let us for the hell of it, or rather for the sake of the argument, assume that it has been announced that Lady Godiva will ride down Fifth Avenue tomorrow morning in her birthday costume. Do you think anything could be done to keep people at home?"

"Oh boy!"

29. *Sheets*

The paper you use to jot down notes for your work is unimportant. It might be old envelopes or letters or menus or whatever is near at hand. But when you then write, and write what is your real and authentic self, you will use your own skin to write on.

30. *The Unvarnished Truth*

We sat together on a bench in Central Park, my friend the famous physicist Hans M. and I, on a late afternoon in May. We had spoken of the youthful years we had spent in Vienna. *"Im wunder-schönen Monat Mai,"* he suddenly said. Well, it was May, but why did he quote the first lines of that poem by Heine? Did he follow it up in thought and continue that in the wonderful month of May when everything blossoms, also in his heart love emerges again? Very unlikely, since we are both seventy-five years old—precisely in May. Or did his thoughts pursue that loving couple walking arm in arm past our bench?

"Are you perhaps envious of them?" I asked. "I hope not. Be your age!"

"I am, alas, I can't be otherwise," he said.

"Thus you envy them that feeling of love; but Hans, you know as well as I that all is illusion."

"And what's wrong with that?"

"I'll tell you. Love passes the time and time passes love. It lasts mere hours, not more."

"Hours? Well, you do not understand, stupid! I am not envious of their love, except perhaps in the sense of the French *amour*. Hours, you say. I am not envious of those happy hours. I am envious of minutes. If I could experience again the tension and release of orgasm, I would, believe me, gladly exchange my fame, my money, all I attained and all I gained for it . . . for a few minutes."

It sounded shockingly pathetic and I felt vicariously embarrassed. I must have looked like a blockhead. We were both silent for a few minutes and then spoke of other things. When I reached home, I suddenly thought of Emile Zola's *Pascal Rougon,* who, much younger than Hans, though already aging, looks back at his youth. I took that book from the shelf and read:

"On certain nights he cursed science which he accused of taking away from him the best part of his masculine vigor." (*"Certain nuits, il arrivait à maudire la science qu'il accusait de lui avoir pris le meilleur de sa virilité."*) I thought again of our youth, misspent in Vienna.

31. *The Displacement to Literary Work*

A writer in psychoanalytic treatment with me was essentially a masochistic character, at this time in a phase of emotional transition with a determined effort to find the way from his neurotic disturbances into the open. Whenever he had finished a short story or an essay and had delivered it to the editor of a magazine, he ran the gamut of emotions from elation to depression. He soon anticipated that the editors would consider his piece very good and then he predicted they would think it horrible. It became clear that he had displaced his self-judgment from the moral area to the territory of literary work. He would think of himself as very kind, then again he would think of himself as a monster and a "son of a bitch." The displacement sometimes took the form: "Who am I to write such a story; I am a fraud, a make-believe."

The shifting to the literary field leaves the core of his problem untouched and only amounts to making the train run on another, parallel track. Its destination remains the same, as is proved by the following episode: He recognized that he had certain weak points in his literary presentation and decided to circumvent them and to concentrate on the subjects which, in his opinion and others', were his strength. "Why should I not?" he asked himself and answered after a pause, "Because when I put my best foot forward I shall perhaps stumble."

32. *The Interfering Agent*

The patient is in a transition phase from a masochistic perversion to a normal sexuality. With a woman to whom he is strongly attracted he feels, as he says, "a mental sexual excitement but it does not translate itself into a physical one." The erection of the penis begins, then subsides, and he desperately awaits what will happen, but in vain: "It is as if it were dead."

He wonders what the unknown interfering agent is and what may be the nature of the inhibiting factor in the transition from feeling to sexual erection. His very wording, "as if it were dead," as well as many symptoms analyzed in the months of treatment, paved the way to the solution of the psychological enigma.

He cannot accept the originally intensive sadistic or cruel component of his sexual drive. Male sexuality has always an aggressive and sadistic component. (A writer recently characterized sexual intercourse as "hostile intrusion"). The patient's early erection fades the moment he approaches the body of the woman because unconsciously he does not want love-making but rape. Strong counterforces in him forbid this aggressive action which nevertheless remains the aim of his unconscious wishes.

The nature of his prohibition is thus the repression of intensive sadistic, even murderous, impulses against which his masochistic perversion was built as a defense like a fortress against the threatening enemy.

Two characteristic features of his attitude confirm this psychoanalytic assumption. He is absolutely unable to approach a woman even in his very shy way if she does not encourage him, if she does not help him by making advances to him. Translated into the language of the unconscious this would mean that the woman must give her permission to be raped. Continuing into the area of the repressed: she wants to be murdered.

The second significant feature is, so to speak, the counterpoint: the patient is compulsively driven to ingratiate himself with the woman whom he desires, not only and certainly not mainly to woo and conquer her but in anticipation of a certain possibility or probability. He foresees that he could become impotent at the most important and decisive moment and reassures himself ahead of time that she will not be angry with him then. If he fails in sexual intercourse she should not feel too disappointed and deceived. He compares in his thoughts this attitude with that of other "normal" men who are not much concerned about the woman's feeling if they should fail. The patient has to be reassured and tries to convince himself beforehand that the woman would love him anyway, even if he fails. She should, he says, "not feel hurt."

This expression as well as the inferences from his previous considerations show that the unconscious train of his thoughts does not refer to the possible case of impotence, but to the motive hidden behind it. The woman should not feel offended, not "hurt" by the unconscious designs of rape or even murder, should forgive him not so much for his failure but for the violence hidden behind it.

Behind the gentleness and even submissiveness of the masochist, he is driven by brutal and violent impulses of whose presence and intensity he is often not aware.

33. *Two Kinds of Breakthroughs*

Shortly after World War I, I treated a neurotic middle-aged man who was—if one can call it that—an embittered masochist. He was consistent in his attempts at self-sabotage, and successful in his iron will to fail in his personal and professional life. He slowly recognized that he was the hidden stage manager who directed the neurotic play on the stage. I convinced him after a long psychoanalysis that an unconscious guilt feeling resulting from murderous wishes against his parents and his brother was the strongest motive for his self-punishment and that he atoned for his wild wishes by his pervasive failures.

The depression into which he sank was sometimes, but rarely, suddenly lifted. It was as if the struggle between the two enemy forces was interrupted by a momentary truce during which the soldiers in the opposite camps indulge in some friendly teasing. The melancholy mood of the patient was then replaced by a strange kind of humor in which he made fun of his neurotic reactions. Once he said, in the middle of his psychoanalytic session: "It's terrible for me and the sufferings I inflict on myself. And all because I killed off a few persons! When one thinks of the many hundred thousand people who were killed during the war, the number of persons I murdered in my thoughts cannot even be taken into consideration."

The memory of that ray of sudden humor that fell into the depression recurred to me when another patient, also a masochistic character, spoke (more than forty years later) of a breakthrough in his neurotic situation. The man, middle-aged as was my patient in Vienna, was unsuccessful and luckless in his relations with women as well as in his practice as a lawyer. Shortly after he returned from a vacation, he told me that his life had been changed. Now several women made advances to him, and many clients came to his office. When he spoke of this breakthrough he compared it to a "push from the trenches," an action in which he had sometimes participated during World War II. Yet his breakthrough was not as successful as might have been anticipated. His attempts to get rid of his neurotic fears and inhibitions resulted only in another form of self-sabotage. He could not concentrate his attention on one of the women who attracted him, and he scattered his energy in the effort to do his best for every client simultaneously.

Picking up his comparison with a "push from the trenches," I was disappointed: the breakthrough, an offensive operation that pierces the enemy's system to reach the area behind it, threatened to become a break-neck for him, since he split up his forces and could not focus on one thing. The common link between the two patients was, of course, the significant parallel they had both drawn between their neurosis and the war situation.

34. *Psychoanalysis of an Obsessional Doubt*

A patient who had obsessional doubts and fears admired the books of a philosopher recommended to him by a relative. He told me that he was enthusiastic about the profoundness and originality of this author whose collected writings he had bought. Some months later a friend asked to borrow one of the volumes. The patient lent him the book reluctantly because he liked to have all the volumes at home. After the friend had left, the patient was troubled by vague doubts whose character eventually became clear: he was concerned that his friend would not treat the book with the solicitude it deserved. Would he, if interrupted while reading it, be careful not to soil the book in putting it down? Superficially seen, these doubts would not be very different in form and content from those of other people about valuable books borrowed.

The continuation of such thoughts leads beyond all doubt into the territory of obsessions. What would happen, he thought, if his friend, fascinated by the original ideas of the philosopher, held the book in his hand while eating? Won't he make a grease spot on a page? What if he, intrigued by a train of thought in the book and unwilling to interrupt his reading even briefly takes the book with him to the toilet while he has a bowel movement? What if he continued reading it while he wiped himself?

Even the layman, not trained in psychoanalytic interpretation, will guess that beneath the patient's extreme solicitude for the book an unconscious mockery directed against his consciously highly esteemed philosopher is breaking through. This unconscious sneering becomes clear in the final conclusion that the friend would turn a page of the book while he wiped himself. The pages of the book would thus be degraded to the category of toilet paper. At this point the horrified patient broke his train of thought because he realized that the esteemed philosopher's books were only fit for something the author had certainly not intended.

The obsessional thoughts of the patient who arrived at an unconscious manifestation of bitter mockery brings to mind the letter that Max Reger wrote to a critic who had written an annihilating review of the first performance of the composer's new work: "Dear Sir, I am sitting in the smallest room of my apartment and I am reading your criticism. I have it *yet* in front of me."

35. *Ellipsis*

The elliptical expression by which words are omitted and have to be supplied by the reader is a special technique in wit. An example of this occurs in Freud's book on *Wit and Its Relations to the Unconscious.*[65] It concerns the Viennese satirist Karl Kraus, who was very aggressive in articles written for his magazine *Die Fackel,* and had often been the object of physical punishment by his enemies. When a new stupidity of one of Kraus's victims was being discussed, someone remarked: "When Kraus hears of that he will be slapped again." The ellipsis is plain: Kraus will then write a very malicious article and will be attacked by the victim of his aggression.

I would like to put side by side with that witty, elliptical remark an obsessional thought connection of a New York woman who was in psychoanalytic treatment with me in Vienna. Her husband, in his last letter, had expressed the wish that she send him a certain photograph showing her half-dressed in a seductive pose. She had at first considered showing me the photograph, but gave up this notion when a "terrible idea" occurred to her, so frightening that she could not tell it to me. Only after repeated urging could she bring herself to tell me: "When I show you the photograph, I must slap your face." The similarities of this obsessional thought with the witty remark just quoted are, in form and content, conspicuous. When you insert the omitted middle link, the psychoanalytic interpretation of the obsessional connection is no longer difficult. Upon seeing the seductive picture I would become sexually excited (as her husband had been) and would make a proposal to her so that she would have to slap my face in indignation.

A significant feature about the married life of the patient and her husband was its sadistic and masochistic preludes to sexual intercourse.

36. *Late Reproach*

A patient reported that she had gotten into an argument with her mother whom she visited in Baltimore. Her mother told her that she had sold her apartment house. The greater part of the money from the sale would be invested in the business of Jack, the patient's brother (four years older than she), while the smaller amount would be reserved for her. The patient, an intelligent divorcée in her late thirties, was violently indignant and poured out her anger in strong terms. She reproached her mother who had always preferred her brother to her. She wept and said: "I always got the short end of things." Afterward, during the analytical session, I reminded the patient of her often expressed jealousy of her brother traced back primarily to the fact that she, as a girl, was underprivileged compared to the brother. I interpreted her expression, "I always got the short end of things," as a belated reproach to her mother that she had borne her as a girl without a penis. I reminded the patient that during the past months of psychoanalysis she had frequently revealed the penis envy every girl experiences in childhood. She energetically protested against my statement, and said that her wording "short end" was an accidental one; she could easily have expressed herself differently.

A few minutes later she told about a childhood memory that had occurred to her. As a little girl she often played that she was a butcher. She took the peelings of the banana she had eaten, closed them carefully and pretended they were fresh meat, then she cut them in pieces with a little knife. In the middle of her tale she was taken aback because she had become aware that the game presented an indirect confirmation of my psychoanalytic interpretation (the banana as penis symbol). She was silent for a moment, then said that an old song hit had occurred to her—"Yes, we have no bananas." She thus admitted that my interpretation had been correct.

37. *The Masochists*

There were people in a previous period who tried to harm and frustrate you, who degraded and humiliated you. Those were the good old days. You had enemies; they fought you and they sometimes succeeded in defeating you. We live in a progressive age. We no longer need aggression that comes from outside. The social masochist provides his own defeat and degradation. His device is: do it to yourself!

38. *An Interesting Misreading*

A correspondent wrote me about an experience he had in 1927. The incident he conveyed to me shows a connection between wit, in its relations with the unconscious, and misreading. The episode, which he told Freud, amused the psychoanalyst very much. I translate the letter from the German:

"As a young man I lived in Paris and had a mistress. She had become pregnant by me, which worried me greatly. I was preoccupied with thoughts in this direction when, as every day, I walked onto a street where I thought I knew every house and every door plate. I suddenly stopped as if I were pinned down because I thought that I had found the solution to my worry. There I read on a shingle: 'Mme. Morin, *sage-femme*' (midwife). Such an address I had hoped to find.

"Regrettably, the title of that establishment proved to be a misreading and a joke on myself. Actually the shingle read: 'Mr. Morin, *prudhomme*' (judge, councilor), which I should have known because I had often seen it before.

"The comic linquistic reversal showed me that I did not wish at all to deal with a *prudhomme* (judge), but I should have rather been myself a '*homme prudent*' or '*prudhomme*.' "

The correspondent, who is not prudish (also a possible association operating in the slip), added that the occurrence had been a warning to him and that he still thinks of his youth with a certain pleasure which he wished to share with me.

39. *What Patients Say*

Middle-aged woman about her husband: "I once sat down on his lap fifteen years ago. He said, 'You know, you are very heavy.' I never sat on his lap since."

"I had a new dress on, a very nice dress I bought just for this evening. I believe he did not even notice it, but he said to Mrs. A. 'That's a new dress you have on.' "

Another woman: "We have been married for twenty years and, let me tell you, he has not the slightest idea what I am like. He is married to an unknown woman."

"He is a cold character . . . in bed and out of bed."

A single woman in her thirties: "I know marriage is a compromise, but it has to be a compromise on my terms."

"My husband pays little attention to me. He is so interested in the different kinds of cars. I told him that he suffers from auto-eroticism."

A young girl: "I told you about Anne. She is my best friend. She was, of course, at the party too. She was dressed to the teeth—a knockout. She is gracious and she wiggles and she flutters her eyelashes when she speaks with a man, and I hate her."

Another girl: "I don't like to be spoken to by strange men. I don't want to be picked up. It's different when you are at the beach or at a cocktail party."

A woman who says that she is just forty years old: "I want to be admired and desired and I want to have those experiences before wrinkles come. Life with my husband is a living death. The only thing he has is his intellect."

A patient about another woman: "She is out for a killing and her battle dress is to strip gradually and slowly."

A woman speaking about the party yesterday: "I smiled so often and so long, especially at women I don't like, that the edges of my mouth ached."

A man after a long silence during the analytic session: "Isn't it remarkable? There we are—two minds without a single thought."

Another man: "She was so ugly that if one were not already impotent, the very thought could make one so—not to mention the attempt."

40. *Displacement from Below*

As a means of distortion that makes the meaning of a memory or of a dream unrecognizable, the mechanism of displacement from the lower part of the body to the upper part is often used. Here, for instance, is the dream of a young girl who had been a tomboy in her childhood and shows even now in her late twenties some distinct masculine features. In the dream she is looking into a mirror, inspecting her throat. "There is a growth inside, hanging out. I am then asking Sandra to look into my throat. Later on I am in a library. I still think of the throat and wonder if that swelling has something to do with the vocal cord."

The interpretation of this dream is facilitated when one considers reminiscences that had emerged in previous analytic sessions, such as that the girl had looked at her genitals in a mirror when she was a child. Sandra reminds her of a girl friend with whom she had discussed the sexes. She had later sought information about sexuality in books such as Krafft Ebing's and in marriage manuals in public libraries. The allusion to the vocal cord concerns the unconscious hope of the little girl of having a penis like boys. In the dream the thought is accompanied by worry or fear of illness. The most important distortion operating in the dream is, of course, the displacement from below to above, from examining the genitals to looking into the throat.

(As a vignette, a recollection should be added here: Freud once told us an episode of the time when he was a young resident working in the nose-and-throat department of the Vienna Clinic. A young girl who came to the clinic with her mother flatly refused to let herself be examined by him. She said: "I shall not let such a young physician look into my throat." Freud told us the story to illustrate the change of mores since the Victorian era when he studied medicine.)

I shall put that dream interpretation alongside the text of a lullaby I often heard sung when I was a child. The lines are by Mathias Claudius, composed by the German Karl Loewe (1796-1869). In the song a mother speaks to her little son in his cradle:

> *Schlaf, holder Knabe, süss and mild!*
> *Du deines Vaters Ebenbild.*
> *Das bist du; zwar dein Vater spricht,*
> *Du habest seine Nase nicht.*
> *Nur eben jetzo war er hier, und sah dir*
> *In's Gesicht, und sprach: "Viel hat er zwar*
> *Von mir, doch meine Nase hat er nicht."*
> *Mich dünkt es selbst, sie ist zu klein,*
> *Doch muss es seine Nase sein; denn wenn's nicht*
> *Seine Nase wär, wo hätt'st du denn die Nase her?*
> *Schlaf, Knabe! Was dein Vater spricht, spricht er*
> *Wohl nur im Scherz. Hab' immer seine Nase nicht,*
> *Und habe nur sein Herz. Hab' immer seine Nase nicht*
> *Und habe nur sein Herz!*

Sleep, dear boy, sweet and mild,
You your father's image.
That is what you are, though your father says
You have not his nose.
He was even now just here, and looked
At you in the face, and said, "Though he has
Much from me, yet he has not my nose."

In my opinion it is too small,
Yet it must be his nose. If it were not
His nose, where is the nose from?
Sleep, child! What your father says is said
Only in jest. Have not his nose,
But have his heart. Never have his nose
But only have his heart.

It is obvious that the song displaces the resemblance between father and son from the male genital to the nose. (The nose of the boy is too small, says the mother.) As one recognizes, the displacement from below to above operates in the song as in the dream.

41. *Psychology*

The phrase "He is interested only in himself" is misleading: it is often used to indicate that a person is extremely egotistic. A man or woman may be very selfish without having the slightest interest in him- or herself and may be very interested in him- or herself without being especially selfish.

When one penetrates to the core of psychoanalysis as a method of research as well as of psychotherapy, one arrives at the following formulations: Psychoanalysis means psychologically exploring and treating others as if they were oneself. Self-analysis means exploring and treating oneself as if one were someone else.

What makes people think that you are interested in what they feel or in what their physical complaints are? Something must drive them to talk about themselves. How compelling this tendency is, one will recognize only when one catches oneself talking about one's own feelings and physical pains to people who are not interested in them.

One could well imagine a dialogue such as the following:

"You will make an interesting acquaintance. I'll introduce you to yourself."

"Must it be? I can live without it. I doubt that it will be interest-

ing. It would perhaps be better to remain superficially acquainted
—just nodding or bowing."

Most people go through life without knowing themselves, yes,
even without being introduced to themselves. And those who do,
sometimes regret it deeply and wish that this acquaintanceship
could have been avoided.

We all sometimes break off the emotional bridges with our past.
But then we must construct emergency bridges in order to understand ourselves.

We all die strangers to ourselves and to others. Others perhaps
know us better than we do ourselves, but they did not know us
well either. The only certainties known about us are the dates of
our birth and death on the tombstone, which means nothing more
than that an unknown person entered life and went out of it. There
is the dead end of our knowledge.

42. *Vicious Circle*

We can observe how atonement, by and by, becomes sin again.
In masochistic characters especially, repentance changes its
character in this way because the repressed drives creep into the
measures of atonement and find their furtive satisfaction within
them. This individual transformation was anticipated and clearly
understood by the early church, which forbade the ascetic monks
near Alexandria violent and repeated self-flagellation when it
became obvious that this atonement led to sexual excitement. The
repressed sexual desires for which the monks punished themselves
sneaked into the penance like thieves in the night.

43. *From First Interviews*

I asked the patient, a student aged twenty-three, about his sexuality.
"Everything is in order in that area," he said. "When was the
last time you had sexual intercourse?" I asked. He blushed and
said, "I am not yet married."

Another patient reports: "Last summer I ran into a young woman. She had three children. She was really ugly. I understood, of course, that she wanted the children. What I did not understand is how she induced her husband so far. . . ."

44. *Feeling Sorry*

People who feel very sorry for themselves have little time, motive or opportunity for other emotions, not even for feeling sorry for other people. Other people exist only in so far as they have shoulders to cry on.

45. *Memories*

Why is it that events live longer in our memory than the emotions accompanying or following them? It is only when those emotions are too painful to remember that the events are also forgotten. They are then also pulled down into the unfathomable depth of the repressed.

46. *Knowledge*

The advantages and drawbacks of specialization in science and in the humanities are well known. He who stares forever into a microscope will perhaps lose some insight in this environment. You must become able to look away from what interests you most and to return to it with a fresh eye. Otherwise you will not see the woods for the tree of knowledge.

47. *Great Expectations—Small Expectations*

My impression is that the experts have neglected some significant psychological features of the aging process. Is it not characteristic that in old age novels, poems, and so on are generally no longer read, or at least rarely? It seems that my contemporaries as well as myself become impatient when they read stories of romance and also novels whose main themes are largely conflicts of love.

This leads to more general considerations. Old age is accompanied by a reduction of the great expectations with which youth is tormented. The extravagant expectations and hopes one has for himself and for others shrink; one recognizes one's own limitations and shortcomings and those of others. The mellowing process in becoming old is intimately connected with the diminishing demands on oneself and on other people. In reflecting on oneself one realizes that one could perhaps have achieved more, but this insight does not result in bitterness but in twinges of regret, the futility of which is felt; and finally, in serene resignation. Considering one's own nature and endowments as well as the external circumstances of one's life, one becomes content with the little one has accomplished. The conceit of our young years recedes and gives way to modesty and moderation. The final attitude is expressed in Goethe's lines:

> *Wieviel bist du von anderen unterschieden?*
> *Erkenne dich—leb' mit der Welt in Frieden.*

> How much are you distinguished from the others?
> Go, know yourself, call all men your brothers.

Also as we consider other people our expectations decrease and the result is a reduction of demands on them, moral and otherwise. We arrive at a state of gentle tolerance with all other human beings.

We old people sometimes look smilingly back at our young selves, and we recognize that we were much too severe with ourselves and that we made too high moral demands because we did not understand or did not want to see the narrow and inevitable limitations imposed by human nature. We all think: "Thus I am, thus I should be," and we unconsciously measure the distance between us and our ideal ego—called superego in psychoanalysis. That is necessary to some extent by the process of moral evolution. To use a comparison: when I have a pistol in my hand and want to fire at that bust on the shelf, I aim a little higher because the recoil presses the pistol downward. But if I aim at the ceiling I shall miss the target altogether. When we are old we understand that we aimed too high in our youth. What right had we to expect that we would not be as cruel, malicious, envious and aggressive as others in our thoughts and wishes? What entitled us to conceive of ourselves as saints who should have no unchaste or immoral thoughts? It was sheer arrogance to think we had to be like Jesus Christ. Why should we not have been "regular guys" like all the others?

And what conceit was in those unnecessary sufferings and self-reproaches we inflicted on ourselves! What waste of energy, and, properly seen in retrospect, what superfluous emotional luxury! To use a comparison: though others go through life with, let us say, fifty pounds on their backs, we thought, Not I! I have to carry a hundred and fifty pounds. I am above being content with the average burden; I must impose a heavier load on myself. Thus we inflict unreasonable and stupid suffering on ourselves. In old age we learn to think much more tolerantly of human nature, including our own. The span of life we see for ourselves is very small, and we obtain, in becoming old, a new virtue, namely humility.

48. *Nail-biting*

The frequent nail-biting of children and grownups is often explained by psychoanalysts as a manifestation of oral sadism. Sometimes you hear it conceived of as auto-cannibalism. Here again, the content of the package is more important than its label. In many cases of nail-biting the original impulse to bite a certain person is turned against oneself. There are at first external and then internal reasons for this change.

A remarkable observation has been made by many psychoanalysts. Often girls who indulged in nail-biting for many years easily give the habit up when they become vain and wish to be attractive to one or many men. Vanity, thy name is woman.

49. *Face-lifting*

In certain cases psychotherapy can only be compared to psychological face-lifting. The work is long, and has only limited success. Finally the true face re-emerges.

50. *Flight into Illness*

We know that even very serious neurotic disturbances vanish when a severe organic illness, for instance cancer, seizes the patient. A kind of indirect confirmation of this significance of organic illness is implied in the fantasies of some neurotic patients who consciously wish to be taken ill. They want to be removed from circulation and avoid the serious conflicts in which they are now engaged.

51. *Fantasies*

Experiences of many psychoanalysts show that fantasies of a sexually perverted kind lose their ability to arouse the person when they are repeated over a long time. They have then to be replaced by new ones or by variations of the old ones. They are subjected to the law of diminishing returns.

52. *Togetherness*

It seems that Americans consider it very difficult to be alone, which need not mean feeling lonely. The recent trend toward togetherness is quite informative in this respect. The consistent and consequent pursuit of togetherness will, I am afraid, make some people so fed up with it that there will remain only one cure: escape into aloneness.

53. *The Alternative*

Julius von Wagner-Jauregg, the Viennese professor of psychiatry, had a whimsical kind of humor. On one occasion, surrounded by the physicians, he was making the rounds in the psychiatric ward, when an insane patient shouted at them: "Either you all lick my ass or I shall shit in the bed." Wagner-Jauregg quietly replied, "Well, in that case, only the second possibility will remain."

On a similar occasion the professor wanted to prove to his students that the orientation of an insane patient was not impaired. "Where are you?" he asked the patient. "I am at a hospital," answered the patient. "Who are these gentlemen?"—pointing to his students. "They are doctors," answered the patient. "And who am I?" asked Wagner-Jauregg. "You're an idiot" (in broad Viennese jargon, *"Sö san a Trottel"*), replied the man. "You see, gentlemen," said the professor, "that the patient's sensory apparatus is not blurred."

53a. *On Emotions*

Certain emotions, like democratic and totalitarian regimes, cannot coexist for any length of time. The emotions depression and rage belong to this group. When you, as a psychoanalyst, succeed in bringing a repressed anger or wrath from the netherworld to the surface and make the patient experience it as actually and vividly felt, you will observe that a certain kind of mysterious depression into which the patient was plunged has been banished. There is, of course, the possibility of a relapse, but for the time being the melancholy mood has vanished as if by magic. This kind of psychoanalytic experience amounts to a verification or confirmation of our theory. Such depression originates in some process of repression or disavowal of a recurrent rage, or of consuming anger that had been turned within the person and whose symptomatic manifestation is the depression. Those secret storms must be brought to the surface and must become articulate, and then they will lose their grip on the patient in violent explosions.

54. *Fantasy*

A divorcée who is at the age of menopause says in her psycho-analytic session: "You know, I have a fantasy in which I am a millionairess, have all the dresses I like, and go abroad. I have many servants who are well paid. Among them are two young men who have—how do you call it?—satyriasis. One of them appears when-ever I want it, during the day or night."

55. *Marriage*

From the report of a woman patient about the failure of her marriage life: "I knew that our marriage was on the rocks. It was all over but the shouting. This began from the very start. He yelled at me on every occasion."

56. *Mirage*

The great illusions of life, love, happiness, and so on, resemble the Fata Morgana seen by wanderers in the desert who enjoy the sight of an oasis and the promise of its water. These illusions are wonderful only as long as the wanderer is a distance away. When he approaches and finally when he gets there the mirage melts away.

57. *The Way*

The straight and narrow path has led many people into an un-happy life. One has to follow one's own road, not that which guide-posts indicate because guideposts have merely the function of warning signs for superior minds and exist only to guide the mediocrities.

58. *The Link*

The part of the human body that most resembles in form and function that of animals are the genitals. With respect to them there are, however, essential differences: we are ashamed of them, attribute a greater and permanent importance to them, and have lost the innocence which animals show in their use. We do not connect their function with the animal part of us except with bad conscience.

59. *Future of Psychoanalysis*

Freud sometimes spoke about the future of psychoanalysis and foresaw that the new science he had founded would in the end, despite many and various modifications, be victorious. I think he was still too optimistic. Now, not twenty-five years after his death, he would be greatly astonished at what is being called psychoanalysis. If he could see it in a few decades, let us say about the year 2000, he would not recognize what had become of his science. He would be as deeply shaken by attending a psychoanalytic session in New York as that Rabbi of Nazareth would be if he were present at a Roman Catholic Mass.

60. *Deep Groan*

If it would be only possible to keep to oneself mentally! If one could only put up a sign "No callers!" for the area of thought. One should be able to send an SOS when in danger of an influx of thoughts in which we are not interested at the moment.

61. *Mother's Love*

Real mother love cannot fully develop when the baby is brought to mother only to be fed while another woman—a nurse, for instance, takes care of the baby, loves him and talks to him. It appears then to this mother as if she were only a kind of cow and she begins to hate feeding time since it means that the baby will be taken away from her immediately after. Mother love is like appetite that comes when you eat (*"en mangeant"*). In the described case the only dependence of the baby is that it is fed by her. She has no opportunity for loving and taking care of the child.

A thirty-nine-year-old man complained that his mother weighed him down with her affection and deprived him of freedom of action. He reversed his role in calling her love "childish." "Don't you think that a mother should be adult with her son?" the patient asked. "It is sickening when a mother asks her thirty-nine-year-old son, 'Do you love me?' "

62. *Peace of Mind*

Early morning alone on the hotel porch, looking at the mountains and forests, at the meadows and flowers. . . . Birds hop on the road and baby squirrels chase each other. One attains here moments of inner peace which are due to the deeply felt experience that nature is unconcerned with and indifferent to us. The same summer breeze that moves the leaves and produces quivering waves on the lake plays around our forehead. You are not something apart, but part of everything. You are not outside, but included in all life. All is in the process of creation and dying.

For some moments you are free from the tyranny of the self. The thought of the closeness of death has no terror for you. Those are only moments, but memorable ones in which you are at peace with yourself and all pride of your individuality has vanished.

Oneself is not important any more. In such moods you understand the man who was asked "How are you?" and he answered "This does not concern me." We are only parts and "fufill great Nature's plan," to quote Robert Burns.

63. *Freud the Spectator*.

There is a great difference between the observer and the spectator. The observer is a careful, keen, and experienced scientific expert. He has a system and knows beforehand what he wants to examine. That system leads him to a certain direction and keeps his field of study within definite and definable bounds. Nothing observable, therefore, eludes his attention or deludes his observation. The spectator has no system. He watches the phenomena as a curious person looks at a spectacle, unprejudiced, impartial, and patient. The observer will see his theories verified and confirmed, although sometimes with modifications. The spectator will find new things in events often observed and will also watch what goes on at the fringes of things. Small features attract his attention and often astound him. He is frequently astonished by what he sees and is taken by surprise, whereas the observer is usually prepared for it.

Freud was rarely a true observer, but he was a genius as a spectator. His scientific findings are, to the greatest extent, results of his watching psychological phenomena without taking part.

64. *Facetious Exegesis*

I suspect that the story in Genesis 3:11 is a later tendentious elaboration. The Lord God did not call unto Adam but unto Eve, and asked her, "Who told thee that thou wast naked?" It is also very likely that the Lord God did make coats of skins unto Eve and clothed only her. Since those primeval times, men have had to worry about women's dresses.

Another conjecture: The original text spoke perhaps not of God, but of a dress designer whom Eve called divine or God, after she found that the dress was very becoming to her.

I further suspect that the version in Genesis 3:19 is a later elaboration, based perhaps on a misunderstood text. God did not say unto Adam: "In the sweat of thy face shalt thou eat bread," but "shalt thou win bread." Adam was the first bread winner, and since the time of our first ancestor every husband has had the same task.

65. *Blasphemy*

Only religious people can be subjected to the temptation to blaspheme. To atheists, blasphemy would be as senseless as to strike at the empty air. There is a long way even from agnosticism and doubt to sacrilege, but from prayer to blasphemy is only a step.

66. *Inheritance*

The meek shall inherit the earth, that is certain, but at the present time they must pay such high inheritance taxes that they will be financially ruined when they come into their legacy.

67. *No Accidental Expressions*

A woman whose sexual life was unsatisfactory and who lived in an unhappy marriage began a psychoanalytic session with the word: "I am at the end of my rope." After some sentences about a recent argument she had had with her husband she reported an experience from her teens. She had first felt sexually aroused during the gymnastic hour in her school when the girls had to glide down a rope after they had climbed up. She was not aware that these two sentences had any connection, nor did she know that she had only clitoral sensations. She had never experienced a vaginal orgasm.

68. *Return of the Repressed*

A patient who had been a masochist in his sexual life reported a strange experience during the last week when he tried to overcome his sexual perversion in which he wanted to be beaten by a woman. Walking with a young girl whom he liked, he had affectionately held her throat. He suddenly thought of himself as Jack the Ripper and was surprised by a sudden impulse to strangle the young girl. In this transition phase he sometimes caught himself thinking how delicious it would be to rape a woman. All this was in utter contrast to the masochistic perversion to which he had been enslaved and signified the return of repressed sadistic tendencies. He thus experienced the emotional force of the original drives and understood that his masochism had developed as an extreme reaction to their power.

69. *Counterphobic Actions*

The process of psychoanalysis was sometimes—even by Freud himself—characterized as a re-education. Are there attempts of re-educating oneself outside of psychotherapy? There are, for instance, the so-called "counterphobic actions," meaning activities that deny the phobia or anxiety by convincing the person that the imagined dreadful thing in certain situations does not occur. The feared situation must be sought again and again because the patient must convince himself that the imaginary expectation will not materialize. The most famous example of such counterphobic actions is that of Goethe who was afraid of heights (arcophobia). In *Truth and Fiction* the poet described how as a young man he compelled himself to climb the Cathedral of Strasbourg and to stand there purposefully to master his fear. This was an attempt at self-re-education that was successful. In other cases the attempt fails.

70. *Abstract Desires*

Men and women sometimes have sexual fantasies about a person of the opposite sex who appears very attractive when absent while in actuality he or she has certain peculiarities and mannerisms that take "the heat out," as a patient called it. He could masturbate, aroused by the fantasy of a certain woman and yet feel not the slightest sexual desire when he was with her. He did not attribute this block to emotional or mental inhibitions but to the fact that the fantasy alone is seductive while the reality is unpleasant. He often spoke of those "desires in the abstract" and felt unable to accept reality.

71. *Discoveries and Surprise*

The powerful resistances encountered by many new discoveries, such as those of psychoanalysis are, properly considered, not astonishing. The revelation of Copernicus that the earth rotates around the sun once awoke a similar fierce opposition. And so too did Darwin's theory of evolution. This antagonism is, of course, to the greatest extent emotional since many new discoveries hurt the pride of men and offend their vanity. But this effect is also due to the fact that the discoveries come quite unexpectedly and surprise people who did not anticipate them. They often appear from an unforeseen place.

When you follow their history it sometimes conveys the impression of a very good detective story in which the criminal at the denouement is revealed as a person no one suspected. Yet many indications of him as the criminal must have been cleverly concealed and disguised, presented in the story before the solution of the plot. It is likely that we shall have such an impression, for instance, when a cure for cancer is found. I don't remember now where I once read that truth is improbable—*"La vérité n'est pas vraisemblable."*

72. *Dream and Technical Progress*

Flying in dreams has the unconscious significance of the erection of the penis. Falling with the airplane has the unconscious meaning of loosing the erection. I wonder if the excursions into the stratosphere will not occur in our future dreams as unconscious representatives of extramarital affairs. Will the attempt to land on the moon be some day interpreted as making a pass at a woman?

73. *Marriage*

It seems very significant that, in Western civilization, the woman takes the man's name when she marries. It may be argued that this change of name is not very significant. Yet the custom had an enormous meaning in all ancient and primitive civilizations. In the puberty rites of savage tribes a youth adopted a new name. He is supposed to have died and been resurrected as another person. He has been reborn.

In the case of a woman, the taking of her husband's name symbolizes the drastic change she undergoes when she marries. After the event, she is not the same, but has been transformed into another individual. She is no longer just a woman but a wife, which implies an advancement.

Marriage does not have the same meaning for the man. The transition from bachelor to husband is not an advancement but, rather, a regression. How implausible that a man who marries should adopt the name of his wife!

74. *Point and Counterpoint*

"You say that men often achieve happiness only when they sleep. Yet what about dreams—anxiety dreams, for example?" "You have a point there. 'There's the rub,' as Hamlet says. Let us qualify my statement and say that men reach happiness in dreamless sleep." "Accepted. No. I remind you of your other statement that happiness is restricted or limited to hours, perhaps even only to minutes." "You are right. Thus we perhaps attain happiness only in those minutes when we glide from the waking state into sleep. In this short time we throw ourselves into the soft arms of Mother Nature and we are relieved and redeemed since we no longer feel the burden of self."

75. *Masochistic Relapse*

Psychoanalytic experiences taught us that almost every progress in the treatment of a masochistic character is followed by a relapse. The character of that "negative reaction" is variable in measure, but in many cases it follows the sequence: two steps forward, one and a half steps backward. The shadow of unconscious guilt feeling haunts each step forward in psychotherapy.

76. *The Nature of Thought*

"But how can thoughts have such fatal consequences, how can their repression lead to neurotic and even psychotic disturbances?" asked a philosopher who should, one would assume, have more respect for the power of thought. I first pointed out to him that not the repression of thoughts or impulses, but just the failure of repression, their return from repression, is the cause of neurotic disorders. "But they are only thoughts, not actions!" he replied. The key to this door is provided by Freud's assertion that thoughts are actions in small quantities, that thoughts are half-actions, near-actions.

Sometimes one grasps this meaning better by substituting a more appropriate expression for a well-worn word. Everybody speaks, for instance, of aggressive tendencies. One learns in clinical psychoanalysis that violent impulses would be a much more appropriate word for those impulses re-emerging from the emotional netherworld. Only when one adheres to the notion that thoughts are near-actions or substitute actions does one acquire true insight into the psychology of neurotic patients.

77. *Night Thoughts*

The things that cloud our judgment during the day sometimes evaporate during the night when we lie awake, unable to sleep.

Those confusing and misleading thoughts serve perhaps to conceal things from ourselves and others. Things sometimes look clearer in the night and we see our way. Some thoughts resemble the clouds into which the Lord wrapped the children of Isreal on their sojourn in the desert during the day, while during the night a pillar of fire illuminated their way.

78. *Death Wishes and Guilt Feelings*

We know from numerous neurotic cases that unconscious death wishes concerning members of one's family and close friends produce guilt feelings. Those death wishes need not even be unconscious, but can emerge and become repressed.

Imagine that you are walking on Broadway and a man in front of you steps on your toe, where you have a corn. His clumsiness has caused you pain. The thought that occurs to you at this moment is "Drop dead!" This death wish will generally not bother you later. But if such a murderous wish arose toward your father or mother or wife, it would percolate and develop its subterranean effects—producing symptoms, doubts, and anxieties.

What are the essential psychological differences between the two cases? That stranger is a matter of indifference to you, but you care for your father, mother, or wife and this emotional factor comes in conflict with the violent and murderous impulses that emerged in you.

79. *The Two Regrets*

When an old man looks back on his life, his memories are accompanied by two regrets. The first is that he has not enjoyed life enough and has let many opportunities slip by. The second is that he has often cruelly hurt some people's feelings. There was certainly a possibility to attain one's goal without hurting people's feelings.

There are only a few cases in which ruthlessness is the only way to one's goal. The Eastern Jews had a saying, "He wants to slaughter a hen without hurting her," thus making fun of an exaggerated and inappropriate delicacy of feeling. In the majority of cases it would have been possible to avoid inflicting grief on those near and dear to us. Such unnecessary cruelty is a two-edged sword: we become aware that we were hurting ourselves too—only much later.

80. *Prepared*

Is it true, as Hamlet asserts, that "readiness is all"? Is it not rather neurotic to be prepared for all eventualities and possibilities destiny has in store for us? It is perhaps neurotic to be always forewarned because it means to be forearmed. Sometimes one has to meet all events as they come without forseeing them.

81. *Broken Chains*

We sometimes overlook the connection between a forbidden deed and self-punishment and thus deprive ourselves of the advantage of unexpected psychological insight. The events appear then simply as one following the other as if they were unconnected. Assume that a man slaps the face of another whom he hates. Pulling his arm back, he collides with a table and smashes his elbow. We see two events without recognizing the link between them and do not realize that the second has all the earmarks of an unconscious self-punishment and atonement for the first action.

82. *America and Youth*

Among the criticisms to which the American mentality exposed itself, one was, in Freud's opinion, its idolatry of youth and an ill-concealed contempt for old age. Freud once told me that he overheard two men speak of him as an "old codger," on a visit to Niagara Falls in 1911. Freud was then fifty-five years old.

We should, I think, pay more attention to the dependency we all have on childhood food preferences and dislikes. I assume that the preference men show for the way their mothers cook certain dishes is to be traced back to being fed at their mother's breast. Freud thought that people who dislike the skin of the milk developed this peculiarity as an unconscious reaction from having been weaned suddenly. The skin reminds them unconsciously of mother's breast. Children who show a distinct distaste for spinach are still unconsciously under the influence of toilet training that was too early and too severe. Spinach reminds them of the color and subtance of feces which as babies they put into their mouths or with which they played before being taught cleanliness. A similar reaction can be assumed in people who dislike strong-smelling cheese; it reminds them of unpleasant body odors. The fact should not be overlooked, of course, that many people conquer food dislikes in later life. (I remind the reader of the story of *Struwelpeter,* "Naughty Peter.") Many children do not like soup, whereas in later life, especially in old age, they enjoy soup as food.

I can imagine the possibility of dying for one's children if necessary, but I am unable to conceive of dying for one's country, for religion, or for the salvation of mankind. Those are all empty abstractions, indefinite, illusive, and evanescent. They are as mythical and as meaningful for us today as are the Gods of ancient Greece or Rome.

Part IV : *Of Life and Letters*

PRELIMINARY REMARK

I spent last summer at Lake Mohonk Mountain House, an excellent hotel near New Paltz, New York. The following notes are the fruits of my reading during those months. I had taken some new scientific books with me. Otherwise I was prepared to read at my leisure whatever the hotel library had to offer. It is quite a library, containing all kinds of works in the social sciences, in history, in biography, and so on. There are also mystery stories to read before falling asleep.

To my delight I found the complete works of Anatole France in the hotel library and read them again and again, volume after volume. I have always loved this writer. Reading his wonderful French prose affects me in the same manner as listening to Mozart's music. It quiets and soothes me and fills me with serenity. Such reading leads me to some thoughts and dreams that reach beyond my usual sphere of observation. It is not astonishing that many of the following notes prolong the echo of those experiences.

Other books, picked at random, touched old experiences, thoughts, and emotions and revived them. Is it not one of the best functions of reading books that they awaken such feelings and ideas that were dormant?

1. *Old Persia and Old Vienna*

Yesterday I picked up the quatrains of Omar Khayyám interpreted by Edward Fitzgerald, and opened the book at the well-known lines:

> A Book of Verses underneath the Bough,
> A Jug of Wine, a Loaf of Bread—and Thou
> Beside me singing in the Wilderness—
> Oh, Wilderness were Paradise enow!

I vividly experienced a kind of emotional protest against the old Persian epigrammatist and freethinker, and some other of his quatrains proving this evaluation came to my mind. My grievance was directed against his rather modest conception of Paradise. My dissent expressed itself in my next thought association, namely, the memory of a Viennese folksong I had heard as a boy. The words of the song, whose melody I had remembered before the lyrics, portray a Viennese, a good Catholic, of course, praying to God in broad Viennese dialect:

> *Du liaber Himmelvater,*
> *I brauch ka Paradies,*
> *I bleib viel lieber dader,*
> *Weil Wean mei Himmelreich is.*

This is perhaps translatable as:

> Thou kind father of Heaven
> I don't need a paradise, see?
> I like it much more here,
> 'Cause Vienna is Heaven to me.

I believe the native Viennese would be more selective with regard to the woman of the Persian quatrain. He always made fun of a certain kind of *"homme à femmes,"* saying, *"Er hat Glück bei Frauen. Es g'fallt ihm a jede."* ("He has luck with women. He likes every one of them.") A jug of wine certainly would not be enough for him, as he says in another song:

> *Trink ma noch a Flascherl,*
> *Solange ma hab' noch Geld im Tascherl.*

> Let's drink another bottle,
> As long as there is money in my pocket.

And a loaf of bread? Man does not live by bread alone, not even by *"panis angelicus."* The native Viennese has a significant phrase, *"Ich bin ein komischer Kerl. Mir schmeckt ka klans Gullash nicht."* He confesses that he is "a funny guy. I don't like no small goulash."

The only common feature between the Persian poet and the native Viennese is the avoidance of all possible activity and the love of leisure. There is a story of old Vienna, dating from World War I, which is significant of the spirit of my native city. In the campaign of 1914, an Austrian field gun was stuck in the mud in East Galicia. A Viennese regiment was ordered to dislodge the cannon and move it. The soldiers put their shoulders to the heavy cannon and loudly shouted, "Ho!" They continued their efforts for some time, but in vain; the cannon would not move. It so happened that a Prussian regiment came marching by. When the Prussian Lieutenant observed the loud but lackadaisical efforts of the Viennese soldiers he became indignant. "You slovenly Viennese!" he yelled, "I'll show you how *we* work!" He ordered a few of his men to move the cannon. They shouted "One, two, three," and the gun was freed from the mud and could be moved. The Viennese soldiers, who had looked on with great interest, shrugged and said, *"Ja, mit Gewalt!"* ("Well, if you're going to use force. . . .")

I once heard an old Viennese citizen praise the wonderful spectacle of Austrian troops in a parade, pridefully reporting how the soldiers marched in straight line past the Kaiser, how their eyes moved simultaneously to the right, and with what precision they presented arms. He boasted that the soldiers all marched in perfect unison, and that not a split second elapsed before an order was carried out. When I reminded the man that the Austrian army had been defeated by the Prussians in 1866, he said, "Well, in war . . . that's quite a different thing." I have always said that the Austrians (I served in the Austrian army as an officer in World War I) were the most belligerent people. They always drifted into war, and they fought against most of the nations of Europe. There is scarcely a European country that cannot boast of having defeated the Austrian army.

2. *Voices*

The annoying habit of thinking in antitheses sometimes leads to unpleasant contrasts. Romeo, called by Juliet, says:

> How silver-sweet sound lovers' tongues by night,
> Like softest music to attending ears!

You imagine a startling contrast: Romeo and Juliet, married many years later, he impatiently shouting at her and she shrewishly shrieking "Drop dead!" in the night. Their tongues have entirely lost their silver-sweet quality.

3. *God*

The deification of self is rapidly progressing. One could venture to predict the creed of the future. It will be: "Number One is the one and only God."

To conceive of God as a father figure is an old custom. Yet Leopold Kompert, a now forgotten Austrian-Jewish novelist, wrote more than one hundred years ago: "God cannot be everywhere;

therefore He created mothers." That is the most beautiful praise ever bestowed upon women.

4. *Reading and Sleep*

There is an intimate connection between therapy of insomnia and reading habits. Since the production of effective drugs that make people sleepy, many of the recent novels have become superfluous. While you put them aside because they are so boring, you wonder how their authors could have written them without having been overcome by drowsiness.

5. *Teaching History*

Teaching history in our schools is still mainly the celebration of wars and the conquests of nations. We still erect monuments to victorious generals. If we were as civilized as we pretend to be, we would rather honor the memory of those men who prevented wars and conquests. They should be considered the true educators of man.

6. *To Be Wise*

"To be wise and to love exceeds man's might," says Shakespeare. There is no choice given to men. The only question in the minds of those who are old and wise is whether all the wisdom of the world is worth the illusion of happiness which love gives. "Oh, to be foolish and blind again!" some old men will sigh.

In a moment of insight Louis XI said that one is no longer happy after sixty years of age. (*"On n'est plus heureux après soixante années."*)

7. *The Zipper*

What a wonderful invention the zipper is! With a simple movement, a woman can step out of her dress. Anatole France complained of the fashions in women's clothes when he was young,
saying that he remembered that dresses had an immense number
of buttons, and added that "fashion was very cruel to lovers."

8. *Self-centeredness*

William Hazlitt wrote, "The least pain in our little finger gives us
more concern than the destruction of millions of our fellow beings."
This is shockingly true. As we are on the subject of physical pain,
we should add: When we have a toothache, we do not love any-
body.

9. *Hymn to Women*

Friedrich von Schiller's praise of women begins:

> Honor women! With roses grown in Eden's bowers
> They intertwine this life of ours.

This is so beautiful that only hardened realists would remind us that
there are no roses without thorns.

10. *Lovers*

Shakespeare said that "the lunatic, the lover, and the poet are of
imagination all compact." Since then people in love have often
been compared with psychotics because of their abundant imagination. Such a comparison is still flattering. Yet to some, a man in
love resembles an idiot much more, a person born with the lowest
I.Q. of 25. As long as one compares a lover to a person with
delusions or likens him to a poet, all mankind loves a lover. But

when he seems to be acting like an idiot, he is more to be pitied than envied. What does it matter that he is happy? Insane asylums are full of idiots who are deliriously and radiantly happy.

11. *Only Afterwards*

In Anatole France's *Histoire Comique,* Félicie Nanteuil meets her lover and they compare notes about their love. He says, "I would never have believed that I loved you so much—it came later. It always comes later." She said, "What you say is true, Robert. One does not know it beforehand." The "it" is, of course, sexual intercourse and the meaning of those sentences is that sexual gratification is re-experienced in one's memory and creates the illusion of love. We assume this is the case with the woman, but it is often similar with the man. Robert de Ligny, the lover of the novel, is transferred to a diplomatic position in The Hague. While he is in Holland, he has several experiences with other women that prove to him the power of his love for Félicie in Paris. None of those women, who differed in age, appearance, and position, gave him the full satisfaction he had with Félicie. Being with them he missed her, and discovered that he desired only her. But for the sexual experiences with these women he would never have known how much he loved Félicie. Anatole France says, "When one pays attention to the literal sense, one will say that he was unfaithful to her. . . . But when one sees deeper, he did not deceive her. He searched for her. He searched for her outside herself and understood that he could find her only in herself." He even experienced some angry feelings because he had "to put the multitude of his desires into so little of substance and into a unique and fragile place."

12. *Spirit of Revolution*

The actress Félicie Nanteuil rehearses the part of a young girl during the French Revolution. Her lover asks her if she knows the

Revolution. "Of course," she says. "I don't know the data, but I have the feeling of the epoch. For me, the Revolution means to have a proud breast below a crossed fichu and the knees quite free below a strapped skirt and to have a little rouge on the cheeks. That's it." One realizes from this what the actress imagines the spirit of the Revolution to have been.

13. *The General*

Anatole France recalls a lullaby his mother used to sing to him:

> . . . *Le voilà général*
> *Il court, il vole, il devient marèchal*
> . . . . .
> *En attendant, sur mes genoux,*
> *Beau général, endormez vous.*

Freely translated:

> . . . Here is the general,
> He runs, he flies, becomes a marshal
> . . . . .
> While waiting on my lap,
> Beautiful general, take a nap.

Is it not charming? It reminds us of the psychological theory that women are fully reconciled to their femaleness only after they have given birth to a boy. In daydreaming of his splendid future they fulfill vicariously their own masculine wishes of which they are often unconscious.

14. *Remarkable Prediction*

In his *Penguin Island,* published in 1908, Anatole France predicted the holocaust that now threatens to annihilate civilization. He describes the illustrious idealist Professor Obnabile who for sixty years had led a solitary and retired life in his laboratory and who was convinced that the barbarism of war would be abolished as civilization advanced. After a visit to America this learned professor becomes convinced that war is unavoidable and concludes, since the folly and wickedness of men are incurable, there remains but one good deed to be done. "The wise man will gather enough dynamite to blow up the planet. When its fragments fly through space, an imperceptible amelioration will be accomplished in the universe and satisfaction will be given to the universal conscience."

Anatole France died in 1924, almost forty years ago. He could not have foreseen the Second World War and Hiroshima, nor the H-bomb and its improved successors. At the end of *Penguin Island* a clerk of the Electricity Trust blows up a whole district—not with dynamite, but with a new material made from radium, a material of unheard-of concentrated energy and power.

15. *A Buddhist Story Psychoanalytically Interpreted*

An old story tells of two Buddhist monks who came to a river. A woman stood on the bank, afraid to cross. One of the monks carried her over, and then the two monks continued on their way. The gallant one sang cheerfully, while the other became gloomier and gloomier and finally exclaimed, "How could you, a monk, take up a woman in your arms?" The first one answered, "Oh, are you still carrying her? I set her down back at the ford."

When you interpret that little story psychoanalytically as if it were a dream, its latent content means just the opposite of what its manifest surface says. Carrying the woman over means symbolically to have sexual intercourse with her. (Compare the custom of carrying the bride across the threshold of the house.) The monk who did so feels cheerful since he is freed from tension. The other monk is sad because he is not relieved and also because he is envious of his more fortunate brother. He blames him for something he himself was too virtuous or not courageous enough to do.

16. *Epigrams*

An epigram is the result of thoughts that have been thought to the end or the precipitation of many accumulated experiences. At all events, one has to leave home and to walk to arrive there. Lookout towers are usually not part of our lodgings.

17. *A Life-Lie*

The life-lie of which Ibsen spoke may concern only a part of a person's life, but often it is of central and far-reaching importance. It may even be a misrepresentation of long duration, for instance, the person's denying he is Jewish and the pretense that his ancestors had come to this country in the *Mayflower*. Such consistent and continual make-believe deteriorates and finally destroys the character because it eventually robs the character of all authenticity and genuineness.

18. *Symbolism*

In a session of our seminar we discussed sexual symbolism in dreams, that universal forgotten language of the unconscious. My students and I searched for analogous symbolisms in myth, folklore, literature, and so on. When tooth-pulling as a symbolic representation of castration was mentioned, I pointed out that in the puberty rituals of some primitive tribes a tooth is pulled instead of the older rite of circumcision.

A student referred to the fear of tooth-pulling, almost always to be met in boys and sometimes also in adults as unconscious manifestations of castration anxiety. None of us could, however, remember having read something akin to those symbolic representations in literature.

Before falling asleep this evening I took a volume of Anatole France's works and began to read in bed as is my bad habit. I happened to open the book to the story called "La Signora Chiara."

The outline of the story, which encompasses just a few pages, is as follows: Giacomo Tedeschi was a renowned Neopolitan physician who performed all kinds of simple operations on his big couch. Tedeschi believed that his wife, Chiara, was as virtuous as she was beautiful, but he knew as a physician the weaknesses to which the nature of women is subjected and he therefore experienced some uneasiness when the young and handsome tailor Ascanio Ranieri of Milano became a frequent visitor, usually in the doctor's absence. Once, Tedeschi returned home earlier than expected and caught Ascanio and Chiara embracing. When the Signora left the room, Tedeschi approached Ascanio with the utmost solicitude. "My friend," he said, "I see that you are suffering and it was good that you came to see me." He assured the young man that he would do something to ease his terrible toothache. So saying, the old man pushed Ascanio into his office and onto the couch that had seen forty years of Neapolitan illnesses.

"I see that you have an agonizing toothache!" the doctor stated, whereupon he took up an enormous dentist's forceps, opened the patient's mouth wide, and pulled a tooth. Ascanio ran away spitting blood into his handerchief as Professor Tedeschi shouted cheerfully after him, "A beautiful tooth! A very beautiful tooth!"

It is obvious that the tooth-pulling is meant as a castration symbol. ("Let the punishment fit the crime," as *The Mikado* proclaims.)

As far as I know, this short story by Anatole France is the only one in modern literature that presents tooth-pulling as symbolic castration. In its displacement of the operation from below to above, it is, in the context of the story, so convincing that even skeptics will acknowledge the reference to sexual symbolism by the French writer long before the name of Freud was known to him.

19. *Philosophy*

Father Lorenzo points to philosophy as "adversity's sweet milk," but young Romeo impetuously answers:

> Hang up, philosophy!
> Unless philosophy can make a Juliet.

These lines bring to mind some sentences of practical wisdom I heard in my boyhood in Vienna, lines that illuminate the relation of philosophy to the vital powers governing our life.

> *Über ein gutes Essen*
> *kann man jede Philosophie vergessen,*
> *Aber über die beste Philosophie*
> *Vergisst man das Essen nie.*

> Over a good meal, on the table set,
> All philosophy you might forget,
> But philosophy, however good,
> Never makes you forget your food.

20. *Temptation*

Women are subjected to sexual temptations as are men, but perhaps not of the same intensity and urgency. However, there are days in which their sexual drives are as intense as those of the males. The difference between the sexes in this respect is owing to the diversity of education and early training. Women are educated to resist those temptations whereas men are not supposed to resist, at least not as effectively and resolutely. Even when men struggle with their passions, they sometimes regret their victory over them. Women would not cynically confess, as Heinrich Heine did:

> *Himmlisch war's,*
> *Wenn ich bezwang*
> *Meine sündige Begier,*

Doch wenn es mir micht gelang,
Hatt' ich auch ein gross Plaisir.

Perhaps translatable as:

'Twas heavenly when I could conquer
Desire of the flesh, to me so dear,
But when I did not succeed,
I had still a great plaisir.

21. *Eros and Thanathos*

Almost two hundred years ago Friedrich von Schiller let his Karlos say:

Ein Augenblick, gelebt im Paradiese,
Ist nicht zu teuer mit dem Tod bezahlt.

A moment, lived in paradise,
Is not too dearly paid with death.

The poet whose hero burst out with this enthusiastic exclamation assuredly was not thinking of certain species of animals who, during copulation, are unaware of the hunter; nor was he thinking of the many men who die of a heart attack during sexual intercourse.

22. *Immigration of Ideas*

The renowned Judge Jerome Frank once wrote that each specialist group "when functioning as such and in the interest of its special concerns, creates its own sub-universe and sets up immigration laws which bar alien facts from entering."

From time to time those immigration laws, directed against the invasion of alien facts, have to be changed and their severity mitigated. Then an influx of alien ideas takes place as, for instance, now in the realm of law where psychology is being given greater and greater consideration.

23. *Luxury*

It is a time of relative luxury we live in. In a biography of Schubert (who was very poor) I read that someone advised him to buy unlined paper and draw the lines himself, since it was cheaper. Are we not ashamed, hearing of such poverty of great composers, when we compare our situation?

Freud, who wrote on long sheets, once told me (when I asked about them): "When one has to restrict himself in other ways in life, one wants to have at least plenty of space when one writes." He never forgot that he was poor in his youth.

24. *Religion*

Brotteaux, in Anatole France's *"Le Dieux ont soif,"* which presents a splendid picture of the French Revolution, complains that the Jacobins want to replace the old religion with a younger and more malicious one—the religion of liberty and equality. He had observed, he said, that religions are most violent and cruel in the vigor of their youth and that they become more peaceful when they are aging.

Is there not here a prediction of the future of the new religion of our time—communism?

25. *The Army*

If one can believe the reports, each army consists of brave patriots. An army has neither cowards nor murderers. If there were many cowards in it, it would no longer be an army but a band; and if it contained killers it would be a gang of criminals. An army is therefore composed of heroes and patriots who are eager to die defending the just cause of their country and to destroy the enemy who threatens the natural order.

26. *Puberty*

Goethe's lines

> *Wo ist einer in diesen Tagen*
> *Der das trug,*
> *Was wir getragen?*

> Where is the lad these days
> Who endured
> What we had to suffer?

concern really the years of puberty, which is the time of the most cruel emotional stress. All the sufferings of manhood are, compared with them, tolerable. Never is the power of women stronger than in the imagination of male adolescence, never the frustration of sexual desires more torturing.

27. *The Jews*

I read an article whose author, like so many scholars before him, complains about the Jews' resistance to assimilation. He points out that all the friendly advances, the obliging, complaisant, accommodating spirit of the Western Christian nations are in vain. All their efforts to absorb the Jews are frustrated. These stubborn people refuse to become merged in other nations and to be absorbed within them.

I am of the opinion that the deepest roots of Jewish characteristics must be traced to their early, prehistoric period, comparable in its consequences for later vicissitudes to traumatic events of early childhood in individual life. I don't know if it was that train of thought, connecting the destiny of Jews with their origin in Africa, but reading that magazine article with its complaints about the unassimilability of the Jews made me recall Anatole France's story about Monsieur Du Chaillu in *"Sur La Pierre Blanche."* The complaints of that magazine writer resemble the serious grievances

Monsieur Du Chaillu had against his gorilla. Du Chaillu killed the mother of a gorilla with a shotgun in the African forest. Dying, she clasped her infant in her arms. Du Chaillu carried the young animal with him across Africa in a cage in order to sell it in Europe. But the young gorilla gave him good reason to complain. It was anti-social. Du Chaillu said: "I was unable to improve its bad character." I suspect that the Western nations have similar grievances against the Jews.

28. *Destiny of the Jews*

After reading some novels with a Jewish milieu from England, France and America, a profound impression of their basic similarity remains. It is as if the Jews of various countries have something in common—beyond religion or irreligion—something deeply rooted in their past and binding them together. Those groups, often separated by thousands of miles, stumble toward each other, just as strayed members of an excursion party grope toward each other through the underbrush, over roots and around tree trunks. They are guided by the sound of their voices, speaking different languages, and meet finally on the same path.

To the superficial historian it may seem as if the vicissitudes of the Jews in the various countries had always been different. Such a variance already appears in prehistoric times when not all the Hebrew tribes wandered into Canaan and some remained in Egypt. That disparity of vicissitudes was observed in the history of ancient times as well as in our modern age. Yet the explorer who penetrates to the core of the problem will recognize that there is merely a time difference of decades or centuries. In the end, the Jews of different countries share the same fate—one group earlier, the other later.

This common destiny has perhaps its roots in the earliest pre-historic period of the Hebrew tribes.

A dutch proverb says: *"Zame ouit, zame thuis"* (Together out, together home), and is often applied to excursionists. The wanderings and migrations of the Jews are perhaps comparable to such excursions. I believe that the future of the Jews of all countries will be the same in the end.

29. *Litttle Boys*

The notions of the world held by little boys are by no means vague and senseless. They might be erroneous and founded upon false premises that lead to mistaken conclusions, but they are definite and often clearly expressed in words. Anatole France reported that little André was not easily deceived by grownups. "Mommy, do you know what Grandfather told me? He said that the hens produce eggs," André informed his mother. But he knew that this was not so. He knew that the grocer of the Avenue de Neuilly made the eggs, "then they were taken to the hens that warm them." "How could hens make the eggs, Mommy?" he asked. "They don't have any hands!" The boy's mistake is due, of course, to his incomplete information about the facts of life. The concepts of the world acquired by children are often blurred by the ambiguity of words adults use in their explanations. There is another example from the same book (*Le Livre de mon ami*). A boy, much younger than André, liked to visit a woman who sometimes gave him a cake. *"La dame en blanc,"* he called her when he later wrote his autobiography. In that woman's apartment the little boy met a man who brought her news of her husband who had a position in a far-off land. The child heard that the husband had been appointed "First Secretary." "On this day," the writer recalled in his memoirs, "I asked my father at dinner what this is—a Secretary." His father did not answer, but "my mother told me it was a piece of furniture in which one keeps papers." A boy in kindergarten said, "I have a writer-daddy," and another boy said, "I have a lawyer-daddy"—a form of introduction by denoting the profession of the father, and an emotional manifestation akin to aristocratic pride.

30. *Supplement*

Confusion is natural when children first encounter words in a foreign language. There is a charming example in the *Reminiscences* of Supreme Court Justice Felix Frankfurter. When he arrived in this country as a boy, he could speak no English. It was his notion that Mr. Laundry must be a very rich man because he had so many stores in the city.

31. *The Maid*

Anatole France remembers from his childhood (in *La Vie en Fleur*) that his father called the maid, Justine, *"la catastrophe"* because she often unleashed all the elements—water, fire, and air—around her when she dropped everything she laid her hands on.

FRIGHT

Freud (in the *Interpretation of Dreams*) speaks of *"Gedankenschreck"* (fright at one's thoughts), meaning the terror we experience when thoughts that are alien to our conscious thinking suddenly emerge to the surface of our mind.

All demons and monsters seem to appear when we think something that is alien to all the people we know and with whom we feel akin. Only occasionally, when we recognize that thought as original and fruitful, if led to the end, do we feel a great satisfaction—in the case of the great innovators a feeling of triumph. But first they must conquer those demons, lay those ghosts to rest.

As for new and unexpected thoughts, are we not also subjected to *"Gedankenschreck,"* an emotion comparable to the fear experienced by small children who feel deserted when they see strangers' faces instead of familiar ones?

32. *Writing*

Ibsen's remark that writing means to sit in judgement upon oneself is correct, but incomplete. The necessary continuation is: and to acquit oneself.

33. *The Two Roads*

"The road to success is to march with others; the road to glory is to march against the others." On the second road you will be alone; it will be a lonely march and you will search in vain for companions in your wandering. At the end you will be tired and ready to give up.

34. *The Pen*

"The pen is mightier than the sword." A writer deprived of the materials to write with—pen, pencil, typewriter, and so on—resembles a warrior going on his way to the battlefield without a weapon, or a man going to bed with a woman without his genitals.

35. *Education of Mankind*

We have arrived at the point where we no longer believe that punishment of a naughty child will improve his morals. Why do we not draw the inescapable conclusion that punishment of criminals will not change them in the direction we wish? Abbé Coignard in Anatole France's stories did not believe in such vaunted effects of punishment and he considered it hopeless to make prison a place of virtue. (*"Il désperait de faire de la prison une école de vertu."*)

36. *Formation of Legend*

There was a school of comparative mythology which conceived of the biblical figures as presenting the sun, the moon, many planets. The interpretation went beyond this point. The scholarly librarian Agen Jean-Baptiste Peres proved that Napoleon never existed and that the story of the great conqueror was nothing but a solar myth.

I don't doubt that the making of legends has not ended. It merely takes other forms, but remains as fantastic and fanciful as the interpretations of comparative mythology. Whoever has known Freud and now reads some recent American books about his personality will admire the extravagant and inventive imagination in which the writers revel.

37. *What Remains*

What will remain of us after we are dead? Nothing; but for a short time people will remember what we said or wrote.

My daughter Miriam has a bookplate on which a sentence of the old Belgian scholar Justus Lipsius (A.D. 1606) appears: "You are a voice, nothing else" (in the original, *"Vox es, nihil praeteria"*). Such a voice we are for a very brief posterity. This voice becomes, by and by, fainter and fainter until it can no longer be heard. Newer voices will reach the ear of the coming generations and then those voices also will be lost in eternal silence.

38. *Before Freud*

From Heinrich Heine's poems:

> *Acht engeschrieb'ne Seiten,*
> *Ein kleines Manuskript!*
> *Man schreibt nicht so ausfuehrlich,*
> *Wenn man den Abschied gibt.*

Eight closely written pages,
A small manuscript, O my!
One does not write too explicitly
When one only says good-bye.

A bit of anticipated applied depth-psychology—nearly a hundred years before Freud.

39. *The Plays and Life*

There is now a pervasive complaint about the presentation and discussion of sexual themes in the plays and movies of our age. This is not the place or the occasion to consider the pros and cons of that debate, but it should at least be considered if that presentation of sexual themes corresponds to life's experience, if it truly reflects the sexual processes of men and women. As far as I know only one modern play mentions the important part of menstruation in the sexual life of women: *Fräulein Julie* by August Strindberg in which the sudden sexual surrender of the twenty-five-year-old leading figure to her valet is made probable by the monthly cycle of the woman. No modern play discusses, as far as I know, the far-reaching consequences of contraceptive measures for sexuality. Compare this absence of treatment on the stage (and in novels) with the significance of contraceptives in sexual relations. Freud once remarked, that the man who invented contraceptive devices or pills that are reliable and easy to use as well as comfortable would be a benefactor of mankind and worthy of a monument in every city.

40. *Lady Chatterley's Lover*

D. H. Lawrence's description of the sensations and emotions a woman experiences before, during, and after sexual intercourse is certainly admirable, but admirable in the way that a violinist plays a concert piece on one string. I am more impressed by Lawrence's insight into feminine psychology in other directions, for instance, in the observation that the woman is afraid the man might leave her shortly after intercourse. She begs him, "Don't leave me! Hold me! Hold me fast!" Lawrence describes her ludicrous attempts to imitate the man's dialect in order to incorporate him also emotionally, to become part of him.

41. *The Sense of Smell*

One must be allowed to follow a psychological speculation to a certain length and then break it off until it can be verified, or at least supported by evidence from other fields. In preceding remarks I pointed out that woman has not removed herself as far as the man has from the soil. In the words of the poet Richard Beer-Hofmann (*Der Graf von Charolais*):

> Only the man was weaned; woman is still allowed to dream
> On earth's breasts, nearer to creation; not yet freed
> From those primal and mysterious contracts,
> Subject still to the same nocturnal planet
> Which commands the sea.
> What appears as an enigma, is that
> . . . she is still close to the elements,
> Is, herself, perhaps the youngest of them all.

Is it true that women have a keener sense of smell than men and that they react sooner and more perceptively to odors? That they relish certain smells and loathe others more than men do? It is unlikely that they have keener olfactory nerves, but probably odors do affect them more powerfully. Do they discriminate, discern, and recognize scents better than men? They are certainly more occupied with perfumes and deodorants than men. Yet some of the best perfumers in the world are men.

Let us assume that women react more perceptibly to good and bad odors. What is the origin of that superior sense of smell? It is easy to theorize that it results from the awareness of the changing smells of their own bodies which are also determined by vaginal secretions and by the blood during menstruation. In other words, that better developed sense of smell results from the education of the girl by her mother, who taught her not only her toilet training but also how to behave during her monthly period. Girls are toilet trained earlier than boys and become earlier and more acutely aware of the smells of their own bodies. Under the influence of their education to womanhood, girls exhibit immediate reactions to the smells of their own bodies and of others' as well, to odors in rooms and in their surroundings.

Freud pointed out that the decrease of the distinctiveness and importance of the olfactory sense was determined when the human animal, in contrast to the others, learned to stand and to walk erect: that reduction of the sense of smell depended on the distance from the soil on which animals recognized the nature of the world. The sense of smell became less necessary and a less certain guide to primal man who no longer moved so close to mother earth. This evolutionary speculation neglects, of course, the area of sexual differentiation between men and women, but its continuation leads to interesting aspects of the problem. As Beer-Hofmann said:

> Only the man was weaned; woman is still allowed to dream
> On earth's breasts, nearer to creation. . . .

Are there also olfactory sensations in those dreams? Do women also remember certain scents better than men? In Marcel Proust's *Remembrance of Things Past,* the narrator recalls many experiences with the help of odors.

42. *Forward, Backward*

Catskill Mountains, Summer, 1962: Spending my vacation here awakens the thought of Rip Van Winkle who played ninepins with strangers and then slept for twenty years. If we were to awaken after twenty years, like Rip Van Winkle, we would be in an alien world and at our wits' end. We would have lost our bearings and be unable to find our way in this strange land. If, in the manner of

H. G. Wells' time machine, we were to move a few hundred years backward in time, after some confusion we would remember things and social institutions. Traces of race-memory would be revived and help in our orientation. If, like the characters of Sir James Barrie's *Dear Brutus,* we received a second chance to live our lives from a certain time forward, we would perhaps make the same indolent decisions and mistakes and would commit the same stupid acts and blunders as long as we had the same character and temperament as before. It would perhaps be better if that second chance were given us when we were old, but then we would have little desire to do something about it. And who can know if we would not commit the same blunders even then? There is no fool like an old fool.

43. *The Observers*

Why is it that women are amused but more often annoyed when they observe that a man is bashful or timid in his approach to another woman? There is, of course, the factor of jealousy of this other woman. Along with this emotion there is a clear understanding that the woman anticipates the approach with great tension and enjoys the man's bashfulness as if it were a token of his high esteem for her.

Another question: Do women really believe that men woo them because they are intellectually brilliant? I should think that such an attitude on the part of the male would be highly offensive to women, because it would be possible only at the cost of the man's admiration for the woman's loveliness or beauty. Fortunately, no woman believes, deep within her, that a man is much impressed by her brilliant intellect. She attributes no more value to it than as an accessory to a beautiful dress. I refer, of course, to a woman in her right mind; but when is a woman in her right mind?

Where are the days in which a woman spoke of herself in the words of Portia in the *Merchant of Venice?*

An unlesson'd girl, unschool'd unpractis'd
Happy in this, she is not yet so old
But she may learn.

Our Portias have all been to college and have studied law.

44. *Justice*

"The insolence of office" of which Hamlet complains is by no means common to all positions. The lower the officer's rank, the greater is his insolence, and becomes atrociously arrogant at the nethermost ranks. The Viennese satirist Karl Kraus once wrote, "We live in a state in which the highest officials are sometimes amiable with us, while the office messengers are, at best, condescending."

Poor and ambitious as I was as a boy, I had some early sad experiences on this account and they left deep traces. They even helped me to resist the pressure of my family who wanted me to study law when I was eighteen. I recall two impressions of that period that influenced my decision not to yield to my family. The first was the inscription on an arch before the Imperial Palace, the residence of Franz Joseph in Vienna: *Fiat justicia, pereat mundus* (Let Justice be done though the world goes to pieces). I knew from those sad experiences how hypocritical that principle was and how its highfalutin sentiment was contradicted every day in old Austria. The other influence was a quotation from Anatole France, whose works had then fallen into my hands for the first time: "The law, in its majestic equality, forbids the rich as well as the poor to steal bread and to sleep under low bridges." The gentle irony of the French writer enchanted me for the first time.

45. *That Pig of a Morin*

I have retained the bad habit of reading in bed before falling asleep. I am unable to read serious scientific work, preferring light literature, such as detective stories. I still like Inspector Maigret,

Georges Simenon's hero. Sometimes such reading is, in spite of its diverting character, "educational," as we Americans call it.

In the last analytic session of the day, a patient complained about his wife who, after many years, still claims that he had a sexual affair with one of her women friends—despite his angry protestations and the furious denial of the suspected woman whom she once confronted. The patient complained that his wife still speaks of him as of a seducer, as a kind of obstinately incorrigible Don Juan. She calls him this not only when she discusses him with her women friends, but whenever she speaks of him. Yet the patient's character is very far from that of the famous courtier and libertine. He is, on the contrary, a timidly shy man in the company of women and is uneasy and bashful in his approach to them. How did his wife arrive at her erroneous opinion that was soon shared by many persons in the couple's social circle?

Was it accidental that I reached for Maupassant's short stories that evening and opened it to the story *Ce Cochon de Morin?* You perhaps remember the tale of the very shy storekeeper Morin from La Rachelle who spent a fortnight in Paris. Excited by the amorous atmosphere of that city, he returns home on the night express and shares the car with a charming young woman. He does not dare to speak to her when she wakes up in the morning and smiles at him. He still cannot think of anything to say and, "seized with a coward's courage," grabs her and kisses her. She screams in terror and tells the guards rushing up that "that man wanted—wanted to"—and faints. The gendarme on duty arrests Morin and the poor linen draper faces prosecution for an outrage of morals in a public place. In his despair, Morin asks the help of his friend, the editor Labarbe. This journalist and colleague, moved by pity, calls on the magistrate, on the uncle and aunts of the girl, and finally meets the girl herself. Morin's wife gives him a beating and abuses him by calling him "that pig of a Morin," an epithet gradually pinned on him by everyone who heard of the adventure. Labarbe himself talks with the girl, the victim of Morin's supposed brutality. The clever journalist, who later became a deputy, flatters and courts her and finds his way to her bedroom, where he spends the night with her. On his way home he runs into many people who ask him, "Have you settled the affair of that pig Morin?" Everywhere he goes he hears that epithet. Labarbe meets the offended young lady again, who has become the wife of a notary. This man thanks Labarbe for his tact and delicacy in the affair "of that pig of a Morin." Years later, after the malefactor had died, Labarbe can never speak of him without calling him *"ce cochon de Morin."*

As I reread this masterful story of Maupassant my thoughts returned to my patient whom his wife persists in calling a Don Juan. The false rumor of his amorous adventure had made the rounds just as the incident of *"Ce cochon de Morin"* and just as undeservedly. In the end he persuaded his wife that he was not a Don Juan. However, a woman convinced against her will is of the same opinion still. And not only a woman, as the story of *"Ce cochon de Morin"* shows.

46. *Two Mystery Stories*

The other day I picked up a mystery story in the public library. I began to read it the same evening, in bed. The story began with a description of a cocktail party, with the usual hustle and bustle and fragments of conversations heard here and there. On the first page of this vivid presentation, a woman is speaking to another woman whose name she does not remember. She notices that this person is wearing a pink chiffon dress. The author, in rendering the dialogue between the two, defines one only by her dress. For example, " 'At home so much of the time,' Pink Chiffon said."

I had not looked at the name of the author on the dust jacket, but I was ready to bet it was a woman. No man would identify a person merely by her dress.

As a matter of fact I was partly mistaken. The mystery story was by Frances and Richard Lockridge, *Murder Has Its Points* (Philadelphia, J. B. Lippincott, 1961). But I am still convinced that that sentence was written by the female half of the partnership.

Opening another mystery story in the library, I read its first sentence: "I had been sitting in the cushiony brown leather chair for ten minutes, crossing and uncrossing my green suede pumps and trying not to chew my lipstick." This, I thought, was a woman writer. But could not a man have written that "I" sentence, trying to imitate the observation of a woman? Well, I thought, it would be possible for a man familiar with women's mannerisms. I read on. The first person narrator remarked that her skirt was "the merest trifle too snug around the hips this morning," and thought she had "better give it a tug when I stand." No, it is almost impossible that a man could have written this. The book is *Garment for a Lonesome Corpse;* the author is Ruth Reeves (New York, Phoenix Press, 1951).

47. *First Educators*

Goethe says in his *Torquato Tasso:* "And when you want to know what's suitable, you had better ask women of nobility." (*Und willst du wissen, was sich ziemt, so frage nur bei edlen Frauen an.*") Here the part of women as educators for social tact, for what is suitable, is expressly stated. The educational role of women did not start with matters of social etiquette, but much earlier and on a lower plane, namely, in the period of toilet training and feeding. It's a long way from breast feeding a baby to the question of which fork to use at the dinner table, but it is a direct line from the one to the other.

48. *Psychological Literature*

Reading some books and articles in psychological journals reminds me of a German book, published more than forty years ago. I have forgotten the name of the writer but not its title, which was *Die Wissenschaft des nicht Wissenswerten* (The science of what is not worth knowing). Many American psychological books and journals contain a collection of exact nothings; they are crammed full of the most precise and minute nullities.

Freud remarked that a certain American mentality is characterized by "unthinking optimism and empty mental activity." The influx of European scientists and writers has improved that mental attitude. It modified and changed it for the better, but was still unable to reform it.

Many Americans still believe in the perfectibility of man and still believe, ever since Jefferson, that men are created equal. They believe that science is sacred even when the scientists write or talk undiluted nonsense.

49. *God and the Jews*

Jehovah is supposed to be heard and not seen. The Jews who conceive of themselves as His children should be seen and not heard —except in praising Him.

50. *The Dead*

According to an ancient Roman proverb, in speaking of the dead one should say only good things (*"De mortuis nil nisi bene"*). I do not doubt that at the core of this pious advice is the unconscious fear of the dead, the continuation of an old, now consciously discarded belief that the dead would punish those who spoke ill of them or who did not praise them. It is astonishing that a false kind of loyalty still makes us say untrue things about the dead.

51. *Talent*

To speak at great length without saying anything is a social talent many people possess, but to write books without saying anything is a rare gift bestowed only upon some poets and quite a few scholars.

52. *The Wall*

"Yes," said Gustav Mahler, when he was told he ought to give up his fight against the outdated tradition of the Vienna Opera, "I am pounding my head against the wall, but only the wall gets dented." If he singlehandedly and single-headedly reached his result, is it then not likely that the wall of prejudices would finally crumble and collapse, if millions of heads were simultaneously to run against it?

53. *Personification*

Many women call the penis "he," personifying the male genital organ and attributing to it a life of its own, independent of the man. Some women give the penis a special name. A patient whose husband had the name Charles called his penis "Carlos." Another woman addressed the penis as "Master," thus differentiating "him" from its owner whom she called "Mister."

On a Sunday afternoon, a woman suddenly felt sorry for the penis of her husband and said to him: "Think of the poor little thing, how he is shut in between your narrow pants. One must set him free." Saying, this, she undid the fly and took the penis out. She then stroked it gently and affectionately until it stood free, head proudly erect. She then brought him "home," or, as she said, "where he belonged." She did not consider that she had released it from jail in order to transport it into another hot and humid prison. She was justifiably convinced that it would prefer this to the previous dwelling place. Later on, she remarked: "He is so restless. He has scarcely arrived at a place and he wants to leave already. He has the spirit of a wanderer." Her husband corrected her: "You should rather say pilgrim, since he visits a sanctuary." "I'm afraid," said the wife, "that he is eager to go from one sacred place to another holy shrine." The wife then spoke of the initial phases of sexual arousal of the penis as "Pilgrim's Progress."

The husband did not personalize his wife's genital organ, but he once surprised her when he suddenly burst into song, praising it with the well-known words,

> My country 'tis of thee,
> Sweet land of Liberty,
> Of thee I sing.
> Land where my fathers died,
> Land of the Pilgrim's pride. . . .

54. *The Reverse*

Anatole France, in one of his short stories, described a young man, Emile Vincent, who fought in the campaign of 1870. He was generally admired. He once approached the enemy advance guard with the composure of a hero and the shortsightedness of a myopic. (*"Il fut admirable durant toute la campagne. On le vit un jour s'approcher des avant-poste ennemies avec la tranquillité d'un heros et d'un myope."*)

Anatole France loved such contradictory word contrasts that reflect the combination of human strength and weakness. He does not restrict himself to such verbal associations of nouns and adjectives, but presents images in which the reader recognizes both sides of human nature in its paradoxical and contradictory complexity. There is, for example, the description of the behavior of a young woman at whom a man made an ardent pass. "She saw her garments in such disorder that modesty itself compelled her to undress." The writer thus attains the ironical and the comical aim he strives for.

There is a serious side to this kind of presentation, namely, the psychological concept of human nature expressed in psychoanalytic theory. In that "defiant courage of truth," of which Freud once wrote in a letter of 1920, he asserted that our virtues are intimately connected with our vices, that "the best" in our emotional life is unconsciously "interrelated with the worst" of it—if one can speak in psychological research of moral evaluations in such popular terms. There are, from a psychoanalytical viewpoint, two sides to every story regarding our kind actions. The other side remains mostly unconscious, in the dark; but the conscious side, isolated and separated from the other, presents a somewhat false picture of human nature. It is too good to be true.

55. *From the Frying Pan*

My daughter had told me that one of the older girls in her college wanted to consult me, but I knew nothing more than this and was not in the least prepared for what this girl revealed to me. After she left my office, I paced the room reflecting on the strange interview, or "encounter," as the existential psychoanalysts would call it. It was certainly a rare and interesting case, I thought, trying to remember if I had encountered similar ones in my long psychoanalytic practice.

In the midst of this search a story by Anatole France that I had read many years ago surprisingly occurred to me. Where had I read it? Was it in *Le Jardin d'Epicure?* No, I must have read it in one of the books in which Anatole France's conversations with his friends and secretaries are reported. It is a story of medieval times, and I remember its details only vaguely. A knight saw a beautiful Coventry girl, rode over to her and propositioned her in the most courteous manner. She rejected him, saying that she did not want to lose the salvation of her soul. Since she remained reluctant, the knight suspected her of belonging to one of those abominable sects that heretically overestimate virginity and ascribe too high a value to the purity of the flesh. The maid was put on trial and condemned to burn at the stake.

Only after I had recalled the outline of that precious medieval story did I recognize how its meaning was connected with the interesting psychoanalytic interview with that college girl. In it she had admitted that she had become indiscriminately promiscuous. When I expressed my astonishment that an extremely well-bred intelligent girl had drifted into a desolate life of this sort, she answered that she could not have avoided it because she was afraid of a greater sin. The girl had been reared as a practicing Catholic and was told in pre-puberty that masturbation, in which she had indulged, was a deadly sin. In order to avoid this, she had begun to sleep around with men indiscriminately.

The parallel between the girl's behavior and the attitude adopted in the medieval story is obvious. There are striking analogies to this attitude in the views of certain early sects of Christianity, for instance that of the Cainites, who proclaimed that the flesh must be mortified by plunging into sexual orgies. I now recall other neurotic cases that show that similar dynamics sometimes govern the emotional life especially of obsessive patients. They vacillate between yielding to their sexual desires and maintaining complete abstinence until they are driven into an impasse in which they wallow in self-degrading orgies.

It might be of interest to the psychoanalyst why I first thought I had read that medieval story in Anatole France's *Le Jardin d'Epicure,* where it is not to be found. There is, in this book, a piece on Judas Iscariot that shows a reversal akin to that operating in the medieval tale of the knight and the chaste maid. In it, France defends the betrayer of Christ. Without Judas, there would be no salvation of mankind; without his kiss, no Passion of the Savior. The first Vicar of the Parisian Cathedral, Abbé Degger, could not tolerate the thought that Judas should suffer the eternal tortures. He searched for a sign given by the Lord to show that Judas, the most cursed sinner, now sits at the right-hand side of God. The miracle happened and the abbé proclaimed that he had become the priest of compassion according to the order of Judas, *secundum ordine*. This abbé represents, as Anatole France called him, "the gentlest of the Cainites." Here then is the tie-in with that early Christian sect that appeared later in my train of thought.

The common denominator in the case of the patient, the medieval story, and this last tale is that the person who wants to avoid a sin is in danger of committing a greater one. One must be tolerant toward one's own weaknesses too, not only toward those of others.

It is not true, as the philosopher wrote, that the self is hateful (*"Le moi est haissable."*) [66] Just as with the religious thinker, such an idea should not be permitted, because, as Goethe remarks, "If God had wanted me different, He would have created me otherwise."

56. *Vision of the Future*

The scene is an office at Columbia University in New York City on a late afternoon in May, 19——, seventeen or eighteen years after my death. Dr. Bendiener, Professor of History, is speaking with Sam, the student whose doctoral dissertation he is directing. "Well, Sam, how far are you with your thesis? Are you still concentrating on the puberty rites of ancient Israel?" "I am coming along fine," Sam replies. "I am still working through the literature, and the basic idea becomes clearer every day. By the way, what is your opinion of the biblical tetralogy by Theodor Reik?" "You mean his books *Myth and Guilt, Mystery on the Mountain, Creation of Woman,* and *Temptation?* I can still recall that they were attacked by the theologians, and otherwise received with silence twenty years ago. However, they are now almost universally acknowledged. That means that the general correctness of their fundamental notions is established. Of course, these works contain many mistakes. As a matter of fact, they are almost obsolete. You know, the new excavations in the Nile Valley and the new inscriptions found in Palestine. . . . I hope you bear these discoveries in mind when you write your thesis." "Of course I shall. But the books of Reik are still interesting, are they not? And they are quite readable, too." "Well, they are written in the style of the late fifties. . . . All right, Sam, go ahead with your thesis research as you have been doing. Goodbye."

Half an hour later. The scene is the Columbia campus. Daniela Reik is walking with Sam along the path toward the campus exit. She is a sophomore, studying comparative literature. Sam: "By the way, Daniela, are you related to Theodor Reik? I was just discussing his work with my thesis adviser." Daniela: "I am his grand-daughter." Sam: "Do you remember him?" Daniela: "No, I was a little girl when he died." Sam: "You still are. . . . By the way, that new summer dress is very becoming. You look beautiful in it." Daniela: "Is that your new line? Do you tell that to all the girls?" Sam: "Really, Daniela. . . . "

At this point, John, who is studying at the Jewish Theological Seminary, encounters Sam and Daniela and greets them: "Hello there! What are you two up to?" Sam: "We're just talking. Did you know that Daniela is the grandchild of Theodor Reik?" John: "You mean the psychoanalyst? He wrote some rather frivolous books on love and sex, didn't he?" Sam: "Yes, but he also wrote some well-known books on biblical archeology, or rather archeo-logical psychoanalysis." John: "Yes, I know. He was an atheist. . . . Well, Daniela, have you read your grandfather's books? I mean, of course, those on love and sex. I saw a paperbound book of his, *The Need to be Loved,* in a bookstore the other day, and bought it. It's quite interesting, and sometimes even amusing." Daniela: "I'll read it during the summer vacation. Look at the lilacs over there! They smell so sweet!" John: "Well, I must rush off . . . so long!" Sam: "Will you come with me to the cafeteria for some ice cream?" Daniela: "I'm sorry, I can't. It's late, and my parents are expecting me for dinner." Sam: "How about tomor-row? It's Saturday. Let's drive out somewhere, to Rye perhaps, and have dinner there. . . . It's a date. I'll pick you up at your home at five-thirty." Daniela: "That would be fine. Do you smell the lilacs?" Sam: "Do you know what occurred to me when you said that, Daniela? Some lines of a poem by Heine:

> "*Im wunderschoenen Monat Mai*
> *Wenn alle Blüten sprangen*
> *Da ist in meinem Herzen auch*
> *Die Liebe aufgegangen*

> "In the wonderful month of May
> When flowers start

> To blossom, there love emerged
> For you, my darling, in my heart."

Daniela blushes. They leave the campus and walk down Broadway. It is rather warm for May.

57. *Uncanny Experience*

It was in 1919 that Freud asked me to look up all the literature on the uncanny I could find for him in the libraries of Vienna. I did not find much, but I copied extracts from magazine articles and dictionaries. (Freud gave me credit for this help in a footnote to his article, "The Uncanny," published in *Imago*.[67])

I thought of Freud's paper today again when I received the message of Fritz's death. It is a pity that I could not tell Freud about the experience that Fritz reported to me when I saw him after some years had passed. Freud was dead then. I am sure he would have welcomed with great appreciation this contribution to the subject contained in the story of Fritz's experience. As a matter of psychological fact, it is, as far as my knowledge of psychological and psychoanalytic literature goes, the most beautiful example of this kind met with in real life. Freud would have seen in it a complete and splendid confirmation of his theory that the haunted in experience can always be traced back to something familiar that has been repressed. The strange coincidence of wish and fulfillment as well as the problem of the double or second self appear in Fritz's experience, and their psychoanalytic interpretation adds the weight of confirmation to Freud's theory.

The beautiful material should not be lost, since it contains the most convincing verification of the psychoanalytic concept of the uncanny.

I must tell the story here from the beginning, since the prelude itself creates a strange impression.

We had run into each other on Fifth Avenue, and for a moment we stood still as if we had both seen ghosts in the middle of the street and in broad daylight. "Fritz!" I shouted, and he called,

"Theodor!" We stared at each other as if we could not believe our eyes.

I took him to dinner and we talked until long after midnight. We had not seen each other for more than forty years, but we had been in touch by mail and we had shared our youth in Vienna. Fritz is much younger than I; I had introduced him to the girl who later became his wife, and I knew that she had died after having borne a daughter.

He told me that his parents had been killed by the Nazis and he had been in the concentration camp in Dachau. He had gotten an immigration visa to the United States somehow and he was now employed as a clerk in a lawyer's office. He had been a good and busy lawyer in Vienna, but what could he do here with his knowledge of Austrian law? But he was happy to get the job, which provided him with a livelihood at least.

An hour later he told me about the first months after his arrival in New York. He had been almost penniless and had taken whatever job he could get. "I was a dishwasher and elevator man and lots of other things. It was horrible. . . ."

He suddenly became lost in thought and looked at me again as if I were a ghost. He shook himself and said, "I'll tell you of an experience which haunted me for a long time." He interrupted himself and asked, "Do you remember, Theodor, an evening we spent together in the Prater, when we were lieutenants?" "There were several," I said. "I know, I know, but I mean the one when we each had a girl and went over from the Hauptallee into the Wurstelprater." "What were the names of those girls? Mitzi and Anna?"

The memory then vaguely came back to me, not of the girls' names, but of that evening. The memory of that summer evening came back with the help of a waltz melody that occurred to me— *"Im Prater blüh'n wieder die Bäume."* The image of the Prater, a park somewhat comparable to Central Park . . . on one side the Hauptallee, a broad, cultivated avenue of several miles of chestnut trees; on the other side an amusement area with shows and stalls, comparable to Coney Island.

Fritz and I, arm in arm with two pretty girls, had strolled along the Hauptallee first and had then, joking and laughing, turned to the right to the Wurstelprater. We had stood a little while looking at a puppet show and had then arrived at the stall of a fortune-teller or crystal-ball gazer.

Fritz reminded me that one of the girls wanted to enter the stall and insisted that he should see the fortune-teller. The other girl and I had waited outside. "Do you remember that fellow?" Fritz went on. "He was an old Italian with a long pointed beard. He made some mysterious preparations and looked at me and then into his crystal ball for a long time. He then described to me what he saw in my future, or rather, how he saw me thirty years or so later. He described how I would look. I would then be, he said, a general in the Austrian army. Seeing my lieutenant's uniform, he perhaps thought that I was a professional soldier. He saw me in a gold-braided uniform with epaulets, and with red pants and boots. The guy, who had perhaps never seen an Austrian general, imagined that I would look like that. . . . But that experience . . . you know, in the winter when I arrived here, I got a job as doorkeeper and car-opener at the Russian Tea Room. Well, it was really cold that winter and I am an old man. It was on a Saturday evening and I had been on the street opening car doors a long time and felt thoroughly frozen. I decided to hurry into the kitchen to ask the cook for a cup of tea. I opened the door and I suddenly saw myself in a mirror in the same uniform as the fortune-teller had predicted—gold braid, red pants, boots and all. For a second I thought his prophecy had become reality or that I had gone crazy. That was, of course, the impression of an instant. I got another job soon after, but I often remembered that moment of shock."

Fritz fetched a cigarette from his pocket and lighted it. His hands, I observed, were trembling. He really did not look well. No wonder, after the many sufferings he had experienced.

He died a few days ago.

58. *Laughter and Age*

It seems to me that what we laugh at is determined not only by individual temperament, environment, and culture, but also by age. Small children laugh when they see someone fall down, which is, as Freud pointed out, an expression of their superiority feeling. ("He falls down. I can walk without falling.") Later on in life, as Anna Freud observed, children laugh after they have been frightened and recognize that there was no reason for their fear. Even as grownups, we burst into laughter when we hear a good joke or an excellent witticism, an attack on respected persons, or upon highly esteemed social institutions. This explosion results primarily from the congruence of an initial anxiety at hearing the joke. This anxiety is recognized as superfluous.

Traces of previous phases still remain when we have progressed in our development. We no longer laugh when we see someone fall down—except the clown in a circus—but there are still vestiges of hilarity and malicious joy at the misfortunes of others expressed occasionally in laughter.

Just as I write this, a scene from a comedy I had seen in my early twenties comes to mind. I still remember that I roared with laughter at the wonderful Viennese comedian Max Pallenberg, in a scene where a man passionately woos a woman. He had thought he had taken a love potion that was supposed to make him irresistible, but instead had swallowed a powerful and quick-acting purgative. His horrified astonishment at his physical sensations during his declarations of love to the lady made me roll with laughter.

If seen today, the same scene would scarcely make me smile and I would perhaps feel sorry for the poor fool. (It is not unlikely that the scene would ultimately evoke some thoughts about the biological connection between the processes of evacuation and of sexual emission.)

A short time after that performance I saw Max Pallenberg in

another comedy, entitled, if memory does not fail me, *"Die Sache mit Lolla."* In this play he took the part of a man who visits a girl and, descending the stairs afterwards, runs into his wife who is going to a dressmaker in the same house. His confused and confusing attempt at explaining his presence there was perhaps not as comical as in the previous play, but the humorous effect was of longer duration. It still gives me pleasure to remember the way the husband, caught in an impossible situation, got out of the impasse. (Such enjoyment is colored by the satisfaction at observing the cleverness and inventiveness of the victim, a quality experienced by the audiences of the incomparable Charlie Chaplin.)

As we get older, we do not laugh as often or as uproariously as in our youth, and we do not laugh at the same things. We are no longer frightened by dangers in our thoughts, and we need not conquer that anxiety by the explosion of laughter. Horace Walpole, the fourth Earl of Oxford, declared in a letter to the Countess of Upper Ossory (August 16, 1776) that "the world is a comedy to those that think, a tragedy to those that feel." Just as we do not laugh as often when we become old, we do not weep as frequently as when we were young. The world is neither a comedy nor a tragedy to us. It is a tragicomedy. We do not laugh anymore. In the best instance, we smile.

59. *Think*

Exhortations such as "Think!" which you sometimes see in offices, and others such as the ancient Greek inscription, "Know Thyself," are very useful. They remind us primarily of the futility of conscious searching and trying, and awaken a salutary doubt concerning our ability to think and to know ourselves.

60. *Speculative*

One is surprised, again and again, at the unconscious determination and overdetermination of our train of thoughts. It is as if they are striving for certain results independent of our will, while we swim in the stream of consciousness.

Take the example of how I arrived at a tentative biological-psychological hypothesis. (It is at the moment irrelevant whether this hypothesis is accurate. It is also not up to me to form an opinion about it.) My train of thought had its point of departure in a fleeting impression. During my walk after dinner I passed the window of a well-known New York restaurant. I saw that the head-waiter was leading a young couple to a table and that he moved the chairs for them to be seated. The young lady was, it seemed, in an advanced stage of pregnancy. (I shall come back to this point later. My attention was first focused on the smiling and welcoming waiter.) What occurred to me next was a memory of Vienna where I was born and bred. The Viennese sometimes made fun of the *Grüsser* (greeter), who received the guests in the better restaurants and clubs of the city, welcomed them, and showed them to their table with friendly words. In later years this male person was often replaced by a hostess who fulfilled the same function.

At this point my thoughts returned to the young lady. It was almost a playful idea that occurred to me: It is right that a woman should be the "greeter." Does she not first welcome the newborn baby into the world? And does she not take him to the place where he will be fed?

Then a line from Goethe's *Faust* occurred to me. Gretchen declaims about a girl, "She now eats for two," indicating that the girl had become pregnant. The transition from the subject of pregnancy to the theme of food was surprising, but I did not notice it then, since the young couple entered the restaurant with the purpose of having dinner there.

But what happened now in my train of thought would have been more surprising had I paid attention to my mental processes. My ideas suddenly turned to my psychoanalytic practice. During the last few years I had had the experience that young women who were obese or too fat lost weight in a very short time when they fell in love. I had found two tentative explanations for this strange phenomenon. The first was purely psychological: that change took place because of the conscious or unconscious wish of the woman to appear attractive to the man with whom she was in love. According to the (lamentable) taste of these times, slender female figures are fashionable. That explanation simplified that change, the loss of weight, as a result of the girl's control of her appetite. The other interpretation offered is the transformation of the female figure by a combination of biological and psychological factors. It appeared possible to me that the libidinous appetite, the desire to be loved and to love, had in those cases replaced the gluttonous appetite for food.

The sight of the pregnant young lady must have unconsciously renewed and actualized my theories; but what now occurred to me was not a continuation of them in the same direction, but involved jumping the track of previous thoughts. That quotation from *Faust,* stimulated by the sight of the pregnant woman going to dinner, was, so to speak, the jumping-off point for the new idea. "She now eats for two" alludes, of course, to the state of pregnancy. In continuation of these thoughts I arrived at the conclusion that pregnancy combined with increased alimentation forms, so to speak, the natural aim of women. It is the unconscious goal of their wishes and the fulfillment of their emotional and biological potentialities. A pregnant woman has, if the expression is permissible, "arrived." She has arrived, namely, at the fulfillment of her biological function as the guardian of the species. Here is the tie-in with the previous thought I had of woman as the "greeter" of the new generation.

Returning to my tentative theory about loss of weight in women who fall in love, I had to change its central point: it was not (or not only) the libidinous desire that replaced the appetite for food, but the unconscious longing to have a baby from the beloved man that caused the loss of weight. The decrease in her weight was thus the unconscious expression of a wish to become pregnant, indicating what she unconsciously craves. It shows her subterranean readiness and willingness to be big with child. All this is expressed, so to speak, in a negative way; her getting slender would thus betoken her unconscious desire to be filled by the man.

This represents an attempt at explanation of the surprising loss of weight of women who fall in love. It does not, however, explain the phenomenon of overweight and of obese women. But it does, if one is only willing to accept and acknowledge the psychoanalytic principle that an unconscious attitude can be expressed by two, opposed means. Those women who are not in love, have, of course, unconsciously the same wish to be big with a child. With these women, the only difference is that their wish has no hope of being realized in the forseeable future; it is frustrated. In eating too much and in becoming obese, they transform their figure in an autoplastic manner as if they had thus fulfilled the unconscious fantasy of being pregnant. They have unconsciously realized that wish; they also "eat for two" and without knowing it play-act at being pregnant. In the one case, that of the girl losing weight, the transformation indicates the wish to become big. In the other, that of the obese woman, there is an unconscious impersonation, a make-believe pregnancy. It is as if that wish that had been frustrated shaped the figure of the woman in the desired sense and form.

But are there in fact such unconscious wish-fulfillments expressed in physical symptoms and changes? One should not really doubt this in our age of hormones. There are such physical transformations in the direction of unconscious wishes. For example, there is a phenomenon from the same emotional area. I refer to the forces that produce "false pregnancy." It should not be forgotten, moreover, that we are dealing here in the area of the fantastic and of mockery that expresses itself in demonstrative and grotesque absurdity. The perplexing abstruseness of an interpretation of obesity as the unconscious impersonation of pregnancy is thus explainable. Patients themselves sometimes come close to such a concept in their thoughts. A simple woman who was very obese explained to me that her overweight figure gave her dignity by voluminosity.

All the preceding might sound as fantastic and as paradoxical as other theories that deal with autoplastic tendencies of the organism. (Sander Ferenczi assumed for instance that giraffes grew their long necks autoplastically in order to reach fruits hanging on high trees.) My intention here was to show through a very illustrative example that our trains of thought are unconsciously overdetermined. The character of the hypothesis was under consideration only secondarily. That tentative attempt might make a funny impression, but this need not prevent its being correct. When Freud first talked about the sexuality of children, his listeners, mostly physicians, roared with laughter in disbelief. Freud, remembering those occasions, used to quote his teacher Charcot in Paris, who did not acknowledge that certain minor contradictions prevented a process from being true, and who repeated the phrase: *"Ca n'empêche pas d' exister."*

61. *Masochists*

The original violent impulses at the bottom of masochistic attitudes should never be overlooked. Masochists are people who changed their spears into boomerangs that, returning, struck them.

62. *Wit and Attack*

Wit often attacks persons or institutions, but attack and wit are sometimes confused. Sometimes society considers a man a wit because it would be too painful to take his offensiveness otherwise.

63. *What Patients Say*

A woman about a friend: "She only has a lover, but I have a child."

A woman about her much older husband: "Our sex-life? Well, he talked a lot about his health at first. We paid strict attention to health foods and also to health in a sexual way. Later on it became a starvation diet."

A man who has an older and more experienced mistress: "She is very generous. I mean she takes care of me and does everything to get me sexually aroused."

A woman about her husband: "I sense what mood he is in when he walks over from the garage to the house, when I hear him walking, and I know what mood he is in when he looks at the letters on his desk and brushes some aside."

An older woman about another one who is an actress: "If she were able to act that scene she made to me *on* the stage, she would be the great actress she imagines she is."

A middle-aged woman: "Dinner with him in a restaurant was nice. The light was not very bright, but flattering."

64. *No Choice*

You can as little choose the persons who will be the most important in your life as a traveler who enters a railway car can choose his fellow travelers.

65. *Hats*

The saleslady said to her customer: "I am sure your husband will like this hat!" What clerk would say a similar thing about the wife of a customer who chooses a hat?"

66. *Utopia*

Oscar Wilde said that "a map of the world that does not include Utopia is not worth even glancing at, for it leaves out the one country at which Humanity is always landing." He should have added that such maps show Utopia in Russia, in the U.S.A., and in various other countries. They remind us of the world maps the old Romans built around the Mediterranean. Utopia is where the cartographer sees it.

67. *Origin of Shame*

In a recent French novel [68] a woman visits her friend who is of shapeless and grotesque ugliness. The woman asks herself how one could connect this sight with *l'amour*. "What does a woman who is impossibly ugly say to a man before she undresses? Does she hope that the naked truth of their bodies, that brutal flesh, will wipe out that of the face?" She imagines that such women are shameless (*"impudique"*).

68. *Prophets*

The prophetic vision is as little infallible as other human gifts. A prophet who is without honor in his own country is often astonished to discover that he is greatly honored in other contries. As a prophet, why could he not foresee this?

69. *Imagination*

It is obviously ludicrous to attribute rich imagination to poets only. A conscientious survey of famous scientific books of our time would prove that the scientist has an abundant and ardent imagination. And what about lovers? What else than the poor enslaving fantasy in which they revel makes them bestow upon their sweethearts (poor women, full of shortcomings) all the beauty and charm of the world and to see them as paragons?

70. *Summer Hotels*

In this hotel you only see old people, sometimes accompanied by their grandchildren. My daughter asserted that no person under sixty-five is admitted here as a guest.

From a letter of last summer: "The quality of the hotel guests gets worse from year to year. Next year's guests are already here."

71. *The Pun in Dreams*

In his "Interpretation of Dreams" Freud pointed out that dream-fragments have often the character of wordplays. The dream-distortion is then accomplished by the unrecognized pun. Here is an instance of such a dream-fragment, reported by a young girl. She dreamed of the air-conditioner in her room. No helpful thought-associations contributed to the interpretation of the dream. The latent significance of it becomes clear when one understands a pun is used here. It is an "heir-conditioner" which meant the female genitals that produce an heir, a child.

72. *A Comparison of Freud*

A psychologist, Armond Maddaloni, reminds me[69] that I once mentioned that Freud discussing the psycho-therapy of neuroses sometimes used a picture postcard of the most ordinary kind for making his point. A picture showed, for instance, a hillbilly in a hotel room trying to blow out the electric light like a candle. Freud explained: "If you attack the symptom directly, you act in the same way as this man. You must look for the switch."

73. *Dependence on the Psychoanalyst*

One frequently hears the complaint that the patient remains dependent on the psychotherapist. A psychoanalyst who is worthy of his name will, of course, try to make his patient independent of him, but in due time. The emotional tie between the patient and him is at first necessarily binding, but will be later more and more relaxed. Let me use a comparison: a mother who has a little boy or a little girl will at first take the child to the door of the classroom. Later on she will accompany the child only as far as the stairs in school, then only to the corner of the street until finally the child will leave home alone to go to school and will safely arrive there. The comparison will perhaps illustrate the patient's gradual gaining of his independence of the analyst.

74. *Woman's Language*

A middle-aged woman rejected the pass a man made at her and told him: "I don't need a boy-friend, but a friend." Every woman hearing this would understand what it means, namely that she needs a boy-friend and a friend united in one person. The man did, of course, not understand this.

Notes

[1] I attempted then to analyze the course of that romance in a book *Fragment of a Great Confession* (Farrar, Straus and Company, New York, 1949).

[2] *The Distinction between Loving and Being Loved.* The Psychoanalytic Quarterly. Vol. XIX, 1950. No. 3.

[3] Harcourt, Brace and Company, New York, 1960

[4] Thomas Yoseloff, New York and London, 1962

[5] In *New Outlook*

[6] *Anaclitic Depression* in Psychoanalytic Study of the Child, Vol. II, 1946; *Hospitalism*, Vol. I, 1945; *The Psychogenic Diseases in Infancy*, and others.

[7] *The Psychiatrist and the Dying Patient*, New York, 1955.

[8] *Jewish Wit.* Gamut Press, New York, 1962.

[9] *Final Contributions to the Problems and Methods of Psychoanalysis.* Edited by Michael Balint. Basic Books, New York, 1951.

[10] *The Neurotic Personality of Our Time.* N. W. Norton & Co., New York, 1937, especially p. 102 ff. Compare also Clara Thomson, *Psy-*

choanalysis, Evolution and Development. Hermitage House, New York, 1956, p. 182 ff.

[11] *The Neurotic Personality of Our Time,* 1937, p. 102 ff.

[12] Dr. Rado elaborated on and qualified this theory later on in his valuable paper "Rage, Violence and Conscience" included in his *Psychoanalysis of Behavior.* Collected Papers, Vol II, New York, 1962.

[13] In my book *Masochism in Modern Man,* 1941.

[14] *Elements of Psychoanalysis,* Cleveland and New York, 1950, p. 231.

[15] "Les délires passionelles," *Soc. Med. Mentale,* Feb. 24, 1921.

[16] *Lehrbuch der Psychiatrie,* 10, Auflage, Berlin, 1960, p. 450.

[17] "Les anomalies, les abérrations et les perversions sexuelles," *Annal. Med. Psychol.,* May 1, 1885.

[18] "Etude psychoanalytique d'un cas d'erotomanie," *Annales Médicaux Psychologiques,* 1950.

[19] *Les causes affectives de l'erotomania,* Paris, 1937, p. 29 ff.

[20] "Les délires passionelles," *Soc. Med. Mentale,* Feb. 24, 1921.

[21] *Les Causes affectives de l'Erotomanie, principalement chez l'homme.*

[22] "Uber einen autobiographisch beschriebenen Fall von Paranoia." *Ges. Schriften,* Vol. VIII, p. 415.

[23] Thomas P. Parrot, *Shakespeare's Comedy,* New York, 1949, p. 188.

[24] Cumberland Clark, *Shakespeare and Psychology,* London, 1936, p. 120.

[25] *Die Welt als Wille und Vorstellung,* paragraph 36.

[26] In his letter to Mathilde Wesendonck, April 15, 1859.

[27] Albert Bielschowsky, *The Life of Goethe,* Putnam, New York, 1905, Vol. I, p. 3.

[28] *Neues über Goethes Liebe,* Berlin, 1921, p. 3.

[29] Karl Victor, *Goethe the Poet,* Cambridge, Mass., 1949.

[30] Wilhelm Weygandt, *Abnorme Character in der dramatischen Kunst,* Hamburg und Leipzig 1910, p. 160.

[31] *Erzählende Schriften,* 11 Band, S. Fischer Verlag, Berlin, 1922, p. 202.

[32] *Theology Today,* III, 1946, p. 187.

[33] *The Biblical Doctrine of Election,* London, 1950, p. 13.

[34] Yehezkel Kaufman, *The Religion of Israel,* University of Chicago Press, 1960, p. 163.

[35] *The Biblical Doctrine of Election,* London, 1950, pp. 147 ff.

[36] *The Faith of Israel,* Philadelphia, 1953, p. 68.

[37] *Jacob's Dream,* Philadelphia, 1946.

[38] First published in *Sexology* magazine, October, 1962.

39 *Claudine Married,* Farrar, Straus and Cudahy, New York, 1960, p. 77. Originally published under the title *Claudine en mènage,* Mercure de France, Paris, 1902.

40 *Le Livre de mon Ami.*

41 Compare S. Freud, "The Acquisition of Power over Fire," *Collected Works,* Vol. XII.

42 "An Outline of Psychoanalysis," *International Journal of Psychoanalysis,* XXI, 1940.

43 *New Introductory Lectures on Psychoanalysis,* New York, 1933, p. 5.

44 *McCall's,* June, 1962.

45 *Encylopaedia Sexualis,* New York, 1936.

46 *The Dark Urge,* Pyramid Books, New York, 1961.

47 *The Sexual Life of Savages in North-Western Melanesia,* New York, 1929.

48 *Les Opinions de Monsieur Jerome Coignard,* Paris, 1893.

49 There is, as far as I know, only one thorough monograph on the subject: Herman Nunberg's *Curiosity,* International Universities Press, New York, 1961.

50 George Macaulay Trevelyan, *English Social History,* London, 1942. Preface, p. VIII.

51 Herman Nunberg, *Curiosity,* p. 73.

52 *Of Love and Lust,* Farrar, Straus and Cudahy, New York, 1957, p. 563.

53 In two books, not translated into English, *Lust und Leid im Witz* (Vienna, 1929) and *Nachdenkliche Heiterkeit,* 1933.

54 The *Three Essays on Sexual Theory* appeared in 1905 (*Gesammelte Schriften,* Vol. V); the paper on fetishism in 1927 (Vol. IX).

55 John Charrerd's preface to Louis Barras, *Le fetishism,* Paris, 1913, p. x.

56 Emile Laurent, *Fetichists et érotomanes* (Les Perversions Sexuelles XII) Paris, 1905, p. 46.

57 In *Cultes, Mythes et Religions,* Paris, 1905-1912, Vol. IV, pp. 105 ff.

58 *Vie des dames galantes* (ed. Vigneau, Paris), 3ᵐ Discours.

59 Emile Laurent, *Fetichists et erotomanes,* Paris, 1905, p. 47.

60 For instance, Louis Barras, *Le Fétichism. Restif de la Bretonne fut-il fétichiste?* Paris, 1913.

61 Reinach quotes an article in the *Saturday Review,* October-December 1902.

62 Frank Capiro in *Encyclopedia of Sexual Behavior,* New York, 1961, p. 434.

[63] Moffard Yard, New York, 1917. I prefer the new translation in the Standard Edition of the *Complete Psychological Works of Sigmund Freud,* Vol. IX, Hogarth Press, London, 1919.

[64] Quoted in *The Times Literary Supplement,* October 28, 1944.

[65] English translation, Moffard Yard, New York, 1916.

[66] Pascal in *Pensées,* II, 434.

[67] Vol. V, 1919. *Gesammelte Schriften,* Vol. X, p. 378. (English Translation in *Collected Papers,* IV, Hogarth Press, London, 1924.)

[68] *Journal d'une Bourgeoise,* by Geneviève Gennari, Paris, 1959.

[69] Reprint "Psychology and Wholeness," School of Living. 1958.